Prais

'Like everything the incr[...] whether it's in speech-wr[...] [...] of music – this is erudite, interesting and, above all, entertaining.'
Alan Johnson, author and Former Home
Secretary of the United Kingdom

'In a world filled with division and anxiety, Simon Lancaster unlocks a treasure trove of advice on how we achieve meaningful and lasting connections with others through our written and spoken communications. And he makes it all sound fun and easy – which is exactly how it should be.'
Viv Groskop, author of *How to Own the Room: Women and the Art of Brilliant Speaking*

'One of the world's best speechwriters unveils the arts of persuasion with the help of some brain science. A racy, engrossing read.'
Professor Ian Robertson, author of *How Confidence Works: the new science of self-belief*

'A rollicking read, jammed full of inspiring insights and examples, showing how we can all use humour and playfulness to become better communicators. Great fun!'
Neil Mullarkey, comedian and author of *Seven Steps to Improve Your People Skills*

'In this highly entertaining guide to communication, Simon Lancaster provides rich insight into how to instantly connect with audiences. His anecdotes and familiar cultural reference points ensure that he always practises what he preaches, and so his ideas connect with readers.'
Jonathan Charteris-Black, Emeritus Professor of Linguistics, University of the West of England.

'Simon Lancaster dives into the language that dominates public debate to argue that the opinions many of us assume to be instinctive are actually the product of others manipulating words and phrases to provoke the reaction they desire. A thoroughly entertaining and highly relevant read.'
Sir Peter Wanless, Chief Executive, NSPCC

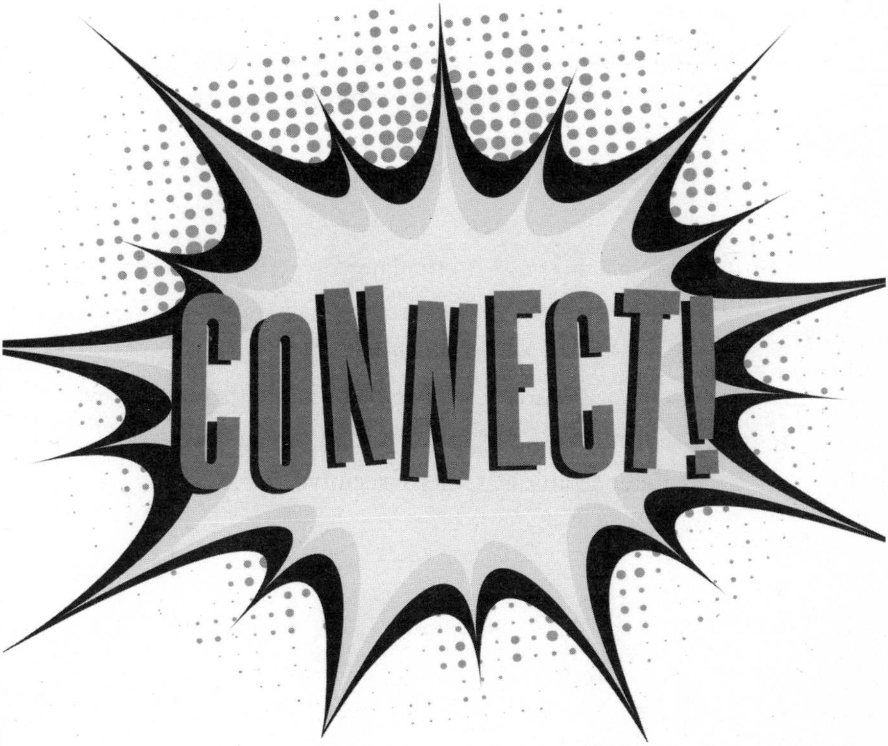
CONNECT!

Simon Lancaster runs Bespoke Speechwriting Services Ltd, a global speechwriting agency.

SIMON LANCASTER

Heligo
Books

First published in the UK by Heligo Books
an imprint of Bonnier Books UK
4th Floor, Victoria House
Bloomsbury Square
London, WC1B 4DA
England

Owned by Bonnier Books
Sveavägen 56, Stockholm, Sweden

facebook.com/bonnierbooksuk/
twitter.com/bonnierbooksuk

Trade paperback – 978-1-78870-643-8
Ebook – 978-1-78870-644-5
Audio – 978-1-78870-642-1

A CIP catalogue of this book is available from the British Library.

Cover and prelims designed by [Sophie McDonnell]
Typeset by IDSUK (Data Connection) Ltd
Printed and bound by Clays Ltd, Elcograf S.p.A

1 3 5 7 9 10 8 6 4 2

Heligo Books is an imprint of Bonnier Books UK
www.bonnierbooks.co.uk

To my brother Brendon, for always inspiring,
influencing and energising me

Contents

Connections

It's the evening of Wednesday 9 March 2016 and I'm leading 30 speechwriters from around the world down the steps into The Comedy Store Theatre in Leicester Square, London. Among us are speechwriters to Fortune 500 CEOs, prime ministers, monarchs, celebrities and billionaire philanthropists. As we push open the double doors to the theatre, we can instantly feel the buzz of energy that crackles through these places in the moments before showtime.

I've always loved comedy clubs. I think it's the prospect of the completely unknown: you never know what's going to happen or where things will go. This is especially true when The Comedy Store Players are performing. They are the in-house improvisation group who have performed on this stage since the early 1980s, and many of the original troupe are performing tonight – Neil Mullarkey, Josie Lawrence, Andy Smart, Richard Vranch. Their act is based around taking random suggestions from the audience and somehow connecting them all together to create a show. As you'd expect, the audience deliberately throws them the most incongruent ideas in the hope of seeing them flummoxed, but invariably they take whatever they're given and turn it all into something smart, funny and totally unique. It's not every day you see a Shakespearean tragedy about a prostitute and a prime minister under attack from a flying panda with nothing to protect them but a pepperoni pizza.

The Comedy Store Players may be exceptionally good at it, but this ability to take random pieces of information and rapidly make connections is an essential skill for life. Every day, we are constantly bombarded with new people, new places and new pieces of information. The only way we can ever make sense of it all is by making quick connections. *This person is like that person. This situation is like that situation. This book is like that other brilliant book – I should buy it right now.* Fortunately, most of the time we make these connections instinctively and, by and large, we do so very effectively.

Imagine you're in your office at the coffee point and you meet a new starter. Let's call her Sarah. What do you do? You look at her face, take a quick mental snapshot and then quickly compare that image against all the other faces you have known in your life, people you knew at school and university, people you worked with in previous jobs, people you liked, people you didn't like . . . until BOOM! You've found a connection.

Ah, Sarah's like Fiona! Well, Fiona's great! I've been out on the town with Fiona dozens of times over the last few years. Fiona's fun, positive and super loyal. Instantly, your brain sparks up at the possibility that Sarah might be as good a friend as Fiona. From then on, the connection between Sarah and Fiona grows in your mind. Before long, you'll start thinking of the two together, and may find it hard to think of one without thinking of the other. Eventually, you may even feel compelled to mention the connection: 'OMG! Sarah's just like my friend Fiona.' And, if the connection between them gets really strong, you might even start to insist, 'Sarah. You *must* meet my friend Fiona!'

Connections like these help us quickly comprehend and categorise new people we meet. According to Princeton psychologists Janine Willis and Alexander Todorov, we decide in a tenth of a second if we trust someone or not – a blink of an eye – and these first impressions are very much guided by similarities to people we've known or met before – family, friends, even people with whom we've only had the most fleeting contact. If someone looks like someone who made us feel warm, we'll assume they'll also make us feel warm. If someone looks like someone who gave us the creeps, we'll assume that they're a bit creepy too.

We think through connections

Our brain works through connections like these and they can frequently be very helpful, sparing us the bother of more rigorous analysis or the discomfort of ambiguity, providing quick and simple signals to how we should act. And these connections don't just shape how we act when we meet people, they determine how we respond in a wide variety of situations. *This workplace is like that workplace. This product is like that product. This issue is like that issue.*

We learn about the world through connections and it starts from the second we're born. Think of a toddler wandering around her living room. She sees a cat in the corner of the room and points at it. To start off with, it's just a big fluffy thing in the corner. At that point, it has no name, it's just an image, a picture in her mind. Then someone says 'cat'. The little girl makes the first connection between the fluffy thing she's looking at and the word 'cat'. This happens a few more times, until eventually the toddler gets that there's a connection between the two. 'Ah! That big fluffy thing is called a cat.' That connection is strengthened as more and more people repeat the word 'cat' whenever a cat is nearby. Eventually, the child can't see a cat without thinking of the word 'cat', nor can she hear the word 'cat' without visualising a big fluffy thing. The connection is made.

From that first connection, more and more connections grow, until eventually a whole network of connections come to exist in her brain around cats, including powerful connections with senses, feelings and memories. She'll think of cats and remember the feel of their fur, the sound of their purring or the smell of their whiskers when they've just had a wash (or the smell of their breath after they've eaten cat food). She may also connect cats with feelings of warmth, happiness and relaxation; and maybe places too: childhood homes, friends' homes, and so on. These connections create a network of thoughts and associations which will, to a greater or lesser extent, remain with her throughout her life, forming part of her deep memory, shaping how she feels and acts around cats. Different experiences will lead to different feelings. Someone who was scratched by a cat as a baby would obviously make very different connections, which would lead to different feelings and behaviours around cats. Either way, it's all about connections.

These connections are not just metaphorical, there are literal connections taking place in our brains. We have around 86 billion neurons in our brains which are constantly connecting with one another, shooting information back and forth at a speed of around 120 metres a second. In the last few years there have been the most phenomenal advances in neuroscience which means that we're now beginning to understand more and more about how the brain works, and what these individual neurons do, with some neuroscientists getting very specific indeed about their functions. One neurosurgeon, Rodrigo Quiroga at the University of Leicester, recently discovered there is a special neuron for Jennifer Aniston: a neuron that only lights up when images of Jennifer Aniston are seen. Other neurons have been discovered for Halle Berry, Julia Roberts, Bill Clinton and the Beatles.

The connections between these neurons determine much about who we are – our character, identity, emotions, thoughts, memories, desires, needs and, most important perhaps, our behaviour. Some neuroscientists are now exploring whether it's possible to map these neurons, much as we have mapped the human genome. Sebastian Seung, Head of Samsung Research and Professor at the Princeton Neuroscience Institute, is developing new computational technologies to map the neural connections in the brain.

It was the Canadian psychologist Donald Hebb who established the idea that when neurons fire together, they wire together; in other words, the more two things are connected together for us, the stronger that connection becomes in our mind. If we're repeatedly exposed to a particular connection, sooner or later, it becomes hard to think about one thing without thinking of the other thing. You are seeing Sarah, but you're thinking Fiona. You're seeing the word 'cat', but you're thinking of a fluffy be-whiskered animal. You see Jennifer Aniston, you're hearing the theme tune from *Friends*.

All day long, we're making connections. The ability to find and make new connections quickly is fundamental to our intelligence. Indeed, the very word intelligence comes itself from a connection between the Latin words *inter* (between) and *legere* (to choose). So, intelligence is fundamentally the ability to choose between different connections. *This is like that. That is like the other. Now is like then.* We're making connections. Intelligent people can make these kinds of connections easily and see links others do not, which helps them solve problems quickly and make sense of complex concepts.

The ease with which we can strike new connections and 'read between' things is an essential element of creativity. Legendary ad man, James Webb Young, said new ideas were often created by simply connecting old ideas and, when you look at the greatest inventions and innovators from the ages, you can see that this may well be true.

New connections mean new ideas

George Lucas said *Star Wars* was basically cowboys and Indians in space. Chemist Helen Diserens invented the roll-on deodorant after looking at a Biro and wondering if the same roll-on mechanism could be used to dispense deodorant.

Connections

Athletics coach Bill Bowerman invented the patented sole on Nike shoes after looking at his waffle iron over the breakfast table and wondering, 'What if I poured plastic in that . . .?' (Don't try that at home.)

David Bowie once described creativity as a big game of 'What if . . .?' In 2001, he delivered a Commencement Address at Berklee College of Music and Drama in which he depicted his own creative experiences as a series of 'what if' questions: 'What if you combined Brecht–Weill musical drama with rhythm and blues? What happens if you transplant the French chanson with the Philly sound? Can Schoenberg lie comfortably with Little Richard? Can you put haggis and snails on the same plate . . .?'

While haggis and snails may not sound too tasty, some random connections can create truly mouth-watering ideas. My wife, Lucy, comes from a family with a long history of making biscuits and cakes. Wright's Biscuits was founded in the late eighteenth century and her grandfather, Nigel, worked there for many years, including after it was purchased by United Biscuits in the 1970s. His company supplied cheesecakes and many other items to Marks & Spencer. One year, the M&S representative asked Nigel if he had any new ideas to liven up their Christmas selection. Nigel scratched his head, then remembered his grandfather once saying that cheese and chocolate went together surprisingly well. Nigel tried the combination again, was delighted with the result, and so it was that he delivered to Marks & Spencer the 'chocolate cheesecake', and it's been a firm favourite with customers ever since.

Connect!

Random connections represent the very essence of creativity. Steve Jobs once described creativity as 'just connecting things' and he certainly made some unusual and profitable connections during his life. Much of Apple was based on playing the game 'What if . . .?' The iPhone was the answer to the question: 'What if we connect an iPod, an internet Explorer and a mobile phone?' The Apple Store was the answer to the question, 'What if we connect high-street retail with the amazing experience you get when you walk into the Ritz-Carlton Hotel?', which is why Apple Stores have unusually high ceilings, helpful concierges and a 'bar' at the back. The reason we have a wide range of fonts on our computers is because Steve Jobs asked, 'What if we connect calligraphy and computing?' Jobs described the process as 'connecting the dots' in his legendary Commencement Address at Stanford University in 2005, saying 'this approach has never let me down, and it has made all the difference in my life.' Indeed, 'just connecting things' didn't work out too badly for Apple or Steve Jobs. It was a case of 1+1 = $3 trillion.

The same principle also worked well at Steve Jobs' other great company, Pixar. All the most memorable Pixar movies were also based on playing the game 'What if . . .?'. *Toy Story* was, 'What if toys had emotions?' *A Bug's Life* was, 'What if bugs had emotions?' *Monsters, Inc.* was, 'What if monsters had emotions?' *Cars* was, 'What if cars had emotions?' And so on and so forth, right up to *Inside Out*, which arguably pushed it to the limit – 'What if emotions had emotions?'

Much Comedy Store humour comes from embracing this game of 'What if . . .?'. In one of the Players' most enjoyable on-stage japes, they take a household object and consider other uses for it, as featured on the 'prop round' of popular show *Whose Line Is It Anyway?* Such a challenge can send them off on a rapid brain trip in which a plain old bathroom mat is quickly transformed into a wig, a tutu, a flag, a car wash, a pet dog, a window, a tongue and possibly ending as a particularly virulent case of belly-button fluff. It's great fun, and we are all very happy to go along with these flights of fancy. We all have the capacity to enjoy two worlds simultaneously: the real world which we can see before our eyes, and that imagined 'what if' world which exists only in our heads.

Some people think that creativity – this capacity for making connections – is a trait we're either born with or not. In fact, like most things in life, creativity is a skill we can nurture or neglect. As Edward de Bono argued in his books, the brain works like a muscle and we should exercise it regularly to keep it in shape or it will decline. *Use it or lose it.* After all, many of us will happily spend an hour a day lifting weights to get a slimmer, more toned body. Why shouldn't we spend the same time getting our brain into peak condition?

This is something I've always taken seriously for myself and my speechwriting colleagues. Back in the early noughties, I led a team of eight brilliant speechwriters in Whitehall – many of whom are still working as speechwriters around the world today. Every week, we would get together and do creative exercises to push our minds in new ways. Sometimes we would play random connections, looking for links between disparate objects and the prosaic policy papers piled high on our desks. A sight of the cover of *Hello!* magazine might get us thinking, 'Why does society celebrate actors and pop stars more than teachers?' If someone had on a green coat we might start thinking, how could education be greener? If someone walked in with a particularly unusually personalised Starbucks drink (a quadruple-shot, half-caff, non-dairy, venti, iced Frappuccino with a caramel drizzle . . .), we might wonder if the education system could ever develop a personalised system of learning that was as good at meeting people's unique needs as a company like Starbucks?

It was all about finding new connections that would jump-start our brains and generate interesting angles for speeches, avoiding the risk of groupthink or, even worse, being boring. Sometimes we would improvise speeches in the style of historical figures: Margaret Thatcher, Martin Luther King Jr. or Jed Bartlet from *The West Wing*. I remember once being inspired to write a speech about parenting after watching an episode of *The West Wing* about gay marriage in which Bartlet had argued that it wasn't for politicians to define or ill-define love. It was a case of life imitating art. Other times, we went to the Whitehall music room and improvised songs around policy issues, grouped around a grand piano. Many of our ideas were badly conceived, ill-judged and could have led to all sorts of problems if they'd ever leaked, but every now and then something half-decent would emerge.

I wrote hundreds of speeches for the Labour minister Alan Johnson. He is a massive fan of the Beatles, so often simply connecting policy issues to Beatles songs worked well for him. When he made a speech about the long-running World Trade Organization negotiations known as the Doha Round, it was called *The Long and Winding Round*. When he made a speech about democracy in schools, it was *Power to the Pupils*. A speech about globalisation and innovation was billed *Sgt Pepper Economics*. Alan is very passionate about the Beatles so whenever he spoke about them, he always had a sparkle in his eyes. Alan has retired from politics and now he's writing brilliant books. His first four books – *This Boy; Please, Mr Postman; The Long and Winding Road* and *In My Life* – were all named after Beatles songs.

This creative approach to speechwriting still guides how my speechwriting agency works with clients today. I actively try to stimulate my clients' imaginations by inviting them to make connections. Asking a straight question like, 'Tell me what your company does' invariably leads them into a pre-prepared answer, devoid of feeling and often meaning. Asking a question like, 'If your company was a chocolate bar, what chocolate bar would it be?', gets their brain sparking, generating fresh energy and invariably introducing new lines of thought. *Are we traditional or modern? Are we sweeter/tastier/ nuttier than our rivals? Is it time to change the recipe?*

We're not just coming up with connections for the sake of it. New connections can generate breakthroughs, which don't just change how people speak but the way that they think, feel and act. Studies have shown that changing nothing more than the metaphor in a piece of text can lead people to dramatically shift their opinion on all sorts of issues – from climate change to coronavirus and even conflicts. We'll explore some of these studies over chapters to come in the course of the rest of this book.

Connect!

Change connections, change perceptions, change behaviours

That is why I host these annual speechwriter networking events in London: to help stimulate creativity among speechwriting colleagues. During the day, we write speeches, drink tea and eat lots of biscuits. In the evening, we explore the neon streets of Soho to observe rhetoric in the wild. And that was what took us to The Comedy Store on that evening in 2016. Comedy clubs are always great places to view rhetoric in action (at the time of writing, both the leaders of the UK and Ukraine started their careers doing comedy, performing on television as comic caricatures of themselves). And shortly after we pushed open the double doors that evening, we bumped into Neil Mullarkey, one of the founders of The Comedy Store Players. Neil and I have been paired as speakers at various conferences over the last few years and he is one of the kindest people you can ever meet. He'd organised special seats for us and after meeting and greeting the new faces among us, he arched his eyebrow and turned straight to the issue of the day. 'So. Brexit!' he said dramatically. 'What do you think?'

Only a few weeks previously, the then British prime minister David Cameron had announced that a referendum would be held on Britain's membership of the EU on 23 June 2016. This had sent shockwaves through British politics. Ever since the signing of the Maastricht Treaty in 1992, politicians on all sides had promised a referendum on the EU but none had ever delivered. Now it appeared a referendum might actually happen, but no one seriously doubted the outcome:

all of the polls and most of the pundits confidently predicted a solid victory for Britain to remain in the European Union.

A few people shared their thoughts and theories with Neil about which way the referendum would go but he zoomed right in to one aspect of the debate in particular. 'What do you think of the word "Brexit" though?' he asked. He repeated the word a few more times, with a slightly altered intonation each time. 'Brexit. *Brexit*. BREXIT!' The more he said it, the sillier it sounded. 'It's a weird word, isn't it?!'

Incredible as it might seem now, the word 'Brexit' was, then, a relative newcomer to the English language. Google Trends reveals the word only really began to take off in late 2015/early 2016 and, for a time, there were other words in contention to talk about Britain's future relationship with the EU. One word, specifically, had featured in several articles: *Brixit*. An article in the *Daily Mail* argued, 'Bring on the Brixit!' The *Economist* once warned, 'Brixit looms', while *MoneyWeek* pondered, 'Why Britain's economy would prosper from a "Brixit"'. It's interesting to consider what the consequences would have been if the vote had been called Brixit ('bricks it') rather than Brexit. Would the associations have been quite so positive if every time we'd talked about a 'Boris Brixit!' we'd conjured up images of the blond mop-top leader of the Leave campaign soiling his pants? *Boris bricks it*.

As it was, the name that stuck was Brexit. The word Brexit is itself the product of a connection – a new word formed by connecting two other words: 'Britain' and 'exit'. This sort of word is known as a portmanteau: an expression coined by Lewis Carroll in the poem 'Jabberwocky' from *Alice Through the Looking-Glass*, when Humpty Dumpty explains to Alice the coinage of unusual words like *galumphing* (a connection of galloping and triumphing) or *chortling* (a connection of chuckling and snorting).

Portmanteaus can appear fun when they first appear on the scene, getting the neurons firing in new directions, seeming neatly to capture some new thought or insight. Look at the various portmanteaus that emerged during the coronavirus pandemic. 'Quaranteen' connects 'quarantine' and 'teenager' to describe the frustrated teenager kept at home by coronavirus. 'Doomscrolling' connects 'doom' and 'scroll' to describe the endless misery of scrolling through social media for bad news. 'Pingdemic' connects 'ping' and 'pandemic' to depict a sudden rush of notifications from track and trace.

Portmanteaus are especially common in politics. Margaret Thatcher was, at the peak of her powers, the 'Maggatollah'. Bill and Hillary Clinton were 'Billary'. Donald Trump regularly ranted and riled about the 'lamestream' media. There's also Abenomics (after the Japanese prime minister), Obamacare and omnishambles – the latter a term coined in the fictional political comedy programme *The Thick Of It*.

Portmanteaus can prove equally powerful in business, representing a connection not just of words and but also ideas. The motel was a hotel for motorists. Pokemon was a pocket monster. A spork is a combination of a fork and a spoon. Elizabeth Holmes' infamous business venture, Theranos, was a portmanteau of therapy and analytics. They've also proved influential in the arts, inspiring new genres, such as romcoms, sitcoms or mockumentaries. The word Bollywood brings together Bombay and Hollywood. John Lennon, a huge fan of Carroll, regularly created portmanteaus in his books and songs, including 'slobbed' (slopped/sobbed), 'hulky' (huge/bulky) and 'astound-agast' (astound/aghast). So portmanteaus can do a lot of work in language, making us smile, causing us to think differently, and sometimes even changing our behaviours.

We can all create portmanteaus easily enough. A new song might give you an 'eargasm' or an 'earmare'. We can connect any words we wish, which is why, coming back to the word 'Brexit', it was curious that the two words which were connected pointed to just one outcome in that referendum: *Exit*. This was, after all, a referendum with two possible outcomes, but the name meant that, regardless of whether people were for or against, the beating drum of every conversation was '. . . exit . . . exit . . . exit'. It was like low-level hypnosis, being in the audience at a Derren Brown show. Had it been called the 'Brin referendum' ('Britain' and 'in'), each conversation would have been punctuated with the sound of '. . . in . . . in . . . in'. Surely a more impartial choice would have been to call the referendum 'Breu', marrying together the words Britain and EU? That would have made sense as that was the relationship being debated, although no doubt those who wanted Britain to leave would have objected to that idea.

But there was another aspect to this word 'Brexit' which arose as we chatted together in The Comedy Store. Neil Mullarkey joked that 'Brexit' sounded like a quick breakfast: something you grab as you're rushing out of the house in the morning. His comedic brain had quickly reimagined Brexit as a portmanteau between breakfast and exit. He developed his theme. 'It sounds like one of those little Kellogg's breakfast bars. Like a Graze bar. Or a Crunchie,' he said. 'Mm . . . A Brexit Bar! Have a break, have a Brexit! Brexit – take it one chunk at a time. Brexit – melts in your mouth, not in your hand. It sounds quite tasty actually!'

Brexit is breakfast?

At first, the phonological similarity amused me. It reminded me of how the Beatles' *Sgt Pepper* album originally derived from the sound of 'salt and pepper', the pre-existing phonological connection giving their ground-breaking album an instant ring of familiarity, as if it was something that just naturally belonged in every household. But my amusement rapidly turned to alarm as I considered the implications. If Brexit was breakfast then Brexit was food and, if you want to promote something, food has long been one of the most powerful sources of connection anyone in communication can make. Our brains are hardwired to forage and feed. Along with sex, it's one of our primary instincts, meeting one of our basic needs for survival. This is why so much advertising, branding and web imagery is based around food. From clickbait to so-called 'food porn' and big branding: its pull is irresistible.

We frequently speak about our loved ones as food, from 'honey' to 'sugar' and 'apple of my eye'. And this is not just a phenomenon unique to the English-speaking world, food-related terms of endearment are found around the globe, including *mon petit chou* (French – my little cabbage), *mumu* (Finnish – breadcrumb), *patatje* (Dutch – little chip), *buah hatiku* (Indonesian – fruit of my heart), *media naranja*

(Spanish – half an orange) and *tamago gata no kao* (Japanese – egg with eyes) and don't even get me started about what the aubergine, peach and banana represent in the language of emojis . . .

But the connection to food had a particular relevance to the Brexit debate, because there is also a deep underlying connection between food and wealth. Many of us, consciously or not, regularly speak through the conceptual metaphor of money as food. We might speak about people 'bringing home the bacon', being 'breadwinners' or having a ton of 'dough'. We might say 'hard work bears fruit', while those making easy money could be said to be 'on the gravy train'. Someone with no money might be said to be 'not worth a bean'. Given the Brexit debate was likely to focus on the economy, the connection with food was pertinent. Not a stick, but a carrot.

There's also a strong connection between food and national identity, which was again a prime emotional factor in the Brexit debate. When we think of many countries, our first thought is frequently their national dish. Think Italy, think pizza. Think the United States, think hamburgers. Think Malaysia, think nasi lemak. But there is a hierarchy within foods as well. Some nations can be disparaged for their tastes in food, for example, 'locust eaters' for Afghans or 'salmon crunchers' for Alaskans. In 2022, when the country formerly known as Turkey changed its name to Turkiye, many reported that this was because they were fed up with the connotations with 'turkey', a bird which is served up at Thanksgiving and Christmas dinners, but also defined in the dictionary as 'something that fails badly' or a 'stupid or silly person'. So there is a hierarchy within foods but, within this hierarchy, no one could much deny that breakfast is king.

Breakfast is symbolically one of the most important meals of the day, eaten at the point when darkness turns to light, night turns to day, and we break our fast to feed. It is a time fundamentally associated with renewal, affirmation and optimism, which is why so many of the greatest political campaigns in history have actively sought to connect with those dawn of day feelings, from Ronald Reagan's 'It's morning in America' in 1984 to Tony Blair's 'A new dawn has broken, has it not?' in 1997, to Barack Obama's promise that 'A new dawn of American leadership [was] at hand' in 2008.

Perhaps the most moving moment of Joe Biden's (otherwise quite peculiar) inauguration in 2021 came when 22-year-old poet Amanda Gorman stood on Capitol Hill and read her poem, 'The Hill We Climb'. Biden had spoken extensively about how Trump had 'cloaked America in darkness' throughout his campaign and Gorman provided the resolution and pay-off in the closing words of her poem, when she talked about stepping out of the shade and a new dawn blooming.

Gorman was echoing the imagery which Maya Angelou had invoked in her poem at Bill Clinton's inauguration, 28 years previously, titled 'On the pulse of morning'.

So the breakfast/Brexit connections were potentially extremely advantageous to the Brexit campaign, and it quickly became apparent that many people were indeed making a connection between Brexit and 'breakfast'. A huge number of people erroneously blurted out the word 'breakfast' when they meant to say Brexit, and vice versa, both in everyday conversations, in interviews, debates and speeches, many of these gaffes have found themselves in amusing compilation videos on YouTube.[1] Perhaps the most amusing was when Andrew RT Davies, Leader of the Conservative Party in Wales, ended his speech to the Conservative Party conference in October 2016 with a roaring peroration, 'And conference, mark my words, we will make breakfast . . . BREXIT . . . a success.'

Not only was there a pre-existing connection between Brexit and food, it also became clear that Brexit's principal cheerleaders were actively seeking to strengthen this connection. At the helm of the Brexit campaign was Boris Johnson, who had spent much of his career criticising the EU, both as a journalist and a politician. He'd always zoomed in on the food aspect of EU/UK relations, and these messages went into overdrive as the referendum campaign got underway. *They're banning our bananas! They're stealing our fish! We must take back control!*

In the three weeks leading up to the vote, Johnson made just two reported campaign trips and both were to food manufacturers. One was to a fish-processing facility in Suffolk and the other was to a biscuit factory in Lancashire. At the biscuit factory, to the delight of those present, he played around with the connection between Brexit and biscuits.

---

[1] In fact, there is some data to suggest a phonological connection between the words 'breakfast' and 'Brexit'. A search of the Nexis database of press articles in 2016 showed the word 'breakfast' appeared within five words of the word 'Brexit' in 208 articles, compared to 87 articles for the word 'lunch'. Comparable figures for the year 2019 are 181 and 60, suggesting a ratio of 3:1, implying a pre-existing connection.

Connect!

'I've never seen so much dough in all my life!' he said. 'But never forget – no matter how much dough they have here, it's nothing like the dough we are sending to Brussels every day, 50 million quid's worth! £350 million a week over which we have no control . . .! This is a company that is in total control of its dough. They know to the ounce how much they use. We've lost control of our dough.'

On 23 June 2016, Boris Johnson's Brexit campaign won a resounding victory in the referendum, with 17.4 million voting to leave the European Union against just 16.1 million who voted to stay. It was the largest popular vote ever in the history of the United Kingdom. But the food metaphors did not stop when the referendum result came in.

In September 2016, Boris Johnson gave an interview to Britain's best-selling newspaper, the *Sun*, saying that Britain could 'have its cake and eat it' in negotiations with the EU, simultaneously introducing immigration controls and continuing open trade. The phrase 'have our cake and eat it', a popular idiom, instantly captured the public imagination, perhaps unsurprisingly, for while practically no one understands the intricacies and complexities of trade negotiations, everyone understands cake.

Have our cake and eat it!

Cake dominated Brexit discussions thereafter. The neurons had fired together, the neurons wired together. As Professor Jonathan Charteris-Black revealed in his brilliant book *Metaphors of Brexit*, there were an astonishing 1,273 articles in the British press between 2016 and December 2018 which featured Brexit in the title and a cake reference in the text. A search of the *Hansard* database of parliamentary debates reveals 449 references to cake in the Houses of Parliament between June 2016 and December 2019. Two new words even appeared in the *Oxford English Dictionary* over that period to characterise Johnson's intended negotiating strategy – 'cakeism' and 'cakeist' (the belief that you can have all the benefits of a particular thing but none of its disadvantages, especially in relation to the United Kingdom's negotiations on leaving the European Union).

Eventually, the neural connection between Brexit and cake became so strong even critics of Brexit couldn't help but succumb. Then Chancellor of the Exchequer and ardent Remainer Philip Hammond said, 'I try to discourage talk of cake among my colleagues . . .' before promptly adding, 'We can maximise the size of the cake and enjoy a much bigger piece.' Bank of England Governor Mark Carney also mocked the certainty that Brexit would be a 'smooth path to a land

of cake and consumption', thereby conjuring up the enticing image of Britain on a smooth path to a land of cake and consumption. European Council president Donald Tusk said the UK position was based on 'pure illusion. It looks like the cake philosophy is still alive.' He urged proponents of the 'cake philosophy' to carry out a scientific experiment: 'Buy a cake. Eat it! And see if it is still there on the plate.'

By referencing the food metaphor, they were reinforcing it. The fact they were refuting it didn't matter: the unconscious brain doesn't process negatives. As cognitive linguist George Lakoff points out in his book, *Don't Think of an Elephant!*, 'even by negating an image, we're evoking that image'. It's like telling a child not to press a button – the first thing they'll think about doing is pressing that button, because that's the image you've put in their minds.

Three years later, with the Brexit negotiations still unresolved, a General Election was called, with Brexit a central issue in that election. With prime minister Boris Johnson leading and directing the Conservative strategy, the food metaphors went into overdrive as he talked repeatedly about his 'oven-ready deal'. Johnson has always been a master of metaphor and knows well their power. I'm told that it was Johnson himself who personally coined the phrase 'oven-ready deal' to describe his Brexit deal, and the whole Conservative campaign seemed to be an exercise in strengthening the connection between Brexit and food, with all his campaign visits strategically designed to provide opportunities to talk about food and be seen with food while addressing the issue of Brexit.

Oven-ready deal

Johnson launched his campaign with a speech to activists at the NEC in Birmingham on 6 November in which he talked about his 'oven-ready deal' on Brexit. 'It's there! You just whack it in the microwave [laughter]. Gas mark, gas mark, I don't know! I'm not very good at cooking, you know [more laughter]. It's there! It's ready to go! Prick the lid [laughter].[2] Put it in. Err . . . [more laughter]. And then we can get on . . .'

On 7 November, the first day of proper campaigning, he was filmed chomping crisps at the Tayto crisp factory in Northern Ireland. The following day, he jumped behind the counter of Burns the Bread bakery in Wells, Somerset, where he popped on a pinny emblazoned with the slogan 'Get Brexit Done' before issuing loaves of bread to customers. He was seen scoffing sausage rolls in Milton Keynes, bingeing on brownies at a stall in Salisbury and even eating ice cream on Barry Island – in November. (If you've ever been to Barry Island in November, you'll know how ridiculous that is!)

It was when he went to the Grodzinski bakery in Golders Green that rivals in the Labour campaign realised the power of his messaging.

---

[2] The confusion about the difference between microwaves and gas marks might appear genuine but I understand that many of Johnson's supposed gaffes, innuendoes and spontaneous diversions are actually carefully prepared, scripted and practised in advance. This was more likely an attempt to garner attention and it succeeded, dominating the following day's media.

Connect!

'The moment I most remember was watching Boris Johnson in a bakery in Golders Green. He's in a Jewish bakery and he's making doughnuts and he's squishing "Get Brexit Done" onto the doughnuts saying, "Get Brexit done. Get Brexit done. Who wants a doughnut? Here's a doughnut. Get Brexit done. On the doughnut. In your mouth. Get Brexit done . . ."'

Johnson was actively connecting Brexit and food in the most audacious way imaginable. Midway through the campaign, the Conservative Party released their main campaign video for social media. The video was only brief, but it contained multiple references to mouth-watering foods including fish and chips, Sunday roast, Marmite, steak and chips and a Thai curry, all delivered in less than four minutes, alongside the inevitable message of 'Get Brexit Done'. The video attracted a whopping 10 million views on Twitter alone, comparable with viewing figures for the UK's top-rated TV show, *Strictly Come Dancing*.

The video ended showing Johnson making a cup of tea. When he poured his milk in before he'd removed the tea bag, it generated outrage from many who insisted the tea bag should be removed before the milk is added. A major national debate ensued about the correct way to make a cup of tea, and there are few topics more guaranteed to get people talking than how to make a good cup of tea. Even Fox News reported on the British prime minister's approach to tea-making. Similar controversy arose when Johnson went to Rodda's Cornish Clotted Cream factory near Redruth in Cornwall and he put the jam on his scone before the cream, triggering another grand debate: jam or cream first. The prime minister argued jam first because the jam created an adhesive effect but not everyone agreed. Incredibly, a resulting BBC News article about the correct way to eat a scone became the most read article on the BBC of the entire election campaign.

Boris Johnson was engaging the electorate in a way not seen before. Issues around social care, public service investment and climate change were overlooked in favour of talk about jam scones, doughnuts and cake. It might not have been wholly relevant to an election, but it was all certainly enjoyable and engaging, and these were issues upon which everyone could merrily opine on without fear of falling out. *Tea bag in or tea bag out? Jam first or cream first?* And, from the prime minister's perspective it was all super-helpful, because all the time, he was strengthening the connection in people's minds between Brexit and food.

On 11 December 2019, the critical last day of campaigning before polling, people across Britain switched on their TVs at breakfast time to see images of the prime minister dressed in a milkman's outfit, delivering milk and groceries direct to the doorstep of a beaming voter in Leeds. Then, at dinner time, the evening news showed the prime minister again with food, this time putting a 'Get Brexit Done' pie into an oven. As he explained to waiting journalists, 'This is the perfect metaphor for what we're going to do if we get a working majority. We have a deal. It's ready to go. You saw how easy it is. We put it in, slam it in the oven, take it out, and there it is. Get Brexit done.' That image of the prime minister saying 'Get Brexit Done' wearing his 'Get Brexit Done' pinny, wielding a 'Get Brexit Done' pie became the defining image of the whole campaign.

The constant food imagery was powerful. The 2016 study *Eating with Our Eyes: From Visual Hunger to Digital Satiation* by Charles Spence and his colleagues at the Department of Experimental Psychology, Oxford, shows that just seeing a picture of food induces dramatic physiological and neurophysiological changes in people. The reward system is activated, hormones are released in the stomach and salivation occurs. By connecting Brexit with food, and showing constant images of food while talking about Brexit, Boris Johnson had people literally salivating for Brexit. The strategy was positively Pavlovian but this is how connections are made. The neurons fire together, the neurons wire together. *Get Brexit done. Get breakfast done.*

Making connections

In the event, Johnson won the election with a landslide, winning 13.9 million votes, the largest vote ever achieved by any election candidate in the history of the UK, bar just one (John Major in 1992). He also won the Conservative Party their largest majority in parliament in more than 30 years. In his victory speech, he actively invoked the rhetoric of Clinton, Blair and Obama as he declared 'a new dawn on a new day on a new government'. His speech ended, once again sealing that connection between Brexit and breakfast, three and a half years after we'd noticed it in The Comedy Store. He said, 'Let's get Brexit done. But first, my friends, let's get breakfast done too.'

Boris Johnson may not be everyone's cup of tea but, regardless of your views of his character, his skills as a communicator are indisputable. For decades, the big problem Britain had with the European Union was that people simply didn't care about it. During the early noughties, I went to weekly meetings at Number 10 on European communication. Every week, we went through polls and every week the polls showed the same thing: people just didn't care about Europe. As an issue, it just didn't register with people. Johnson made it an issue by connecting it with things that people did care about. Bananas. Pies. Cake. That was the stroke of genius.

Basically, we have two piles of things in life. In one pile, we have things people don't much care about, like or understand – the mundane, the boring, the serious, the technical, the incomprehensible. In the other pile, we have things people desperately do like, understand and care about – this is stuff that is absolutely crucial to our survival, the stuff to which we cannot help but have an instant and instinctive reaction: sex, love, danger, disease, dirt, darkness and, of course, cake.

Bad communicators unremittingly speak to the 'don't care' pile. We all know people like this. They drone on and on and just listening to them makes you feel like the air is being sucked out of the room. Great communicators, whether consciously or not, habitually take stuff in the 'don't care' pile and connect it with stuff in the 'must care' pile, using a mix of comparison, analogy, metaphor, symbolism, innuendo, pun, rhythm, performance and suggestion. By so doing, they bypass logic and connect directly with some of our deepest instincts and emotions, instantly grabbing our attention and transferring energy from the thing we do care about to the thing we don't care about. In this way, they're able to change the way people think, feel and act. By connecting things people may not care

about with things they must care about, they are able to overcome resistance and create a reaction. It's like hot-wiring a car, firing people up, creating energy, generating power.

It's connections like this that create engagement. They get our brains buzzing, literally. They make neurons fire, creating electrical impulses that rapidly transmit across the brain, generating a literal energy that is visible to onlookers, as people's heads rise and eyes light up, but which can also be measured scientifically. EEG brain scanners monitor levels of electrical activity in the brain to see how engaged people are: delta means sleep, theta means drowsy, alpha means relaxed, beta means focused, and gamma means high insight. Boring communicators hold us down at a delta or theta, whereas great speakers lift us up to a lively beta or a gamma. It is at that point when the mind is opening up to new suggestions and possibilities that you're beginning to inspire, influence and energise.

Connections

The brain works through connections and so does communication. Great connections are fundamental to our cognition so they must be fundamental to communication. Great communicators should work with the grain of how the brain works, rather than against it. This is how marketing and advertising campaigns work: by establishing connections between brands and feelings. People buy products not just for their functionality, but for the promise of the images, feelings and senses connected with that product. Dove is not selling soap, it's selling the promise of peace, honesty and real beauty. Lynx is not selling deodorant, it's selling the promise of seduction, and the romantic rituals that lead to sex. And Boris was not just selling Brexit, he was selling the promise of delight, satisfaction and fulfilment.

But Boris Johnson isn't the only world leader who knows the way to voters' hearts. Let's leave London now and travel 5,000 miles across the globe. Let's head to India, the largest democracy in the world and also home to Indian prime minister, Narendra Modi. Modi is the biggest election winner in the history of the known universe, having won almost half a billion votes in the last two Indian elections.

Modi is not a typical prime minister in India. Since independence, most Indian prime ministers have come from a narrow elite, and one family in particular: the Nehru–Gandhi dynasty. Modi, in contrast, grew up in a one-storey house, a member of what's known in India as an OBC ('Other Backward Class'). Modi is a divisive but dominating figure. A Hindu nationalist, he has pushed forward a dramatic economic reform agenda in India (he is known as India's Margaret Thatcher).

Connect!

However, if there is one word which is now synonymous with Modi, it is that he is the *chaiwallah* – a chai vendor. As Thatcher was the Iron Lady, so Modi is the *chaiwallah*.

For those readers who haven't indulged in chai, it is a rich, sweet drink comprising sugar, milk, tea and spices (generally a variation of ginger, cloves and cardamom). It's a luxurious drink, closer to a dessert than a conventional cuppa. In India, many people enjoy chai with their breakfast and throughout the day as part of their daily rituals; as a result, it's hard to walk five metres in much of India without being offered a steaming hot cup of chai. And, when Modi was growing up, his father worked as a chaiwallah outside the railway station in Vadnagar, a small town in Gujurat. Modi helped out on his father's stall from time to time, hence: *chaiwallah*.

The term *chaiwallah* was originally directed as an insult towards Modi when Congress Leader Mani Shankar Aiyar said, in the run-up to the 2014 Indian national elections, 'I promise you that in the twenty-first century Narendra Modi can never become the prime minister of India. Never! Never! Never! If he wants, he can serve the tea here, but he can never be prime minister.' But, just as Thatcher took the Iron Lady insult and turned it to her advantage,[3] so too did Modi. From that point on, he actively sought to highlight his *chaiwallah* background, using it to show solidarity with the 90 per cent of Indians who work in the informal economy, and to contrast him sharply with the other candidate in that election, Rahul Gandhi.

---

[3] It was the Russian newspaper *Pravda* who first referred to Margaret Thatcher derogatorily as the Iron Lady.

Connections

Storm in a tea cup

On 12 February 2014, Modi took the unprecedented step of announcing that he would be hosting *chai pe charcha* – 'chats over chai' – right across India, putting his *chaiwallah* status at the centre of his campaign. At 1,000 sites in 300 cities, people were invited to come and enjoy a cup of chai and talk about the issues in the election with their friends and neighbours. Visitors were given a warm cup of chai as they arrived – served in a cup emblazoned with Modi's face. Modi then appeared on a giant screen, holding a matching cup of chai, as he set out his political vision and answered questions, via a network of satellite, internet and mobile video links.

The *chai pe charcha* went down a storm and came to be regarded as a tremendous innovation in modern campaigning – commentators referred to it as a 'storm in a tea-cup'. Even Barack Obama referenced it when he met Modi in Delhi, saying, 'We need more of these [*chai pe charcha*] in the White House.' Modi's campaign was unprecedented in its approach and unprecedented in its outcome. Modi increased the vote for his BJP party from 78 million in 2009 to a whopping 171 million in 2014, beating his rival, Rahul Gandhi, by a massive margin of 65 million.

As Boris Johnson's campaign successfully connected Brexit with food and satisfaction, so Modi's campaign successfully connected Modi with sustenance and warmth. For all the different people who attended the *chai pe charcha* and all the different conversations they had, the one thing they all had in common was that they were all talking about Modi while holding a Modi-branded cup of warm chai. So they were all making a connection. *Modi = warmth.*

Social psychologists agree that warmth is one of the prime factors determining trust and it's not hard to understand why. From the time we are babies, we come to connect trust and warmth. When we are babies and are being held by those who we love (and who love us), our body temperature literally rises. When we are put down and left alone, we become colder. So this connection between trust, warmth and loving relationships becomes hard-wired in our minds. Which is why, as adults, we regularly speak about our relationships in terms of temperature. We can all understand what it means to say someone is a bit 'icy', or that we are 'warming' to them. And this connection is not just a linguistic phenomenon, it's also physical. Studies have shown it works the other way around as well. Feelings of social exclusion can lead people to literally feel cold.

So the connection between Modi's speech and a warm cup of chai could potentially have been useful. But is it really possible that a warm cup of chai could influence people to think of a politician as warm? John Bargh at Yale University and Lawrence Williams from the University of Colorado carried out a study in 2008 to check the inter-relatedness of feelings of physical warmth and perceptions of social warmth. A professor gave participants drinks to hold in a lift but some of the participants were given cold drinks, while others were given warm drinks. Later, the participants were asked to rate the personality of the professor who had given them the drinks. Those who were given the warm drink said they believed the person had a 'warmer personality'.

People were subconsciously connecting the warmth of the drink with the professor's personality. Maybe something similar occurred with Modi's *chai pe charcha*. Maybe campaigners in the UK who wanted Britain to remain in the European Union would have fared better if Brexit had been called 'Breu', and voters had been invited to tea parties across the country to discuss the issue. '*Fancy a breu?*'

So far, we've explored some relatively rich and self-indulgent foods and drink – cakes, scones, biscuits, chai and the like. In the interests of a well-balanced diet, this might be a good time to consider some healthier options. So, let's leave behind the sweet and spicy streets of Delhi and zap to the other side of the planet to sunny California, land of constant kale, endless avocado and of course the awesome apple. And I'm not talking Granny Smiths or Golden Wonder, I'm talking Apple Inc., the most valuable company in the world.

The Apple core

As we've already seen, Steve Jobs, the founder of Apple, was a big believer in the power of connections and also an incredible communicator (which is no coincidence). When he decided to name his company Apple, he made several important connections.

Firstly, he was connecting his company with his favourite fruit. We all love apples. They have been associated with good health for thousands of years. There is the famous saying, 'an apple a day keeps the doctor away'.[4] Steve Jobs was a fruitarian, sometimes eating nothing but apples for weeks on end, so these sentiments about apples would have meant more to him than most. Also, after dropping out of college, Jobs worked in an apple orchard, so presumably the apple would spark some happy memories of his youth.

But the apple also had a deeper symbolism for a company breaking into the field of information technology. Just as there is a pre-existing culturally understood conceptual metaphor of food as wealth, so too there is a well-known metaphor of food as information. We might have an 'appetite' for learning, be 'hungry' for information or have an unquenchable 'thirst' for knowledge. A great idea might be 'tasty', 'mouth-watering' or 'go down a treat'. A bad idea might seem 'half-baked', 'indigestible' or 'hard to swallow'. So thought is food. Isn't that 'food for thought'? So the connection was apposite. And the idea of the apple was not just written into the company name and logo, it was also written into its products. I'm writing these words on my Macintosh computer, named after Steve Jobs' favourite type of apple – the Mcintosh apple, the national apple of Canada.

The second connection the apple made symbolically for Steve Jobs was with his favourite band. Steve Jobs adored the Beatles, who also named their company Apple. Jobs described the Beatles as his 'role model in business' saying, 'They were four

---

[4] This actually originated in Wales where it was, 'Eat an apple before going to bed, and you'll keep the doctor from earning his bread'. Another example of the food is money metaphor in action . . .

very talented guys who kept each other's negative tendencies in check. They balanced each other and the total was greater than the sum of the parts. And that's the way I see business. Great things are never done by just one person, they're done by a team of people.' By connecting his new company with his heroes, he ensured he would think of them every day.

The third connection he made was with another of his heroes, Sir Isaac Newton, one of the greatest ever scientists, who famously discovered the law of gravity after an apple fell on his head while he was sitting under an apple tree. The very first Apple logo, designed by Steve Jobs himself, depicted Newton sitting under that apple tree with the quote: 'A mind forever voyaging through strange seas of thought alone.'

The spirit which runs through that quote, and indeed the spirit which runs through the Beatles, Isaac Newton and Steve Jobs, is that of creative thought and adventure. And that is the spirit that runs through the Apple brand, and which has been promoted through many of its campaigns over the last few decades, perhaps most notably in its brilliant and now iconic 'Think Different' ad campaign, which featured 17 iconic personalities from the twentieth century, including Albert Einstein, Alfred Hitchcock, Jim Henson, John Lennon, Picasso and Muhammad Ali. This was like Apple's equivalent of the *Sgt Pepper* album cover, making a statement to the world: this is who we are, this is who we admire. They were all extraordinary creatives, people who had refused to conform, people who had the courage to 'think different'.

For many years, we've seen imagery like this, connecting the Apple brand with creative thought and adventure. Think of the hundreds of times a day that you are exposed to the Apple brand and the connections you make with it at a subliminal level. Every time you pick up your phone, or fire up your computer, or walk into a Starbucks and see the MacBooks around. The apple is pretty ubiquitous now, and its symbolism instantly understood. But what effect might these connections have? Is it possible that the logo might actually go so far as to prompt people to think different?

In 2008, Grainne M Fitzsimons, Tanya L Chartrand and Gavan J Fitzsimons, branding experts at Duke University, did a study where they asked people to come up with different uses for a household object, much like The Comedy Store Players might do with a bathroom mat. This is a common measure to test creativity but, in this study, the researchers added a twist. Half of the people taking part were exposed to the Apple brand before carrying out the exercise, while the other half were exposed to IBM's brand. The study found that those who had been exposed to the Apple brand came up with eight uses for the household object, while those who'd been primed with IBM images came up with just six. Maybe the logo had primed them to be more creative and think different?

This might explain why the Apple brand is now the most valuable in the world, with a value of more than $355 billion. Branding is all about connections. It's interesting to speculate whether Apple's fortunes would have been different if it had been given a different name. Would the company have been worth so much if Steve Jobs had called it Turkey. Or pipe. Or bathroom mat?

Connections

It might be a bit surprising to discover that our cognitive processes are so fallible. Most people imagine that they're immune to such subliminal suggestion. After all, we all like to imagine that, as human beings, we're supremely rational, carefully analysing the logic of each and every issue we encounter. In fact, there is a huge body of research that now shows clearly that we are more motivated by instincts and emotions than logic. Instead of really analysing the logic of most issues, what we tend to do is start with an instinctive reaction and then use our logical faculty to create an argument to support that instinctive reaction. So our logical brain is less concerned with analysis than it is with producing rhetoric to justify our instincts. As social psychologist Jonathan Haidt puts it, 'The conscious brain thinks it is the Oval Office but actually it is the Press Office.' This is what makes subliminal communication so powerful: the fact that most people believe they're immune to it. And that is why it is connections that frequently represent the make-or-break point between communication that flies and communication that fails.

Using your connections

In this chapter, we've only explored one very niche and limited type of connection – connections with food and drink – but, as we'll discover, it is within our power to connect anything with anything. We can connect our relationship to Posh and Becks, Harry and Meghan, Will and Jada. We can connect a corporate strategy with Elon Musk's ventures in outer space, Emma Raducanu's shock win at Wimbledon or the latest BTS album. We can turn our company into a family, a battlefield or a swimming pool. Making connections is the closest we can get to making magic. Different connections can achieve profoundly different effects. The effects can be awesome.

Throughout this book, we're going to look at the different connections you can make to inspire, influence and energise people, whether in speech or in writing, at a networking event or in email, at work or at home. We'll look at all sorts of different connections: between mind and body, the personal with the universal, the moral with the mundane, stories and statements, the past and the present, one thing and another thing, rhythm and reasoning, statistics and symbols, the silly and the serious, and dreams and deeds. Along the way, I'll give you examples of how it's done, explore the science and studies behind making connections and also include some fun and provocative exercises to get your own brain firing. It's all very playful.

Obviously, some connections work better than others. It's often just a case of trying different connections until you find something good that works for you. It needs to feel authentic, relevant to the issue, and resonate with the audience, but when we find a connection that works, the effect can be extraordinary. It give us the power to turn products into friends, apathy into anticipation and a no into a yes. This is a mighty power. Of course, this power can be used to good or wicked intent. My previous book – *You Are Not Human: How Words Kill* – explored the dark side of rhetoric. This book is designed to appeal to people who want to change the world for the better. Rhetoric should be something that everyone has the power to use, not just the privileged and powerful. After all, it shouldn't just be the preserve of Boris Johnson to talk about Brexit as cake. Maybe other issues would seem more appealing if we talked about them as cake? What about if we talked about tackling poverty as cake? *Making sure everyone gets a fair slice.* Maybe fighting climate change could be cake? *We've had too many promises of jam tomorrow when we're hungry for change now.* Maybe a corporate change programme could be cake? *We've got the recipe for success.*

It's up to you what you want to achieve with these techniques. Maybe you want to achieve something specific at work: changing the culture, winning promotion, or becoming a better leader? Maybe you want to create a movement, start a campaign, or change the world? Maybe you want to become prime minister? Your ambition might be personal, professional or political, but staying connected to your own dreams while you're reading will help keep you keep motivated and focused, while also providing you with something tangible you can explore, using the techniques we're covering.

Connecting with your dreams

So write down here what your dream is . . .

I have a dream . . .

_____

_____

_____

_____

We'll come back to your dreams again towards the back of the book. But, as we've seen throughout this chapter, whatever

Connect!

your dreams, if you want them to come true, you're going to have to get connected. You're going to need to connect with your self, you're going to need to connect with others and you're going to need to connect with the world. So what do you think? Can you do that? Yes you can. As Boris Johnson proved with Brexit, it's a piece of cake.

INSPIRE!

Why is it that some people radiate a warm glow, while others issue a chill? How is it that some people appear instantly friendly while others seem shifty? The answer to many of these questions can be found in processes hard-wired deep into our neurology and physiology, evolved over hundreds of thousands of years to keep us and our species safe.

Our instinctive brain works in an extraordinary way, like a super-powerful high-tech CCTV system constantly scanning and assessing people around us, sending us vital signals about whether we should feel safe or scared. It does this automatically whenever we walk into a meeting room, a big open-plan office, a conference centre, a shop, a pub, a restaurant, a waiting room, a railway carriage or when we switch on our computer. Our instincts try to serve our best interests, acting like an invisible hand, gently guiding us in one direction, not another.

Connect!

But how can we connect to these processes in a positive way? What can we do to ensure that the first impression we make is great? How can we present ourselves in a way that leaves people inspired rather than inspires people to leave?

These are the connections we're going to explore in the next three chapters, and we're going to start by examining possibly the most important connection any of us can ever make: the connection between our mind and our body.

Mind and Body

It's 22 November 2003 and more than 80,000 people are packed into the Telstra Stadium in Sydney to watch the nail-biting closing moments of the Rugby World Cup Final between Australia and England. The whole game has been on a knife-edge since the opening whistle. We're now 100 minutes in and, with seconds to go, the score is 17–17 and both sides' defences look impenetrable. It seems inevitable the competition will go to sudden death – something that has never happened before in a Rugby World Cup Final – unless, that is, one of the teams can magically pull a drop goal out of the hat.

I remember watching this game from a pub in West London that Saturday morning. I had a particular connection to the game, not only because I'm English and many of my colleagues at the time were Australian (I was writing speeches for Patricia Hewitt – the Australian-born Secretary of State for Trade and Industry), but also because I'd gone to school with the then England fly-half Jonny Wilkinson. Wilkinson had had a great game, scoring four penalties, but it was in those final moments that he delivered the pièce de résistance.

Connect!

One hundred minutes in, Matt Dawson passes the ball to him from a ruck, Jonny Wilkinson lets it fall to his left foot and then wellies it up the pitch. He's 40 yards back and his left foot is not his strongest, but he doesn't even need to look up to see the ball go over the posts. He's so certain he's on target that he immediately turns around to celebrate with his teammates. He's just given England their first Rugby World Cup win in history. The crowd goes wild.

But what was it that gave Wilkinson the deep inner confidence that he'd scored? Obviously, there were the thousands of hours of practice he'd put in over the years on our old school playing fields, but he also had another secret weapon. In the run up to that World Cup Final, he had regularly practised positive visualisation exercises in which he'd imagine scoring kicks just like that one against Australia. As he put it, he would 'create the sights, sounds and smells, the atmosphere, the sensation and the nerves, right down to the early morning wake-up call and that feeling in [the] stomach. It helps your body to get used to performing well under pressure.'

With positive visualisation, he was making a connection between his mind and his body: between what his body could do, and what his mind wanted his body to do. And that is the connection we're going to look at in this chapter: the mind–body connection. This might sound a million miles away from connecting Brexit with cake, Modi with tea or an iPhone with an apple, but connecting our mind and body is possibly the first and most important connection we must all make. After all, how can we possibly hope to connect with others if we aren't connected within ourselves? The mind–body connection is fundamental to all we are and everything we do.

It's easy to think of our mind and body as separate because we often speak about them that way. We say things like, 'it's all in your mind' or 'sort your head out'. Or we talk about 'mechanisms' and 'systems' in our bodies as if it were a machine. But biologically our mind and body are utterly interconnected and there is a straight flow right between them. Our neurology directly affects our physiology, and our physiology directly affects our neurology. Our mental health affects our physical health and our physical health affects our mental health. Signals are constantly shooting back and forth down this mind–body connection route, sending back and forth vital messages and information. It's worth taking a second to pause and observe in action how it works.

The mind and body connection

If you stretch your index finger out now, that happens because your brain is sending an instruction to your index finger telling it to do that. However, if you press your index finger hard on a drawing pin, you'll feel a sharp pain – and that's your finger sending a rapid message back to your brain. That's a sign messages are flowing efficiently back and forth between mind and body. The mind–body connection is working. Ensuring a strong connection between our minds and our body is vital to our safety and well-being.

But Jonny Wilkinson was turning this mind–body connection to his advantage. With positive visualisation, he was using his mind to trick his body into thinking it was doing things it was not. This meant he could develop muscle memory without lifting so much as a finger (or a foot, more accurately) so by the time he went into the Telstra Stadium, he'd already imagined scoring that drop goal thousands of times. That's why he could walk out on to that pitch with the psychology of a winner.

Our minds are very vulnerable to this kind of mind trickery. Functional Magnetic Resonance Imaging (fMRI) technologies show that when we imagine kicking a ball, the part of our brain that deals with kicking starts lighting up. Likewise, when we imagine holding a ball, the part of our brain that deals with holding lights up. So, as far as our minds are concerned, there is very little difference between imagination and action.

Successive studies have shown that positive visualisation can transform achievement levels across a wide variety of sports including basketball, football and running. Guang Yue, from the Cleveland Clinic Foundation, found positive visualisation increased the weight people could lift by around 35 per cent. Many great sportspeople habitually incorporate positive visualisation techniques into their routine, as an essential accompaniment to physical training. It makes good sense. After all, there's only so much time in the day you can devote to physical training before you wear your muscles out. Why not spend the rest doing mental training?

Many of the greatest sportspeople in history have been devout practitioners of positive visualisation. Muhammad Ali described his go-to self-improvement routine as 'affirmation, visualisation, mental rehearsal, self-confirmation' and perhaps the most powerful epigram of personal worth ever uttered, 'I am the greatest'. World champion golfer Jack Nicklaus said, 'I never hit a shot, not even in practice, without having a very sharp in-focus picture of it in my head.' Gareth Southgate, who has taken the England football team far further in international competitions than any other manager in recent history, also swears by the power of positive visualisation.

One of the most astonishing displays of positive visualisation I've seen in the last few years came in the dramatic closing moments of the title fight between Tyson Fury and Deontay Wilder in December 2018. Thirty-four seconds into the final round, Fury was knocked to the canvas by a brutal left-right-left combination. Fury was laid flat out on his back. He shocked everyone when he got back up again to fight. He explained afterwards, 'I'd had a dream and I saw myself getting knocked down and I saw myself getting back up.' The crowd and the whole boxing community was left breathless. Even seasoned fighters like George Foreman and Mike Tyson (after whom Fury was named) couldn't believe what he'd done. That fight ended in a split draw, but Fury went on to win the rematch against Wilder in February 2020.

It's not just top sportspeople who practise positive visualisation; many stars who have achieved immense success in different fields rely on it. James Corden, Will Smith, Oprah Winfrey, Bill Gates, Roger Daltrey and Russell Brand have all spoken publicly about the importance of positive visualisation. When Simon Cowell hit the big time with *X Factor*, someone asked him if he'd ever envisaged such phenomenal success. With characteristic modesty, he replied, 'Yes, I did actually.'

Connect!

The power of positively visualising events might sound so obvious it shouldn't need saying, yet so many people do not practise positive visualisation; in fact, what they practise is precisely the opposite: negative visualisation. They lie in their beds the night before an important meeting, event or speech, conjuring up all sorts of catastrophic scenarios and images, repeating to themselves negative messages like mantras. *I'm going to be terrible. It's going to be a disaster. Why the hell did I ever agree to this?* For many people, the more important the challenge ahead, the greater the catastrophising that accompanies it. And this stuff matters. As positive visualisation breeds success, so negative visualisation leads to failure. The more we say this stuff, the more deeply we connect to it. We are sending negative messages from mind to body, creating a self-fulfilling prophecy.

Positive visualisation is a much more positive pastime to practise. Our imagination is a tremendous force. We are quite capable of seeing two worlds at once: a world containing the person we are today, and a world containing the person we want to be in the future. We can use positive visualisation techniques to imagine anything we want, in a completely safe and supportive environment. And the more real our positive imagery, and the deeper we connect to it, the more likely we are to succeed and overcome our fears.

Public speaking is a great fear for many people. Indeed, some surveys suggest that public speaking is people's greatest fear, greater even than dying; although, as Jerry Seinfeld has pointed out, that would mean that, at a funeral, people would rather be the guy in the casket than the guy delivering the eulogy. As a speechwriter, I see people who are grappling with this fear literally every day of my working life. Several of my clients who appear filled with confidence in public, can be consumed by fear in private. There's nothing like the prospect of a speech to turn even the strongest leader into a quivering jelly. And this is a fear that I can totally relate to.

I used to suffer from a terrible fear of speaking. And I don't just mean public speaking, I mean I was afraid of speaking. In my early twenties, I suffered terribly from anxiety. There were all sorts of reasons for this. I grew up on a council estate in inner London and working with people from very privileged backgrounds made imposter syndrome almost inevitable. Simply waiting for my turn to speak in meetings would set my heart racing. I remember sitting rigid in meetings, reluctant even to pour a glass of water for fear someone would see my hands shaking. Positive visualisation helped me combat this. I had an amazing self-hypnosis on VHS by Paul McKenna on self-confidence that I went back to time and again through those early years of my career, which helped me build up my self-belief. Through that, my mind sent a new set of messages to my body. It tricked my body into believing I was confident and changed my life.

Mind tricks body

But I've not been afraid to go back to positive visualisation and call upon it again and again whenever I've felt I needed it, and this was the case in spring 2016, as I prepared to give my first ever TEDx talk. The invite came via a friend of mine, Caroline Goyder – who is a brilliant author and expert on confidence in public speaking. I knew this was a big deal. I'd wanted to deliver a TEDx talk for years and I knew what I wanted to say – that tuition in rhetoric should be extended to everyone. But I also knew that if I screwed it up, it would be a disaster for me and my business. I was a speechwriter making a speech about speeches. If I fluffed it, it was game over! And I also knew the video would go on YouTube whether I ended up flying or dying, so the stakes were through the roof.

I engaged in positive visualisation exercises every night in the six weeks leading up to that talk. I lay in bed, imagining myself on the stage, standing on the famous red TED dot looking energised, confident, smiling. I imagined the audience looking back at me, also looking engaged, inspired and entertained. No negativity was allowed in my vision. It was all going to be perfect. I played this vision over and over again, imagining myself going through all the motions.

And that meant that by the time I got to delivering the talk I had that essential quality that you need to give a credible speech: confidence. Confidence comes from the Latin word *confidere*, to trust, and self-confidence is trusting yourself. Because I'd imagined myself giving this speech successfully dozens of times before, I absolutely trusted in my ability to do it well. This was nothing new, just a repeat performance. And there was no risk of failure because I'd done it brilliantly so many times in the past, albeit in my head.

I simply cannot recommend positive visualisation highly enough, especially for readers who suffer from nerves. It's proved transformational for me and for a number of my clients. Create an image of what you want to be and connect to that image as often as you like. The more you connect to that image, the more you'll internalise it, the more you'll believe it. And, as the saying goes, if you believe it, you can achieve it.

I'll walk you through my own simple three-step process for positive visualisation now. It's based around the acronym B-I-G, so I call this 'thinking BIG'. It's a little exercise that I do myself and that I recommend to my clients. The great thing about this is that you can do it anytime, anyplace, anywhere: lying in bed, sitting at your desk, on the train or even in the loo.

It starts with B for BREATHING. You're probably thinking, 'I know how to breathe', but this is not just randomly breathing in and out, it's controlled, focused, deliberate breathing with a big emphasis on the out-breath. Short breath in through the nose for 4. Then hold for 7. Then long breath out through the mouth for 8.

Really tune into that breathing. Let every other sound just pass you by and focus on your breathing. Breathing like this has a magical effect. It automatically changes your brain chemistry, bringing down your cortisol levels while bringing up your oxytocin and serotonin levels; in other words, it reduces stress and makes you feel good. You can see footballers practising this kind of breathing as they prepare to take a penalty. Short breath in through the nose. Hold. Long breath out through the mouth. This is how they get themselves in the zone. Other performers do the same.

For thousands of years, pretty much every major religion in the world has encouraged breathing in this way to relax and induce a state of near trance. They might do it in different ways – through chants, mantras or silent prayer – but the physiological and neurological effect is the same: it gets you really relaxed. So keep this special breathing going for a minute or so. After about 30 seconds, you should be able to feel your body beginning to relax and your heart rate slowing. Now, work through your body from the top of your head down to the tips of your toes, finding any points of tension and letting them go. Really tune into your body, strengthening that mind–body connection. And, when you're feeling totally relaxed, you're ready to move to step two.

Step two in thinking BIG is IMAGINING. Imagine there's a huge movie screen in front of you. Now project on to that screen a big image of yourself just as you want to be. See how confident you are, how positive you are, and see how people are responding to you positively. Make that image bright and make it bigger, bringing that image close towards you.

Then, when that image is really clear, we move on to the next step in thinking BIG: GO! Now, visualise stepping outside of yourself and stepping into that body on the screen. Feel how great it is to stand in that body. See how it feels to walk that way. See how it feels to talk that way. See how it feels to experience the world that way. Really connect with all of those feelings. Enjoy it. Experience it. Engage with it fully. If you don't feel comfortable imagining a transformed version of yourself, maybe start by imagining you are one of your heroes . . . Why not? If a trade negotiation can be a slice of cake, then why shouldn't you be Barack Obama or Amy Schumer?

Now when you've got everything just how you want it to be, tightly press together your thumb into your second finger on your right hand and hold it there for 45 seconds. Then release it. This serves two purposes. Firstly, it connects that image in your mind with the physical feeling in your body. This means that, in future, if you want to take yourself back to this happy place, all you need to do is squeeze your thumb and second finger together and it will instantly transport you back there. But the other benefit is that, by squeezing the thumb and second finger in your right hand in this way, you open up the left frontal lobes of the brain, which puts you into challenge mode, so basically you feel more up for it.

When I was preparing to give my TEDx Verona talk, I did this positive visualisation every night. And every time I did it, the image grew stronger and the experience felt more real. As it got closer to the date of my actual TEDx talk, I could practically feel the stage beneath my feet, and hear the crowd laughing at my jokes and see them applauding rapturously. It gave me feelings of intense joy, occasionally even approaching

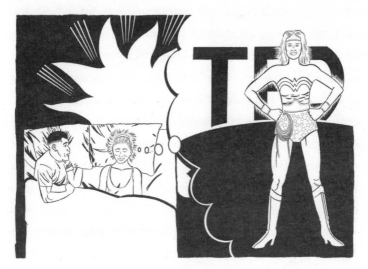

euphoria. I'd be lying in bed, body tingling, a huge smile on my face. My wife once jabbed me mid-visualisation and asked what I was thinking about. She looked relieved when I said I was just thinking about my speech . . .

In the end, it was all worth it. I felt great when I delivered my TEDx Verona talk. Which is not to say the nasty voices of self-doubt didn't creep into my mind from time to time in the weeks leading up to it – they did, but I was able to combat those voices because of the experience of positive visualisation. Could it have been better? Yes, maybe. Could I have prepared better? Probably not. Could I have given any more? I doubt it. It enabled me to reach my best and in the six years since I gave that talk literally not a day has gone by when I did not receive a message from someone, somewhere in the world, thanking me for giving that talk. So it was worth it. As Jonny Wilkinson has said, 'What I'm proud of is that I've searched for the best of me.' And isn't that all any of us can do?

Positive visualisation can help you reach your best too, and it can help in all sorts of professional contexts, not just speeches and presentations. One study in the *Journal of Consulting Psychology* tested its effect on job seekers. They split a group of job seekers into two groups. Each was given career counselling and interview coaching, but one group was given positive visualisation techniques, the other was not. Two months later, the candidates who had received positive visualisation techniques were three times more likely to have got jobs than those who were not.

So far, we've looked at how we can use the mind to trick our body into believing we're experiencing things we're not. Now we're going to flip it over and look at how we can use our body to trick our mind into believing we're experiencing things we're not. This is not positive visualisation – I think of this as 'positive physicalisation'. It's not thinking big, but ACTING big.

Body tricks mind

When we are afraid, we tend to make ourselves small, hiding ourselves away, putting our head down, hoping nobody notices us: this is an instinctive way to defend ourselves, protecting ourselves from predators. Our mind sends a message to our body, saying hide, then our body does that, and hides. By making our bodies big it reverses the message and sends it the other way. It sends a message straight to our mind saying that there's nothing to be scared about, so it's a great way to dispel anxiety. So now we're going to look at some different ways that you can make your body bigger.

First, stand up! That instantly makes your body bigger and is a great starting point. It's a basic principle of communication that, if you've got something important to say, you should stand up. This is why we talk about '*standing up* for our opinions', '*standing up* for one another' or being a '*stand up*' kind of person. Standing up is a statement of solidity and strength, even before we've said a word. So, if you want to feel big, stand up – even if you're just at home doing a Zoom call in your underpants (make sure your underpants aren't in camera view, though).

And when you are standing up, press your feet firmly into the floor. As the advice goes in the movie *Die Hard*, make fists with your feet. Many of our sensory cues about the environment come to us through our feet, so the more you connect there, the stronger you feel, sending the message to your mind that you're on steady ground.

Now, if you want, you can make your body even bigger still. Amy Cuddy is a social psychologist at Harvard University. Millions of people have watched her 2012 TED talk, 'Your body language may shape who you are'. Cuddy famously pioneered the idea of the 'power pose', where you put your legs astride and put your hands by your side like Wonder Woman or over your head, basically making yourself as big as you possibly can. This is the human equivalent of a cat puffing itself up: it makes us look bigger, but critically, it makes us feel bigger as well, sending a message to our mind that we are big and strong.

Cuddy's research showed that doing the power pose even for just a few seconds raises our testosterone levels, reduces our cortisol levels, and increases our willingness to take challenges (the latter was measured by asking participants if they wanted to gamble some money). While some of Cuddy's peers cast doubt over her findings, a major peer review in June 2020 largely vindicated her. So, dear readers, please do 'power pose' away. And frankly, whatever Cuddy's critics say, many of my clients absolutely swear by the power pose, so why not give it a try? It only takes twelve seconds. What's to lose?

But making ourselves big doesn't stop there. Now, make sure your neck is extended and strong and your head is held firmly up. Perhaps imagine you have a string on the back of your head pulling you up. Many people these days who are waiting to do something important instinctively do the opposite of this: they start tapping on their phone, thinking it will provide some comfort and escape from the stress of the moment when, in actual fact, research shows this increases our stress levels. Looking up takes us out of our peri-personal space, our immediate environment, and engages us with our extra-personal space, which is the space of possibilities. This engages our brain's reward network, activating the flow of dopamine, which might explain why looking up is such a simple but affirmative act.

Now, let's add a big smile, as well. Even if it starts off fake, it won't take long for your body to trick your mind into thinking there really is something to be happy about, and then those beautiful feel-good hormones – endorphins, dopamine, serotonin – start pouring in. Dr Fernando Marmolejo-Ramos at the University of South Australia carried out some research in 2020 on fake smiles. He asked a group of people to hold a pen between their teeth. Even though the participants knew they were faking their smiles, it didn't take long before they were feeling great. As Dr Marmolejo-Ramos explained, 'When your muscles say you're happy, you're more likely to see the world around you in a positive way . . . A "fake it till you make it" approach could have more credit than we expect.'

There's one other approach we can use to make ourselves feel bigger, and that's wearing clothes that make us feel big. Don't worry, I'm not suggesting huge, swinging 1970s big flares or 1980s *Dynasty* style shoulder pads; more clothes that make us *feel* big. Some people try and pack themselves into the smallest, tightest clothes possible when they're doing something important because they think they're flattering but it can backfire. Constricting the body can restrict breathing, which sends a message to the mind, warning of potential danger, gently stoking up the anxiety levels further.

There have been several studies now on what's known as 'enclothed cognition', i.e. that we are what we wear. One study showed that wearing a lab coat increased people's attentiveness and care. Another showed dressing up more professionally for interviews gave people extra confidence, while another study found students who wore Superman T-shirts outscored others in mental agility tests. You may not want to don a Superman T-shirt the next time you're doing something important, but you may well want to think about what outfits make you feel at your very best, whatever the reason.

When I did my TEDx talk, I wore an Angelo Galasso shirt and a Brioni suit. The connections these sparked for me were just brilliant. Angelo Galasso makes shirts for the likes of Paul McCartney, Al Pacino and David Beckham, while Daniel Craig wore a Brioni suit in the Bond movies. Dressing like that made me feel like a rock star; maybe I was subconsciously projecting that vibe as well. I remember one surreal moment when, after delivering a speech to speechwriters in Washington, an Obama speechwriter slapped me on the back and said, 'You're a fucking rock star, man!' Whether it was me or my shirts that led him to say that, it was clear I'd come a long way from the young guy who'd been scared to pour a glass of water in meetings.

So far, we've looked at thinking BIG and acting BIG. There's just one more thing to cover and that's 'talking big'. Our words, thoughts and actions are all interlinked so this is the last point to cover in this chapter. We've gone from positive visualisation to positive physicalisation, to positive verbalisation.

As we've already explored, many of us have little internal narratives running around inside our heads that are destructive. We can talk to ourselves in a way that we wouldn't dream of talking to a stranger, or even someone we hate. *You're rubbish. You don't deserve this. You're no good!* Imposter syndrome is a very real and surprisingly common phenomenon. A 2018 study revealed almost 9 in 10 people aged between 18 and 34 had experienced imposter syndrome at some point in the previous 12 months.

We need to convert our narratives from negatives to positives. The words we say to ourselves can make all the difference. The University of Pittsburgh carried out a study in which volunteers were asked to perform mental arithmetic tests in public. Half of the participants were asked to say, 'I feel anxious' beforehand while the rest said, 'I feel excited'. Perhaps predictably, the group who said 'I feel excited' outperformed the group who said they felt anxious. I get quite frustrated with event organisers who run around fretfully backstage before an event saying to their keynote speakers, 'Are you nervous? Are you nervous?' I don't want that word anywhere near any of my speakers before a speech. 'Are you excited?' That's much better.

Think big, act big, talk big

Maybe you can develop a little inspiring mantra for yourself. It doesn't need to be as grandiose as Muhammad Ali's 'I'm the greatest' but simply something that you can rely upon to connect you with your best self. I had three words in my mind when I went on to deliver my TEDx talk. 'Smile. Energy. Idea.' I had those words written on the top of my speech draft together with little emoji doodles to signify them all. They captured the images I'd had in my mind during my thinking big exercise. I still bring those three words and images to mind if I'm feeling a bit flat. It peps me up. I know another client who keeps in mind 'All is well' whenever he goes to speak, and indeed that is exactly the energy he exudes: a sense of serenity. What would your three-word mantra be? What three-word slogan might you rely on to connect you with your best self?

What is your three-word slogan?

I hope this chapter inspired you to think about what you can achieve. Jonny Wilkinson didn't always have the confidence and composure he showed during his incredible performance in the 2003 World Cup Final. In his autobiography, he wrote about his experiences of anxiety and depression. As a child, he was often sick in the hedge before rugby matches. Many of us can relate to those kinds of feelings and experiences. He's come a long way since. He thought big, acted big and he made the England rugby team better and bolder than it had ever been before. Now he can say confidently that he's done all he can to be his best. Can you?

If not, keep those positive messages flowing from your mind to your body and your body to your mind. Keep those connections strong and allow them to belong, so that after a while they are flowing automatically. Once we are connected within our best selves, then we are ready to connect with other people. That's what we'll explore in the next chapter: how we connect the personal with the universal, bringing together 'me' and 'we'.

Me and We

When Ariana Grande went to LA-based hip-hop radio station Power 106 FM in March 2016 to be interviewed by DJs Justin Credible and Eric D-Lux she was at the top of her game. Still just 22 years old, she'd achieved extraordinary success in the worlds of television, musical theatre and pop music. There was no shortage of topics the DJs could have asked her about. Instead, as this edited extract shows, the interview delved into more mundane matters:

Eric D-Lux – If you could use make-up or your phone one last time which one would you pick?

Ariana Grande – Is this what you think girls have trouble choosing between?

Justin Credible – Yeah! Absolutely!

Ariana Grande – Is this *men* assuming that that is what *girls* would have difficulty choosing between?

Eric D-Lux – Yes! Can you really go anywhere without your cell phone?

Ariana Grande – Yes!

Me and We

Eric D-Lux – How long can you go without looking at Twitter?

Ariana Grande – Many hours! When I'm at a dinner party I like to be present and talking. Eye contact!

Justin Credible – Listen and learn, ladies! Ladies learn!

Ariana Grande – Boys learn! Come on! Come on! Boys and girls: we can all learn! You need a little brushing up on equality here. I've changed my mind. I don't want to hang out at Power 106 FM . . .

The interview was instantly picked up by global media outlets and beamed around the world, attracting comment everywhere from *Time* magazine to the *Daily Mirror*. It also went super-viral on social media where the clip still appears so regularly on TikTok that when I played it on my computer my 13-year-old daughter was able to recite Grande's responses word for word.

It's fair to say that Eric D-Lux and Justin Credible are probably not graduates of the Dale Carnegie school of charm, but equally their provocative and challenging style is not especially unusual in today's media environment. Many broadcasters today deliberately cross boundaries and breach social norms, prodding and provoking their guests in the hope of prompting a shock reaction that goes viral.

A disconnected world

It was back in the nineties that Deborah Tannen, a professor of linguistics at Princeton, coined the term 'Argument Culture' to describe this combative media environment which 'urges us to approach the world, and the people in it, in an adversarial frame of mind.' Since then, with the advent of social media and 24/7 broadcasting, the argument culture has escalated. Some describe today's environment as a 'culture war'.

Today, different social groups are frequently pitched against one another – old against young, black against white, men against women, North against South, trans against feminists, urban against rural. We've seen this especially in the last election cycles and through the coronavirus pandemic. Issues ranging from vaccines to climate change, abortion and assisted dying to trans rights and Trump have frequently been presented through the prism of identity, forcing people to pick sides, based less on evidence than on perceived tribal allegiance. Social-media algorithms then exacerbate these divides, promoting ever more provocative content to the warring factions, engaging instincts and emotions, with little regard to truth. Truth and accuracy have no relevance in a battle of identity anyway: the debate is all about protecting your tribe: right or wrong.

This combative culture doesn't just restrict itself to the media; increasingly it is creeping into homes and workplaces as well. In the past, the rule was never to talk about sex, religion or politics in polite company. That's gone right out of the window. A study by YouGov in 2019 showed that today just 14 per cent of people think politics should be out of bounds in conversation. Many of us have witnessed or experienced the consequences of this. In the UK, many families fell apart over Brexit, and similar has happened in other countries, with heated disputes about Modi in India and Trump in the States.

Me and We

So connection is getting harder. And this was all exacerbated post 2020 with the spread of coronavirus, lockdowns and the move to online communication. But the good news is that human beings are bound to be together. As human beings, we are all intrinsically and deeply motivated to connect with one another. We fear and dread alienation, ostracisation and isolation, as much as we crave inclusion, admiration and a sense of belonging. So what can we do to promote our chances of connection in an age of disconnection? How can we connect our personal dreams with a wider audience? How can we turn our best me into the best we?

This is a tricky question and it's one I've long pondered professionally. If speechwriting is about anything, it's about creating connections. It's also a question I've grappled with personally, especially when I got married in 2004. Marriage is possibly the ultimate instance of turning a 'me' into a 'we'. I wasn't sure I had what it takes. I had no idea what a successful marriage looked like. My father was completely absent when I was growing up, living literally on the other side of the planet, while I was brought up by my mum on her own (brilliantly, I should add). My wife's parents had also separated when she was a baby so she was not much the wiser. So, in search of some pointers, I wrote to a hundred celebrities asking their tips on what makes a successful marriage – in truth, I was also in search of a good theme for my wedding speech. Amazingly, a huge number replied, undoubtedly incentivised by the KitKat chocolate bar I enclosed with each letter. Many made kind, long and thoughtful suggestions in response, which I'll come back to later, but the important point to make at this stage is that the way we connect with other people – forming bonds, groups and alliances – is completely instinctive, with its basis lying deep in our evolution, psychology and anthropology.

Forget rationality, forget intellect, when it comes to connecting with others, we're basically still cavepeople prowling around the savannah looking for allies and guarding against threats. Whenever we walk into any new environment, we are carefully scanning around us, processing all the cues and signals coming in, checking that information against our stored memory system and then using those connections to form judgements about whether we should feel safe or scared.

Our senses do a lot of the hard work for us. We've already seen how we make our minds up about whether people are trustworthy in a blink of an eye, based largely on their resemblance to other people. We've also seen how giving people warm drinks can lead people to think someone has a warm personality. Our senses quickly make snap decisions based on such sensory inputs. *Good person/bad person? Safe place/ dangerous place?* Many companies now actively appeal to their customers' different senses, employing sensory designers to advise how different sounds, colours and aromas can shift how their customers feel and act. It can make a big difference. The lighting as you walk into a restaurant. The smell as you walk into a show-home. The music as you walk around a supermarket.

Making positive connections

There's lots of research showing the difference little tweaks can make. For instance, we know that the sound of soft acoustic guitars and sweet harmonic voices encourages collaboration; we know that the smell of fresh flowers makes people more talkative; and we know that soft textures encourage collaboration and generosity. Such insights can easily be applied to create environments more conducive to connection. So, perhaps the next time you're organising a work bash, you might go for marshmallows instead of tortilla chips, round tables rather than square tables, the Brother Brothers playing in the background, rather than the Foo Fighters . . .

We all experience this ourselves all of the time. Just the other week, I met a client in a hotel in London to discuss his speech. The client had a fearsome reputation and the speech we were discussing was complicated for all sorts of reasons but, as soon as I walked in, I felt instantly at ease. The lighting was gentle, the music calm, and I leant back in a leather armchair that was as soft as butter. But, to top it all, there was a subtle perfume being released by little dispensers dotted around the hotel: a heady cocktail of cookies, vanilla and talcum powder. I instantly recognised it as the same perfume found in the Disneyland Hotel, which activated a ton of happy memories of family holidays, which made me relax and feel good. The client came in and, possibly experiencing a similar reaction to the environment, instantly opened his heart and soul, his eyes flashing as he shared with me the many ideas he had for how he wanted to change the world. Our meeting was phenomenally productive. The environment we're in does make a big difference to our chances of connection. But we can't always control the environment. So what else can we do to improve our chances of connection?

Connect!

Here, I think some answers can be found from observing Ariana Grande rather more closely in her more natural habitat, away from Power 106 FM. TikTok is now the world's number one hub for global connection, having overtaken Google as the world's most popular online destination in 2021. In the three years since it went international, it has helped all sorts of stars like Ariana Grande deepen their relationship with their fans, as well as propelling all sorts of previously unknowns to the realms of social-media stardom, giving them fan bases which can frequently number in the tens of millions. It's interesting to explore how the site works, because the speed with which people scan the site, swiftly swiping past videos they don't connect with and staying on videos they do, is like a microcosm of what happens in ordinary social situations anyway. *Good person. Bad person. Safe. Scared. Like you. Don't like you.* It's all totally instinctive. Real tenth-of-a-second stuff.

And when we look at Ariana Grande (26 million followers), along with some of the other top TikTokers, such as Bella Poarch (88 million followers), Khaby Lame (130 million followers) and Charli D'Amelio (135 million followers), we see some common features. The signals they send that enable them to connect are probably not dissimilar to the way people would have connected on the savannah tens of thousands of years ago. TikTok may be a new platform, but the techniques that work on it are as old as time. It's a case of old wine in new bottles. So what are some of the things that make a difference?

It starts with the thing Ariana Grande mentioned in her interview with Justin Credible and Eric D-Lux: eye contact.

Top TikTokers have the most amazing eye contact. They are not looking to the side of the camera, they are looking straight into the camera, which means they're looking us straight in the eye. And when we look into one another's eyes, it stimulates the most extraordinary physical effect within us: our oxytocin levels rise, and so too do our phenylethylamine levels, a hormone associated with attraction. Also, many TikTokers accentuate their eyes with a mix of make-up, camera angles and occasionally filters. Studies show big eyes and larger eyebrows are more likely to engender trust. Baby faces are irresistible. A video of a top TikToker's baby, @daeox, has had 390 million views at the time of writing.

But also, many of the top TikTokers hold the cameras really close to their faces so we feel not just as if we are looking into their eyes, but that we are doing so from a very close distance, very much within their personal, intimate zone, at a proximity we normally only experience with our very nearest and dearest, so we feel deeply connected. It doesn't have to be on TikTok, of course. When we look people into someone's eyes, we're showing interest and offering an invitation to connect. We all get this. Just as we all also understand that if someone is looking over our shoulder they are sending us a signal that they don't want to connect.

There are many studies showing how deepening of eye contact leads to a deepening of social connections. One researcher studying the effect of prolonged eye contact between opposite sex couples probably achieved more than he had bargained for when two of the participants in his study, randomly put together, ended up marrying one another six months later!

Connect!

The other thing all the top TikTokers do is smile fantastically well. Anyone who works in a service or sales role is quickly taught the importance of a smile. Smiling is such a simple and easy invitation to connect. It's well established that smiles promote trust yet so many people still go around in a right grump. A smile is not just an invitation to connect, it also provides the promise of good feelings ahead. When we see people smiling, the instinctive response is to smile back, which gets all those beautiful hormones flowing which make us feel good. Studies have shown this even works on online platforms like Zoom, Teams or TikTok. As laughter begets laughter, so smiles beget smiles.

This might explain why so many great leaders have great smiles, from Blair to Biden, Branson to Boris, Obama to Ardern. I always thought Tony Blair's smile was far more advantageous to the Labour Party than any of its carefully constructed policy positions, which partly explained why his successor, the intellectually gargantuan but intensely grumpy Gordon Brown, ended up being such a dismal failure electorally. Today, every time I see Jacinda Ardern flash her amazing smile, I can't help but feel a warmth towards her, and I'm sure millions of others feel the same: it's a natural human reaction. Smiles are instinctively irresistible. This also explains why signifiers of smiles are so frequently worked into brand logos – like Amazon and TUI – and product designs.

Smiles are universally understood to signify safety. Amazingly, even goats appear to understand this. Alan McElliott at the University of Roehampton carried out a study in which he put two photos beside a field of goats – one of the photos showed a person with a smiley face, the other showed a person with an angry face. Fifty-one per cent of the goats went to the happy face first, compared with 30 per cent who went to the angry face (the remainder didn't show a preference). And those who went to the happy face first spent longer there!

So smiles are important. The other features we see from the big hit TikTokers is open body language. Our body language is the most powerful metaphor for our mood and motives. We can instantly understand from someone's body language whether they are positioning themselves as friend or foe, and whether this is an environment in which we can feel safe or scared. By positioning our bodies as open, we are saying that we are friends and this is an environment in which we can feel safe. If our body language is closed, we are signalling this may be a hostile encounter and there could be threats around.

The top TikTokers' body language is open to the nth degree. TikTok started largely as a platform for lip-synching and dancing, so they're frequently dancing, which is often a metaphor for extremely deep, intimate connection, sometimes even of the sexual variety. Displaying such signals may not be appropriate in all work environments but there are many other ways we can show we are open, without necessarily busting out our best moves or throwing some shapes.

It's all about opening up the most vulnerable parts of our body. This is why the head tilt (which we see often on Tik-Tok) is so intimate. Our neck is the most vulnerable part of our body so, if we leave that exposed, we're showing we feel safe, which sends a message to others that they can be safe. Opening up our hands and showing our palms is also an important statement. It says we come unarmed, which is why classic informal greetings include waves or handshakes: they demonstrate we don't have a weapon. It's also why politicians often wave to an imaginary friend in the audience when they walk on stage. It shows they're not carrying weapons.

Sometimes when we're feeling insecure, our body language can give us away. Avoid self-comforting gestures, such as stroking your cufflinks or your wedding ring, something we might do instinctively if we feel under threat and are seeking reassurance. Likewise, try and make sure your feet are pointing towards the person you're talking to. Our feet naturally indicate our intentions, and people on the receiving end of a conversation are very tuned in to this, and will notice if your feet are pointing towards the door when you're talking to them.

The important thing is to be natural. I'm struck by how some people can go on presentation training courses and come out so stiff and controlled it's like someone has put a vacuum cleaner up their backside and hoovered out their soul. It's not as easy to say: just be yourself, and everything will be ok. The point is to make sure your body language projects your best self; if you do so, people are likely to respond to you by giving you their best selves in return.

Body language is endlessly fascinating and we're barely scratching the surface here. If you're interested in finding out more, I recommend you subscribe to the *Behavior Panel*, which meets regularly on YouTube to analyse the body language of people of the day. You can find them on TikTok too (@thebehaviorpanel). This programme brings together some of the world's leading body language experts, including my friend Mark Bowden, who's worked with many G7 leaders and Fortune 500 CEOs. The podcast is hilarious and incredibly insightful and so are Mark's books, stuffed with further tips for how to win trust, such as the 'eyebrow flash'. The eyebrow flash, a quick lift of the eyebrows to indicate recognition and interest, is universally understood in cultures around the world. It only takes a tenth of a second but it creates a real intimacy.

We've talked about connective body language through the prism of TikTok, but these same factors come into play in all sorts of scenarios: at work meetings, social occasions, in presentations or speeches. Eye contact, an honest smile, open body language. You can remember this through these three words: Eyes Wide Open. In a speech, a speaker arriving at the podium may well work through all these motions almost immediately, within a tenth of a second.

That's just the first tenth of a second; now we might think of the kinds of things we might talk about to deepen that initial sense of connection we've established. Before we get into that, there's a story worth mentioning.

During the 1970s, Robert Levenson and Dr Gottman created what they called a 'love lab' near the University of California. In their love lab, they looked at the behaviour of a number of different couples, analysing their body language, the way they spoke to one another, and a whole array of interactions, to see if they could predict which ones would stay together. They then followed up nine years later to see which ones were still together. Amazingly, they'd correctly predicted which couples would stay together and which ones would divorce with over 90 per cent accuracy.

Connect!

One of the critical aspects that informed their predictions was the share of positive to negative interactions enjoyed by the couple. With the couples that stayed together, the ratio of positive to negative interactions was 5:1 – five positive interactions for every negative reaction. Positive interactions included things like, for example, acknowledgement, interest, agreement, empathy, appreciation or amusement. A negative interaction might be an eye-roll, a contradiction, or a correction. With the Ariana Grande interview, there were more negative interactions than positive, which is why Ms Grande was on the brink of walking out. This was unhealthy communication. As we've established, this is not winning friends and influencing people.

Curiously, this 5:1 ratio is almost exactly the same ratio that politicians will classically go for in persuasion. You make five points that people can readily agree with (nodding points) before throwing in the tricky point. The idea is that people will have built up so much nodding energy agreeing with the previous points that they'll just keep nodding along. People like to look consistent, and you've established a pattern of agreement.

This suggests that maybe the 'shit sandwich' which is often spoken about in business schools, is actually a flawed approach. In the shit sandwich, you start with praise (one slice of bread), then you give the bad feedback (the shit filling), before ending with something nice (another slice of bread). This sounds reasonable but clearly it only represents a 2:1 ratio. If the Levenson/Gottman's 5:1 ratio is right, we need to surround that shit with at least three more layers. Maybe we should turn the shit sandwich into a bacon, lettuce and tomato shit sandwich to ensure it's more digestible?

So what are some of the ways we can connect with other people? Well, one of the first things is to put the other person first. To paraphrase John F Kennedy: think not what it is that you want to say, think instead what your audience wants to hear, and then connect with them using that knowledge. Studies show that 60 per cent of the time people spend talking, they are talking about themselves. This rises to 80 per cent on social media. Let's flip that around. To really connect with people, we must walk into their world.

This is the approach many hostage negotiators take. So instead of beginning a negotiation trying to assert their authority, they usually start with a simple question. *Are you OK, John? Do you need anything? How are you doing?* They're giving the hostage taker the opportunity to speak but they're also finding out information that might be used to their advantage later.

Flipping your role around from being a speaker to being a listener makes life much easier, instantly removing a whole heap of pressure. What's more, by giving people the chance to speak about themselves, you're giving them the chance of great pleasure. People love talking about themselves! Harvard researchers found that talking about ourselves lights up similar parts of the brain to taking cocaine.

And then, once they've started talking, really listen. Many people only half-listen during conversations, and are instead pre-occupied with what they will say next.

When I set up my business, I started recording all my meetings about speeches (with permission, of course). I did this because it was essential to ensure I could accurately reproduce clients' voices in speeches but when I went through the transcripts afterwards I was shocked to discover that there were frequently huge chunks of conversation I had no recollection of, chunks I'd obviously missed in the moment, usually because I was reflecting on something that had been said, anticipating something someone would say or already thinking how this might all come together in a speech.

To address this, I started practising a much more active kind of listening. I tried to focus far more on what was being said to me rather than thinking. I'd acknowledge, admire or interrogate a little further what they were saying. Sometimes, I tried to imagine I was in their shoes, that it was me saying what they were saying, which really helped me build empathy and begin to see the world through their eyes. Listening is key to great communication. As the saying goes, we have two ears and one mouth and we should use them in that ratio.

Active listening is also very much in our own interests because it provides us opportunities to find deeper connections, connections that we can use to convert the 'me' into a 'we'. *Ah! You grew up in London! You've got two daughters! Oh, you watch* Strictly*!* We can connect and find commonality over all sorts of things. A love of music, food, drink, family, travel, movies, theatre, newspapers, art, literature, or even swearing. Friends in common, views in common, clothes in common. Shared views, shared experiences, shared identity. Such connections are really valuable.

All the evidence suggests we like, trust and feel safest around people who seem like us. Around 2,500 years ago, Aristotle said, '[People] love those who are like themselves'.

Today, Edelman PR firm's annual global trust barometer shows the same: we are most likely to trust people who seem like us. We see this on TikTok as well. One of the reasons it has been such a sensation is because it is reassuring to see how similar we all are. It's great to see Hollywood stars or our heroes without make-up, loafing around in their kitchen, dancing goofily, or sneakily snaffling a slice of chocolate cake, à la Reese Witherspoon (5.7 million views).

Common connections

We all have more in common as people than we might imagine. Connections can be found with anyone. When my wife and I got married, we went on a year-long honeymoon, backpacking around the world. It was huge fun and a great way to start our marriage. We went from East to South Africa, top to bottom of India, from Singapore to Hong Kong in Southeast Asia and then right around the whole perimeter of South America. On our travels, we connected with all sorts of people, being welcomed into mud huts in Africa, rice barges in India and tin shacks in Southeast Asia for dinner. We found by the end of our trip we could make connections with anyone anywhere. There are three things that literally everyone in the world can come together over. Food, family and fun – no exceptions at all. Oh, and the Beatles, of course. You can pick up a guitar anywhere on the planet and even people who can't speak a word of English will sing along with 'Hey Jude' (especially the Na Na bit at the end).

Some points of connection are more culturally specific. In Britain, we have a peculiar fascination with the weather and this is often a useful touchpoint that helps people connect. The weather can also be a metaphor for expressing mood or motives and, in a country like Britain where the weather is so swiftly changing, it's a fairly fail-safe conversational topic and can usually be interpreted any which way. A recent study showed 94 per cent of British people have had a conversation about the weather in the previous six hours, with 38 per cent of us having talked about it in the previous hour! For all our differences, social, cultural, and financial, we all share in common the experience of living under the same sky.

The connections don't need to be particularly significant or forged by anything more than serendipity to help start or strengthen a relationship. A 2006 study by Gregory Walton of Stanford University found that when college students believed they shared a birthday with another student they were more motivated to complete that task and performed better on it. Over the last few years, I've had a few other people called Simon Lancaster get in touch with me, for no other reason than to be in touch with their namesake. It's intriguing. I'll never say no to a chat with someone who shares my name. We might have completely different personalities and perspectives, but it genuinely feels as if we have something incredibly important and personal in common – which we do.

These connections can all help connect a 'me' and a 'we', connecting the personal with the collective, the specific with the universal. As a speechwriter, this is invariably what you're always seeking to do at the beginning of the speech. You're actively promoting connections by emphasising shared experiences, shared perspectives, shared visions, shared values, shared histories, and shared ideas wherever possible. By so doing, you are emphasising commonalities, inviting the audience to belong to a bigger group than ourselves, which has a powerful persuasive appeal. Instinctively, we all know that we find safety in numbers.

One of my favourite stories is of Muhammad Ali giving a speech at Harvard University in the 1970s when someone in the audience called out to him to share one of his poems. He paused, looked to the sky and then replied. 'Me? We!' I love that. Just four letters and two words but it says so much and, in communication terms, that is precisely the journey we need to make: from me to we.

One of the easiest ways for speechwriters to turn a 'me' into a 'we' is by actively switching the pronoun from me to we. I'm quite often sent speech drafts to review and if the speech feels a little combative, I'll just 'we' all over it and it will make an enormous difference. It's the difference between saying, 'You've all got to wear masks!' and 'We've all got to wear masks!' When you speak in the first-person plural, you're speaking from an assumption of shared identity. Anyone who keeps saying, 'You've got to do this, you've got to do that,' is bound to get people's backs up. It's only a matter of time.

A comparative study by the University of Sussex of New Zealand prime minister Jacinda Ardern's rhetoric vs Boris Johnson's during the coronavirus crisis showed Ardern's go-to pronoun was 'we' while Boris's was 'you'. And it is fair to say that Jacinda Ardern won greater acclaim for her handling of Covid, with her 'team of 5 million', than Boris did for his coronavirus strategy. It makes a big difference, and not just for big leaders. Dr Justin Lehmiller, a research fellow at The Kinsey Institute, says that the language we use to talk about our relationships can predict a break up, pointing out that the pronouns we choose are 'a sign of how close you feel to your partner'. There's a world of difference between a married man who says, 'I love going to nightclubs' and one who says, 'We love going to nightclubs.'

One of the other ways that speechwriters will build connection is through showing admiration for the audience. In ancient rhetoric, Cicero used to talk about the idea of *captatio benevolentiae* – winning an audience's goodwill – through a combination of humility, flattery and gratitude. Such devices work very well in big keynote speeches, but they also work very well in social situations. They have the same effect. They make people feel good.

Me and We

I love your shoes. That was a great question you asked. I've admired your work for years . . . Christopher Korn, a post-doctoral fellow with the University of Zurich's Computational Emotion Neuroscience Lab, has found that flattery triggers the same reward centres in the brain that light up during sex. It doesn't even matter too much if the flattery is insincere. A 2010 study tested the effectiveness of compliments in which the recipient must have known the flattery was fake, and yet it was still found to have the same impact. It leaves people feeling good. And people will never forget these feelings. As Maya Angelou said, 'People will forget what you say, they'll forget what you did, but they'll never forget how you made them feel.'

There are other ways to make people special. One of the most obvious is to remember people's names. Our names are symbols of our identity and very important to us. Anyone who can't be bothered to learn someone's name is showing they can't be bothered about that person. And, unsurprisingly, people are sensitive to that. It's especially important when names are a little more unusual. The two most senior politicians in Britain who come from a Muslim background – Sajid Javid in the Conservative Party and Sadiq Khan in the Labour Party – regularly have their names mispronounced, both by colleagues and the press. Mayor of London Sadiq Khan's name is regularly pronounced 'Sad-eek' where it should be 'Saad-ick'. He tells a story about once visiting Wandsworth prison as Secretary of State for Justice and hearing somebody shouting out 'Saad-ick'. It grabbed his attention because no one called him that except for his family and close friends. It turned out to be somebody he went to school with, who had been sentenced to prison.

Connect!

It can be hard to remember people's names, especially if we are at a large social function, meeting lots of new people in rapid succession. A great little memory technique to make people's names stick in your mind is to create a connection between their name and one of their features. If their name is Ruth and they have big hair then perhaps imagine their hair as a great big roof. *Roof – Ruth.* From that point on, every time you see them, you'll see their big hair and be reminded of that ludicrous image of a roof on their head, and their name will come to mind. It's learning through connections. Or, if their name is Rick, and they have thick black hair, maybe imagine them with a black top hat doing magic tricks. *Trick – Rick.* The more absurd and incongruent the image, the more likely it is to stick. I've tried this technique a few times, especially when working in the Middle East or Asia, where names can be less familiar for me. I can confidently master a room of 30 people's names in as many minutes.

There are other conversational gifts we can provide. Jokes, stories, gossip, information, fun facts . . . . *You heard about this great new restaurant that's opened? You seen the new show on Netflix? You wanna hear some great gossip?* Different people excel at giving different things in conversation, so exploit what you're already good at, rather than trying something new.

It's worth thinking what gifts you bring to conversation. What are your go-to topics? What things do you do or say that really pull people in and attract them to connect to you? What do you look like at your best? You might even keep a notes file on your iPhone of the conversational goodies you've used that work. Jokes, stories and other delights. Keep updating it. When someone tells you a gag, scribble it down. When something funny happens to you, scribble it down. When you read something interesting in the paper, scribble it down. It's worth building up a list. Having interesting things to share is a great way to get people to lean in and really connect with you.

But what happens if, after all of this, after being as open and welcoming as we can, we still can't connect? What happens if the people we are trying to connect with are relentlessly and remorselessly combative, hostile, on the offensive? This is still a risk. We are living in an age of tension. The Argument Society. Culture War. Whatever you want to call it.

If in doubt . . .

I think the starting point must always be to give people some slack. Try and put yourself in other people's shoes. Many are dealing with mental health issues or other issues we may not even be aware of: bereavement, sickness, debt. Keep trying to connect with them positively. Acknowledge. Affirm. Understand. Empathise. *That must have been awful for you. I can see you feel strongly about this.* Often the people who are quick to go on the attack are the people who feel most under attack.

Another strategy that you can deploy is called pacing and leading. You start by going along with someone's mood or behaviour (pacing). So, if someone is being shouty, maybe match their shoutiness. If someone is being outrageous, maybe be outrageous with them. Match their body language too. If they're waving their hands around, maybe you should wave your hands about. Then, once you've matched their behaviours and connected with them, you can start to shift the mood (leading). At which point, you can lower the volume and calm down the body language.

We all have it within our power to change the energy levels around us. We do not need to take what we're given. If the mood is dipping, take responsibility for lifting it up. Any speaker who comes off the stage and says, 'Oh, they were a bit dull,' is effectively admitting that they themselves were a bit dull. We are all programmed to copy one another's behaviour. If we're lively and smiley, other people will become lively and smiley. If we're happy and confident, other people will become happy and confident. We are all instinctively inclined to follow people's behaviours and this is something we can all use to our advantage.

Often people just need to get stuff off their chest and feel hurt. Show you get it and keep connected with them. *We all want this over as quickly as possible. It's really tricky for everyone. A lot of people are feeling angry about this.*

When you're navigating through a thorny issue, always keep the conversation moving forward. We live in a world in which argument is regularly depicted through the metaphor of war. We talk about 'shooting' our mouth off, 'firing off' an email, of someone's position as being 'indefensible'. This is a naturally negative way of looking at argument because it encourages people to pick sides and go on the attack. A more helpful way to view conversation is as a journey, in which we are on the same side, all looking forward, trying to make progress, navigating around thorny issues, overcoming obstacles and getting closer towards the truth.

Me and We

But it's not easy, and it's something we all need to keep thinking about, especially as we are living in a fraught period in history for all sorts of reasons: coronavirus, climate change, international conflicts, incessant squabbles on social media, the 'culture war'. At the end of December 2021, Pope Francis gave some brilliant advice for couples who were feeling the pressure. He said that there were three words we should never forget in marriage: 'Please, thanks and sorry.'

You can't say it much simpler than that. And it ties beautifully with the advice that my wife and I were given in the run-up to my wedding 18 years ago.

Simon Le Bon, the singer from Duran Duran, urged, 'Don't be scared of compromise or if it comes to it, failure. BE NICE to each other and remember that for it to work you've both got to be happy.'

Lord Carey, the former Archbishop of Canterbury cautioned, 'Life is not always a picnic. Illness comes. Kids come with demands and pressures, jobs pack up and temptations come. But you say to one another "We belong!"'

Gary Lineker, TV presenter and former captain of the England football team, said, 'I believe that you should do whatever it takes to keep your lady happy, because if she is happy, then generally so will you be!'

Comedian Dawn French said, 'Agree on separate shelves in the fridge for your independent chocolate provisions and never pilfer from your partner's shelf. EVER!'

In summary, all of the advice seemed to come back to the golden rule. *Treat others as you would have them treat yourself.* Hopefully it's advice that Ariana Grande will take to heart as she now embarks on married life to real estate dealer, Dalton Gomez, having married in summer 2021. They were married in an intimate setting with just 20 people present (although the picture from their wedding got 26 million views on Instagram). And this is advice that I think is worth keeping in mind no matter who you're dealing with, where you're dealing with them, when you're dealing with them.

Always remember that the people you're trying to connect with are human beings just like you, with a need to belong, just like you; with a need to be involved, just like you; with a need to be respected, just like you; with a need to feel protected, just like you; with a need to feel safe, just like you. So meet those needs. Make people feel safe, make them feel protected, make them feel respected, make them feel involved and make them feel like they belong. If you do that, you'll be meeting some of their deepest needs and, in return, they are bound to give you all of the support you are looking for.

It's the golden rule, so do the right thing, which leads us beautifully into our next chapter . . .

Morality and Mundanity

Imagine you're a police officer investigating a drugs case at a college. A young man has been accused of possessing cocaine. All of the evidence suggests he was guilty – drugs were found in his bag in his college room and he'd been seen hanging around with drug dealers. The young man pleads innocence but it seems a pretty clear-cut case. So, what would you do? Would you arrest the young man? I suspect you probably would. After all, that would be the right thing to do.

But now let's throw in a complicating factor. The defendant was your best friend at primary school. You share with him a bunch of beautiful memories: blowing out candles on cakes at birthday parties as kids, white-knuckle roller coasters as teenagers, even going on double dates as young adults. So, what would you do now? Do you still turn him in? What would be the right thing to do now?

Admit it. You'd pause, at least for a millisecond to reconsider, wouldn't you? What once seemed a straightforward decision is now complicated because of your implied moral obligations to your friend. Yes, he's probably guilty. He probably should be arrested. But what about your friendship? What about loyalty? Doesn't that count for anything?

You wouldn't be alone if you allowed your friendship to cloud your view of the case. Corey Cusimano and Tania Lombrozo in 2021 at the Concepts & Cognition Lab at Princeton University tested people's responses to a number of scenarios like this. They found a sense of morality often interferes with our rationality. Our view of evidence can be dramatically shifted by the force of emotion. We often say that facts are king, but if that is true, then morality may well be the power behind the throne.

Power of morality

Antonio Damasio is a neuroscientist at the University of Southern California. He has spent many years carrying out research on patients who have suffered terrible brain damage – people who have lost the ability to experience joy, shock or pain – yet he's found that they still know right from wrong. So he's concluded that morality is fundamental to our decision-making, guiding our emotions and rationality. He's even identified the part of the brain that deals with morality: the ventromedial prefrontal cortex, which lights up when we are contemplating matters of morality.

From an anthropological and evolutionary perspective, it is easy to see why morals have such importance in our decision-making processes. It's morals that hold us together, creating the codes we all live by, the dos and don'ts of life. *Be honest. Do good. Speak truth.* We can all agree with these sentiments. Such callings guide us to the correct way in all sorts of scenarios, enabling us to distinguish right from wrong. We're all motivated to follow such moral codes, partly through instruction and experience, but also for the self-interested reason that if we follow these moral codes, we expect that others will too. It's the golden rule again, that notion of give and take, which is crucial for trust in society. We all understand the importance of morality. To think morality is anything other than central to the way we live our lives is literally the stuff of comedy.

In the HBO hit show *Curb Your Enthusiasm*, former *Seinfeld* co-creator and writer-in-chief Larry David deliberately crosses moral boundaries and breaches social norms to hilarious effect. Through the eleven brilliant series of this cringe-comedy, David toys with very similar moral conundrums to the ones tested by Cusimano and Lombrozo in their research. For instance, if someone tells you they have cancer, can you be honest about your deep fears that they may not survive, and expose your own (selfish) hopes for a future without them? If someone is embarking on a marriage with someone who is blatantly unsuitable, do you dare to tell them? *Curb* is funny because David responds to these dilemmas in a way that breaks basic behavioural codes. It's absurd to imagine anyone could act that way in real life, which is why it makes for such funny TV.

Our sense of morality lies deep within our make-up. It comes from a range of sources: our upbringing, schooling and background. Much of our moral thinking is shaped in our very earliest years.

From the second we're born, parents or guardians try to teach us the difference between right and wrong through a mix of praise and punishment. *Stop it! Don't do that! Well done! Good boy for telling the truth!* Of course, each family has slightly different moral codes and we quickly become aware of these as soon as we enter someone's house. *No phones at the table. No drinking before 6pm! No feet on the sofa!* Challenge these rules at your peril.

We also get our sense of morality from our schooling. Plato, the founder of The Academy, one of the earliest ever schools, argued that one of the prime purposes of school was to train children in what he described as 'the art of orientation', or what we might call today our moral compass. And this is a role schools still perform. As soon as we walk into a school, we invariably see posters setting out expected rules and behaviours. *Show respect. Be courteous. Be kind.* These codes that are then enforced through a mix of praise, punishment, example, analogy and stories.

We also get our morals from religions, faiths and creeds, if we have any. Most religions offer a rule-book for life. *The Bible says . . . The Koran says . . . Buddha says . . .*

For those who do not have faith, lessons in morality can be found elsewhere, including in popular culture. Early Disney movies stress a morality around honesty, hard work and humility, alongside more controversial ideas, for instance, that the only way a woman could achieve fulfilment in life was by finding a prince and riding off into the sunset. More recently, Disney is offering a new kind of princess, with a new kind of moral outlook: characters like Merida in *Brave*, Elsa in *Frozen* and Tiana in *The Princess and the Frog* promote courage, independence and self-expression. For some people, they are going too far. For others, they are not going far enough.

Hollywood actively seeks to engage our sense of morality. Movie companies now increasingly employ neuromarketing companies to conduct test screenings using fMRI brain scanning technology to check that the ventromedial prefrontal cortex, the part that deals with morality, is being engaged. They talk about the ventromedial prefrontal cortex as the 'money-making part of the brain'. Think of the moral ambiguities involved in your favourite programmes: *The Wire*; *The Sopranos*; *Mad Men*; *Breaking Bad*; *The West Wing*; *Fleabag*; *I May Destroy You*. Such programmes are deliberately designed to engage your sense of morality and get you thinking about what is right and what is wrong.

So morality is crucial. Everyone knows they have to do the right thing. But what's not so easy is working out what is the right thing to do.

Doing the right thing

When I was eight years old, my mum used to smoke around ten cigarettes a day. She had a stressful job and the odd cigarette every now and then provided, undoubtedly, deserved relief. But I didn't like her smoking. I'd read the health warnings on the sides of the cigarette packets. I'd seen the ads on TV. So, one night, when she was making dinner, I took her cigarettes out from her handbag and flushed them down the toilet. I thought I was doing the right thing. It's fair to say my mum didn't agree.

Anyone can tell themselves they're doing the right thing. Even the Mafia believes they are doing the right thing. That's

Connect!

why Martin Scorsese's 1990 gangster film was called *Goodfellas*. That was how they saw themselves, as Good Fellas. As Henry Hill, the real-life Mafiosi upon whom the film was based, explained, 'We were good fellas. We were taking care of people that no one else would look out for.'

Even Prince Andrew thinks he is a good guy. When asked by the BBC why he had visited the Manhattan home of convicted sex offender Jeffrey Epstein in December 2010, he said he went there because he believed it was the 'honourable and right thing to do'.

And, yes, even Hitler thought he was doing the right thing. His dying words were that the world would be 'eternally grateful for what he had done'. It's fair to say his prediction fell a little wide of the mark. There's a hilarious comedy sketch by UK comedy duo David Mitchell and Robert Webb in which they play two Nazi soldiers holed up in the bunkers of Berlin as the Russian Army invades. With hours left to spare, David Mitchell can be seen looking anxious, quietly contemplating the skull on his cap before the realisation finally strikes. 'Hans! Are we the baddies?'

Everyone has to believe they're doing good, even when they're committing the most terrible crimes. We all create internal narratives to justify our own behaviour. And then, once we've created that narrative, we'll go to extraordinary lengths to defend it, even in the face of overwhelming evidence that our behaviour is wrong. As social psychologists Carol Tavris and Elliot Aronson say, we prefer to 'cover up' rather than 'fess up' our mistake: it's more important to falsely convince ourselves that we have done the right thing rather than deal with the cognitive dissonance of admitting we've done something bad.

We'll then form ourselves into groups of people who will justify our sense of morality. We see this playing out *in extremis* every day on Twitter, where everyone groups themselves into their tribes, repeating to one another the same moral mantras.

We are good; they are bad.

We speak truth; they tell lies.

We believe in justice; they are cheats.

It's the argument culture/culture war phenomenon we explored in the last chapter but of course it's nonsense. Decisions simply can never be seen in such binary terms. Nor can people be defined as intrinsically good or bad, much as it might comfort us to believe that is true. As Obi Wan Kenobi says in the Star Wars movie *Revenge of the Sith*, 'Only the Sith deal in absolutes.' In truth, everything is a matter of perspective.

Social psychologist Daniel Sullivan argues that our motive for fixating on enemies is to avoid confronting an even more uncomfortable truth: that we are not in control, that things are not simple, that the world out there is chaos.

And the world out there is chaos, especially when it comes to navigating issues of morality. We speak in terms of 'a moral compass', as if finding our way through dilemmas was as easy as looking down at a compass and seeing which way the arrow is pointing. It's much more complicated than that. Morals can and frequently do conflict with one another, and often send us in different directions. Instead of having one single moral compass that guides us forward, it would be more accurate to depict a huge array of compasses in front of us, disrupted by some sort of magnetic forcefield which has left them all pointing in completely different directions. The challenge for us then is to decide which of these compasses to follow, which we do, but in a fast and fairly haphazard kind of way.

When morals collide . . .

Take an everyday dilemma. We're late for a party. Our partner has spent hours getting ready and asks, 'Do I look OK?' We look up. *Hmm.* . . . It's immediately obvious that their jacket clashes monstrously with their trousers. But do we tell them so? Morally, of course, it is right to tell them the truth: we all value *honesty*. But it is also morally right to show *respect* for our partner's feelings. And we also have a moral obligation to get to the party on time. So, one moral compass (*honesty*) points one way, the other two compasses (*respect* and *punctuality*) point the other. We form a quick calculation – 'Punctuality + Respect >

94

Honesty.' We check our watch again and quickly decide to lie. 'Sure! You look amazing! Let's go!'

Or take another common dilemma. You are invited to someone's house for dinner. Your host has put on the most amazing feast, but you are trying to eat less and lose weight. You've told your host this, but they insist on pushing you to have that extra slice of cake. 'Go on. It won't kill you.' How do you respond? We know that *self-restraint* is a virtue but so too is *respect* for our hosts and *gratitude* for their thoughtfulness for preparing such a lovely dessert. We form a quick mental moral calculation, then we see and smell this mouth-watering, moist chocolate cake, and before we can think anymore, we say, 'Oh go on then!' Yep, as we've already established, cake is enough to tip the scales of reason in any dilemma.

What about if you're on a night out in the pub, getting a round of drinks in and one of your friends says he'd like a pint of 'wifebeater', a slang term for Stella Artois, a lager. You wince and think his use of the term is wholly inappropriate and offensive, but do you call him out on that? *Hmm.* You know that if you do, you'll cause a scene and begin a conflict that may last years, and which will inevitably disrupt the social group. So what do you do? That's tricky. Twenty years ago, I didn't call out a colleague who noisily referred to Stella Artois as wifebeater in the pub on several occasions, and I've regretted not doing so ever since. Studies show we are more forgiving to people who are close to us.

That's the thing. This stuff is not black and white. It's really difficult and we frequently make big mistakes. And these are dilemmas we're constantly navigating, not just personally, but also professionally. *Can I work for a company that is spewing out carbon emissions? Can I work for a company that has a board comprising purely white men? Can I work for a company that promotes and monetises hate speech?* Viewed in isolation, these dilemmas seem straightforward, but they are far more complex when viewed alongside other factors like a sense of loyalty to colleagues and a responsibility to provide for our families. Instead of having one clear path to follow, our moral compasses point in all sorts of different directions. Our courage compass points one way, our loyalty compass another, our compassion compass somewhere different altogether. And this is the way of the world. The truth is that we can't expect our moral compasses to all point the same way any more than we would open up a box of drawing pins and expect all of them to point the same way.

So, in the absence of any single reliable compass, how do we find our way through these dilemmas? Not very well, in truth. In most situations, it's not practical to pause for in-depth deliberation. Nor can we ever hope to find the definitive right answer to these questions because no such thing exists. This is the stuff of stress and sleepless nights.

It is precisely because these moral decisions are so bewildering that we frequently look to our leaders – social, cultural, religious, political or commercial leaders – to provide the breakthrough, helping us resolve these issues, providing us with a sense of moral clarity we crave. It's like replacing our unwieldy huge set of broken moral compasses, which are all pointing in different directions, with a beautiful shiny, new GPS Google Maps which just emits simple, clear instructions to our dilemmas. *Head straight on. Turn left at the lights. You have reached your destination.*

Moral leadership

Since the dawn of time, people have looked to leaders to provide moral guidance. Think of any of the great leaders from history – Muhammad. Jesus. Buddha. Gandhi, Mandela, Reagan. Thatcher, Malala, Greta – all had (and have) a clear sense of right and wrong, and set out clear route paths their followers could easily see. Whether their judgements turned out to be right is a moot point, but at the time, they certainly positioned their motivations as coming from a strong place of moral conviction. Today, many pop stars, sports stars and movie stars fill their Instagram and TikTok feeds with simple moral appeals. *Do something nice today. Call someone you've not spoken to for a while. Make someone smile.* They make life appear simple and virtuous, which is welcome in this age of complexity and ambiguity. This moral simplicity is incredibly seductive.

We are anthropologically, socially and neurologically wired to submit to moral appeals. Because we all understand that society is held together by moral codes, anyone who rejects the prevailing moral argument runs the risk of looking anti-social, as if they are rejecting society. To keep the Mafia analogy going, a moral argument is an offer that can't be refused. Comply, and you'll win approval, inclusion and pride; fail to comply, and you can expect guilt, shame, rejection, isolation and alienation. No pressure then. And we crave the flow of oxytocin that comes from social approval. Oxytocin is described by neuroscientist Paul Zak as 'the moral molecule' and we all crave the warm, fuzzy sense that comes with knowing we're among people with shared views, values and beliefs. The pressure is off, now we can relax.

The most mundane demand can be made more powerful by connecting it to a moral calling. *Would you mind doing the washing up? I did the cooking earlier,* is an appeal to fairness. *We should go to visit Aunty Nora tomorrow. We haven't seen her for ages,* is an appeal to family values. *Don't be too hard on her. She's not having an easy time right now,* is an appeal to compassion.

The moral argument frequently proves the clincher in all sorts of arguments – personal and professional. *They're not playing fair. He needs to be more responsible. Just be kind!* These are clear statements to which we instinctively know we must submit. The moral dimension is frequently enough to completely change the dynamic in an argument, generating a new energy and pressure to comply.

The point you connect to can prove instrumental on basic political questions, like whether or not a rally should be allowed to take place. One study was carried out by the criminal justice charity Transform Justice in which people were asked, 'Given the risk of violence, would you favour allowing a hate group to hold a political rally?' Asked like that, a minority of people, just 40 per cent, thought they should. The question was then asked, 'Given the importance of free speech, would you favour allowing a hate group to hold a political rally?' Asked that way, 85 per cent said yes. Politics is often thought about as being a battle between left and right. In fact, it's more often about right and wrong.

Morality and Mundanity

This is why, when leaders need people to act in a particular way, they frequently connect their demands with moral obligations. During the coronavirus pandemic, governments around the world made unprecedented demands of people, demands that challenged fundamental aspects of the relationship between the individual and the state. *Do not leave the house. Do not visit your loved ones, even if they are dying. Do not go out without wearing a mask.* Making demands like these could, in other circumstances and at other times, have incited an uprising or a revolution. But governments around the world presented these demands as moral responsibilities. *This is the right thing to do. This is the compassionate thing to do. This is the courageous thing to do.* And it worked. Compliance with these instructions was off the chart, which is perhaps not surprising: people's lives were at stake.

But curiously, these moral connections proved equally powerful when people were being asked to act in a way that would spread the virus, potentially risking lives. People in the UK were urged to send their children to school, go back to work and spend money in restaurants in the autumn of 2020, long before the vaccine had been developed. This is about *saving livelihoods. We have a responsibility to our children, our employers, our community.* Behavioural scientists were closely involved in developing the government's messaging to drive the correct reactions.

But perhaps the most brazen appeal to morality came when Number 10 staff were found to be breaking the rules that they had put in place. When the prime minister's chief advisor was found to have driven across the country at the height of the first lockdown when he was actually infected with coronavirus, senior members of the government sought to excuse his behaviour on the basis he was taking care of his wife and child. 'Two parents with coronavirus were anxiously taking care of their young child' (Foreign Secretary – Dominic Raab). 'Taking care of your wife and young child is justifiable and reasonable, trying to score political points over it isn't' (Chancellor – Rishi Sunak). It was an appeal to family values.

Then, when it was revealed that the prime minister had hosted boozy parties at Number 10 during lockdowns, his defence was that he was thanking staff for their hard work. *Gratitude is a virtue.* By focusing on morality rather than the law, attention was being directed away from something which is inherently complex and ambiguous, to something which is innately simplistic and indisputable. Not everyone fell for it, but it certainly bought the prime minister some time.

The moral leaps we witnessed on coronavirus highlight how moral appeals can be used, and abused, as well as the potential immorality of some appeals to morality. But what it also shows is that, in any argument, morality reigns supreme. Arguing facts against someone who's arguing morality is like going against someone who's got a nuclear bomb with a pea-shooter.

In their book *Your Brain's Politics*, George Lakoff and Elisabeth Wehling argue that every political argument should start from a moral position. It does seem like good advice. You can connect almost any mundane argument to any random moral appeal and find it makes the argument stronger.

Take an issue like Britain's proposed new high-speed rail line, which will be the country's second high-speed rail line, known in shorthand as HS2 (HS1 was the link from London to the Channel Tunnel). HS2 is the biggest infrastructure project in Europe, likely to cost more than £100 billion and will provide a high-speed link between the north of England and London. However, as with so many large-scale infrastructure projects, it's over-budget and running behind the original schedule.

You could seek to defend the project with facts and figures, dates and timelines, lists of benefits and so on. But let's try engaging the ventromedial prefrontal cortex, taking three possible moral appeals at random – three which begin with C.

We could position this as a matter of *courage*. HS2 is showing the same courage as the Victorians who built the railway network. It's showing the courage that lay behind the invention of the telephone, the jet engine, the worldwide web. Now today, we must show we still have that courage that has served us so well in the past, the courage of our ambitions, the courage of our aspirations. *We are the builders again!*

Or we could make it about *compassion*. Think about the tens of thousands of people who are working for HS2. Think about the millions of people across the country whose lives will be improved by the new line. Shouldn't we think about them? Isn't it right we ensure that the next generation of rail users enjoy better travel than the last generation? Isn't it right we ensure everyone has fair access to fast travel, based not on wealth?

Or we could make it about *creativity*. Creativity has always been a great strength in our country. HS2 is encouraging a new wave of creativity, investing billions in finding cleaner, greener approaches in construction and transport, as we seek to create a new, clean construction industry that truly cares about cutting carbon emissions. Of course, major projects like this run into difficulties sometimes, but we are finding creative solutions to get the project back on track.

I literally just tried the first three moral appeals beginning with C – courage, compassion, creativity. Some work better than others – for me, the courage-based argument is probably the strongest – but they all have potential. It can be worth creatively trying different moral arguments to strengthen a fact-based argument. Once you've selected which moral appeal you want to pursue, you can very quickly assemble a collection of personal stories, historic analogies, quotations, jokes, facts and stats that you can wrap around the argument to press the point home.

A moral dimension can be used to strengthen all sorts of arguments in all sorts of circumstances. Say you are asking for a bigger budget for your team; instead of simply basing your argument on facts and figures, why not connect to morality? This is about showing *responsibility* to our team members. It's about having *ambition* for the future. It's about keeping *faith* in our strategy. The introduction of a moral element instantly gives the argument greater power. We must be *resilient*! Isn't it right we demonstrate *patience*? Shouldn't we show *grit*?

Such moral appeals can establish a good base of support. And, while our views on rational issues can vary, our views on morality tend to be shared. We might all argue about whether the company's strategy is the right one, but we can all at least agree with the need to show respect, kindness or generosity.

Morality and Mundanity

Connecting to morality provides a strong, universal and deep-felt starting point from which to move forward and build consensus.

It's not just politicians who must expose the moral dimension to what they do. Business leaders also need to show that they're doing the right thing. The world is facing a multitude of environmental, societal and economic challenges and businesses must also increasingly demonstrate to their customers, employees and shareholders that they are led by more than simply commercial imperatives. Many companies are now keen to demonstrate that they are doing the right thing.

Nike was seen as the ugly face of capitalism for many years in the 1980s, following allegations of child labour in Southeast Asia. In recent years, they turned their company around, establishing their brand as a force for good, taking a clear stance on a range of moral issues, including Black Lives Matter. In 2018, they marked the thirtieth anniversary of their *Just Do It* campaign with a TV advert showing American football player Colin Kaepernick taking the knee to protest police shootings of unarmed black men. The campaign was launched with a quote from Kaepernick – 'Believe in something. Even if it means sacrificing everything.' The campaign attracted the ire of some (including the then president Trump), but Nike's revenue went up 10 per cent afterwards and its profits rose by 7.2 per cent.

Uber was also seen as the bad boy of corporate life for many years, criticised for bad employment contracts, unfair trading practices and increased carbon emissions. The founder and former CEO, Travis Kalanick sometimes delighted in Uber's reputation, even enshrining it in the company's written values, one of which was 'always be hustling'. The new CEO, Dara Khosrowshahi, actively sought to clean up the company's image, abolishing Kalanick's values and replacing it with a simple six-word mantra. 'We do the right thing. Period.'

An element of morality can make a huge difference to a company's brand value. Companies like Ben & Jerry's have become inextricably linked with doing good, which provides benefits for the company as well as the consumer. It makes eating ice cream an act of virtue, which is good news in so many ways.

Good businesses need to know they're doing good things. We often think of businesses as abstract, anonymous, amorphous entities, but they're not: they're full of people who need a reason to get out of bed in the morning and give their best. A strong moral dimension helps them achieve that. Which is not to say it's not without risk. Companies that take the high ground can be easily knocked down, and there is a backlash now against companies which are seen to be embracing social agendas, with critics making the case to companies that if they 'go woke, [they] go broke'. This stuff is hard: it requires resilience, persistence and determination. But when you get it right, it can create enormous value to a company and a brand.

We've already seen how simple exposure to the Apple brand can now lead people to 'think different'. They're not the only brand to achieve this kind of effect. A separate experiment explored whether exposure to the Disney brand could lead people to behave more honestly. Participants were asked a range of questions in which they would be invited to admit to socially undesirable behaviours (as we all have in the past). It's a classic study of honesty. Some of the participants were exposed to the Disney brand beforehand, others were exposed to E! channel. They found that the participants who had been exposed to Disney were more likely to be honest. And perhaps the most important thing about morality is honestly acknowledging that this stuff is complicated.

So, we've established moral arguments are powerful in all contexts. We've also established that a range of different moral appeals can be made. But what are the moral appeals which you might make? What morals matter most to you? These are questions that I frequently ponder with my clients, when we are considering how to position a speech or an argument.

To start with, there are some moral arguments that resonate deeply with everyone, because they are deeply embedded in our ancestral wisdom. These are moral arguments which have tremendous power because they form the basis of our social groupings as human beings. Social psychologist Jonathan Haidt has codified five of these in particular, which he describes as our 'moral foundations'.

1. Care is good/harm is bad – which derives from the natural empathy and connection we have for one another. *Do no harm.*
2. Fairness is good/cheating is bad – this derives from the evolutionary process of reciprocal altruism, aka the golden rule. *Play by the rules.*
3. Loyalty/betrayal – which derives from our history as tribal creatures, forming shifting coalitions. *One for all and all for one.*
4. Authority/subversion – which derives from our history as hierarchical creatures. *Do what you're told!*

Connect!

5. Sanctity/degradation – which derives from our need to protect ourselves and our communities. *The body is a temple!*

Arguments based around any of these themes can prove compelling and universal. But I try to tease out from my clients which moral themes matter most to them, to ensure they speak from a point of conviction and authenticity. There are some exercises I do with them to discover these themes.

One exercise I sometimes do is ask them which five fictional characters they find most admirable – characters from TV shows, movies or novels. Then I'll ask them what attributes they most admire in them. That can elicit some interesting insights about moral priorities.

Another approach I sometimes try is to ask them, if they had just 15 minutes left to live, what would be their message to their loved ones? This can rouse some interesting answers. Sometimes they're a little predictable. *You get what you give. Pay it forward. Live each day as if it's your last.* Sometimes they can be a bit more unique and personal. One of my favourite answers was, 'Have as much f*&^ing fun as you can without f&^%ing up anyone else's fun.'

Alternatively, I might show them a list of different virtues and ask them to rank their top five, saying which traits they most admire in other people, explaining why.

Ambition
Courage
Compassion
Creativity

Morality and Mundanity

Curiosity
Discipline
Flexibility
Friendliness
Generosity
Hard work
Honesty
Hospitality
Humility
Humour
Independence
Innovation
Integrity
Kindness
Perseverance
Resilience
Responsibility
Reliability
Respect
Self-sufficiency
Serenity
Service
Solidarity
Tenacity
Thoroughness

It is intriguing to see the different way people approach these questions. These are huge generalisations, but in my experience different cultures do seem to place a different value on different moral callings. In America, there tends to be a premium on courage and independence while in Asia, there seems to be more of a premium on humility and respect. Right-wingers tend to value self-sufficiency and responsibility while left-wingers value hard work and solidarity. Those who work in tech industries lean towards independence and innovation while in energy industries, there seems to be more of a premium on reliability and responsibility.

What would be your top five from that list? Knowing which morals you give priority to can help you in all sorts of ways. It might help the next time you are trying to navigate your way through a moral maze. It might also suggest some themes you should speak to. Some of my favourite speeches are built around just one word. Respect. Resilience. Responsibility. And those are just the ones beginning with R. There are other possibilities as well. Humility. Honesty. Hard work. And so on. . . . Speeches which explore these themes are bound to release a huge energy within a speaker, and the dilemmas and contradictions contained within them can prove engaging and comforting to audiences.

Morality in practice

It can also be good for you to celebrate the morals that matter most to you in different ways. If you value kindness, and it's World Kindness Day, why not start your team meeting on that day by talking about kindness, sharing a story about something kind you've seen someone do recently and inviting others to share similar stories? Perhaps write about the things which matter most to you on LinkedIn, or speak to them on TikTok.

Celebrate as well when you see members of your team demonstrate moral virtues which you admire. Not only will it make them look better and feel better, it will also reflect well on you. If you choose to see people positively, other people will see you as positive. Just as, conversely, if you're constantly highlighting people's negative traits, other people are likely to view you negatively.

Connecting to your morality will inspire you and it may well inspire others. If you don't have a moral calling, try and find it. It could give you the energy to do something new and make a difference to the world, even if that's just in a very modest way.

Shortly after I set up my business, I had a call from Westminster Council. My office was based in Westminster and they asked me to run a speaking workshop for a group of disadvantaged youngsters in the borough. The lady at the council explained that these were young people who'd been completely excluded from the formal education system for several reasons. Many came from impoverished and violent backgrounds; some had suffered multiple and severe abuse. She couldn't promise that the students would be cooperative or compliant and warned the session could be quite challenging.

I walked into the makeshift classroom, a damp garage under old railway arches in South London. At first, none of the youngsters looked me in the eye, all eyes were fixed on the floor. They were about 14 or 15 years old, from a variety of ethnic backgrounds and were mainly, but not exclusively, boys. I opened up and shared a few stories about my own background. I emphasised we had some things in common

Connect!

and leant into those points of connection. Slowly, I could feel they began to relax. Heads started to lift. Eyes connected. Their body language started to open up.

I talked about some of the people who inspired me and then showed them a video of Barack Obama making his legendary speech at the Democratic National Convention in 2004. This was the speech that introduced Obama to the world. He started by talking about growing up with a father from Kenya and a mother from Kansas. He then talked about what binds America together: his belief that 'we are connected as one people', saying, 'I am my brother's keeper, I am my sister's keeper, that's what makes this country work.' He ended with the promise that 'Out of this long political darkness, a brighter day will come.'

I shared my thoughts and feelings about the speech and then outlined the speech structure he was using – MY STORY; OUR STORY; WHAT NEXT – a standard structure for emotional campaign speeches. I asked them to write their own speeches using that same structure. An hour or so later, those pupils stood up and delivered some of the most powerful speeches I've ever heard in my life. Some told stories of abuse, some told stories of friends lost to gang violence, some told stories of exclusion, alienation and abandonment but all of them connected their own individual stories to the universal story of the world around them right now, and presented visions for how this world could be put right. It was deeply moving. When the class was over I walked out through those railway arches with tears in my eyes.

Morality and Mundanity

But I also left that building inspired, with a new sense of purpose. I've since gone and spoken in dozens of schools about the art of rhetoric, walking them through similar exercises to the one that I took those youngsters through. The more I've become involved in this area, the more committed to it I've become. In my 2016 TEDx talk, I argued that 'Instead of telling children to sit down and shut up, we should be teaching them to stand up and speak out.' It's a moral argument that I strongly believe myself, but which also resonated with others.

Discovering a moral direction enabled me to connect with my business and my work in a different and deeper way. It's enabled me to connect with many other people who share that sense of mission: including in philanthropy, academia and even in publishing. The publisher of this book, Heligo, has a commitment to reach groups that have traditionally been underserved by publishers.

It's not easy. This stuff is hard. There are always tensions, conflicts and ambiguities in trying to do the right thing. We're all of us always balancing between profit and passion; money and meaning. But if we find something that inspires us, something that gets us leaping out of bed in the morning, something that we want to change in the world, there's at least a reasonable chance that we might be able to inspire others to do that as well.

INFLUENCE!

Tens of thousands of years ago, people sat around campfires, looking up into the night sky, studying the stars. And then they began to connect those stars, creating shapes and constructing grand stories of heroes and villains. Stories of Perseus cunningly using his shield to deflect the lethal gaze of Medusa. Prometheus courageously stealing fire from Zeus to bring to earth. Or Pandora, whose curiosity led her to open the infamous container that unleashed catastrophe. These stories engaged, entertained and inspired people to come together, but they also helped establish a moral framework, creating a system of values, beliefs and expectations that have influenced the way people have thought, felt and behaved ever since.

Today, of course, instead of looking to the stars in the sky for our heroic stories, we look to our screens, and the stars of pop music, sport and entertainment. Stories from the stars guide our values and suggest ways we should behave. When we see Tyson Fury getting up again after being knocked to the floor, we learn the importance of resilience, of keeping going, no matter what obstacles stand in our way. When we see Ariana Grande pluckily snapping back at mansplaining interviewers, we learn we don't need to put up with being belittled, we should stand up and speak up. When we see Jonny Wilkinson speaking candidly about his battles with mental health, we learn about the value and power of honesty.

But it's not just stars in the sky or stars on our screens who guide us, there are also the everyday stars who surround us – our friends and family, colleagues and clients, acquaintances and associates – each of whom share their stories with us, about how they overcame challenges in their life, how they managed grief, recovered from illness and maintained hope in the face of challenges.

That's what we're going to be looking at in this part of the book: the incredible power of story to influence how people think, feel and act. We're going to explore all sorts of types of stories – personal stories, historic stories, metaphorical stories. We're going to examine how they are told, how they are found and how we can use this mighty power to create change.

By the time you've finished this part, I hope you will have your own collection of stories you can use and refer to forever after, your own unique storybook. You can use these stories individually, or you can weave them all together to create a MY STORY – OUR STORY – WHAT NEXT speech, as Barack Obama did in his speech to the Democratic National Convention in 2004. After all, things didn't work out too badly for him . . .

Statement and Story

In the middle of 1993, the president of Procter and Gamble in Cincinnati, Ohio received a letter from an eleven-year-old fifth grade student at the Little Red Elementary School in Los Angeles telling the story of something upsetting that had happened to her the previous week at school. In beautiful handwriting, the young girl explained that her class had been completing an assignment for social studies, analysing television adverts and examining the messages. They'd been watching adverts for cough syrups and laundry powders and then an advert came on for New Ivory Clear dishwashing liquid, a brand owned by Procter and Gamble.

The advert showed women standing over kitchen sinks full of dirty pots and pans. The women then removed their washing up gloves dramatically and threw them out of the window in slo-mo, casting them away as a deep male voice intoned, 'The gloves are coming off. Women all over America are fighting greasy pots and pans with Ivory Clear.'

The young girl was shocked by the stereotyping in the advert, which suggested women were only good for washing and cleaning. Her fears were confirmed when two boys in her class started jeering at her, 'Yeah, that's where women belong – in the kitchen!' Enraged, and with the encouragement of her father, she wrote and asked the president of Procter and Gamble to change the wording of the advert.

The issue of stereotyping in advertising was not new, even then. Studies from the 1970s had exposed, explored and examined the narrow depiction of women in adverts as homemakers and sex objects, dependent on men and incapable of making decisions. No big companies had done much to tackle this, but this young girl's story struck a nerve with the president of Procter and Gamble, causing him to act. Within weeks, the company had agreed to change the wording of the advertisement. From then on, instead of saying 'Women all over America' the advert said, '*People* all over America are fighting greasy pots and pans'.

The young girl became something of a celebrity, appearing on *Nick News*, an educational programme on cable network channel Nickelodeon, where she looked straight into the camera and addressed the viewers directly.

'If you see something that you don't like or are offended by on television or any other place write letters and send them to the right people and you can really make a difference, for not just yourself but for lots of other people.'

The story of the girl who wrote that letter will no doubt have inspired, influenced and empowered many people to speak out. That's what stories do.

Her story inspires us to believe that change is possible. And what a remarkable young girl she was. Today, she is better known as Meghan, the Duchess of Sussex. Opinions on her are divided, especially in the UK, but it is beyond doubt that she is still inspiring many people to speak out about things they don't like or which offend them. We'll come back to her later, but her story demonstrates how stories can and frequently do change the world, both in big and small ways.

A single story on LinkedIn about someone being bullied at work can transform the way we manage and approach our team. A documentary on the BBC about the impact of plastic waste on a small island in Indonesia can change the way we handle rubbish and recycling in our own house. A powerful story on Instagram about someone acting with kindness might prompt us to make a phone call we've been neglecting to make. Stories have the power to change how all of us think, feel and act.

Stories and change

When we hear one another's stories, we cross into each other's worlds and learn what it feels like to live in someone else's skin. We don't have to be an eleven-year-old girl at a school in Los Angeles to imagine how it must feel to be an eleven-year-old girl at a school in Los Angeles. That is the beauty of story. It gives us a passport into other people's worlds. And it is by seeing the world through one another's eyes that we can create shared empathy and intention, breaking down barriers and enabling us to change and grow.

We all understand the power of story and we experience it in various ways every single day of our lives. But still, for so many people, in a professional setting, stories are all but absent. Instead of turning to stories, people instead rely on assertions, facts and statements to influence people. *These are the rules. These are the processes. This is who we are and that is what we do.* You walk into any workplace, and instantly you see the posters on the wall which seek to instruct. *We believe in diversity. We are entrepreneurial. We are FUN.* The posters can be beautifully designed with lurid primary colours and wonderful fonts and pictures, but they don't create change any more than putting a sticker on a banana saying 'I am an orange' causes that banana to change.

This is the thing: assertions score 1/10 for persuasive power. Let me demonstrate. I might try to persuade you that we need to do much, much more to extend opportunities for children from disadvantaged backgrounds. So let me try. *We must do much more to extend opportunities for children from disadvantaged backgrounds.* How persuasive was that? Are you moved? That's the thing. Simply asserting a point is unlikely to convince anyone of anything. It contains zero emotion and, without emotion, you can't move anyone. The clue is in the origin of the word – it's from the Latin word emovere, meaning to move, move out or move through. It almost has the English word 'motion' in it, of course, so that gives a sense of movement too.

So, let me try another approach to persuasion. I have two daughters, Lottie and Alice. When Alice was born, she had a difficult birth. She was born in a small hospital in Wales and, in the first 24 hours of her life, she was struggling to breathe. The doctors didn't know why she was experiencing difficulties, but she ended up being rushed into the neo-natal unit and was put in an incubator, where she spent the first nine days of her life. These were the worst nine days of my life. We didn't know whether she was going to live or die. My wife and I spent every waking moment in there. I was drawing pictures of her because we weren't sure she would make it through. I'll never forget that neo-natal ward: the bright fluorescent lights, the low constant hum and beeping machinery, the hard plastic seats, the smell of antiseptic, and the absurdly small thumb-size paper coffee cups from the vending machine.

But there is one other thing I will never forget: in the incubator next to Alice there were twins, and they were two of the tiniest little babies I have ever seen in my life, so small you could hold them in the palm of your hand. Their skin was as thin as tissue paper, almost transparent, you could see their hearts beating and lungs inhaling. And all the times my wife and I went to see Alice, not once did we see anyone come to visit these little twins. Not once. And, while Alice had her name on her incubator – Alice Elizabeth Lancaster – the twins' incubator simply bore the names A and B, and that's how they were also named on their charts, and on the little plastic bands around their wrists.

I asked the doctor who ran the ward what their story was. She explained that they had been born to a teenage girl from the valleys, a deprived part of Wales, and the mother couldn't look after them. I don't know the life story of the mother, but I could imagine her life hadn't been easy. Alice has recovered completely now from whatever it was that she went through in the first days of her life, but I still think about those twins from time to time. I think about the contrast between them and my daughter: how Alice had everything ready for her – her cot was ready, her room was ready, her family couldn't wait to see her, hold her, and spoil her with gifts. But, for those tiny twins, who knows? But let's face it. Outcomes for kids who are abandoned at birth are not brilliant. That's why I think if we're to do anything with our time on our planet we should try and make sure that kids like those little twins have the same opportunities we would wish for our own children? Don't you agree?

Think of that statement before: *We must do much more to extend opportunities for children from disadvantaged backgrounds.* Now think about the story I just told you. Is that approach more persuasive? Are you feeling the emotion? Will you agree we should do more to extend opportunities for children from disadvantaged backgrounds now? I hope you don't mind me subjecting you to that emotionally fraught experience but I wanted to demonstrate the power of story, and what better way to do that than through story. When I simply made the statement that we should extend opportunities for children from disadvantaged backgrounds, it had zero power. By connecting that statement to a story, we have made our argument irresistible.

When we hear one another's stories, we connect. We actively seek out points of connection between the story and our own lives, from the big dilemmas to the tiny details. *My child had a difficult birth as well . . . I was born in Wales . . . Don't you hate those little paper coffee cups as well . . . ?* These connections bind us together. It's comforting to know that we're not alone in the world, and particularly that we are not alone in our experience of pain. You can see people coming together as stories are shared. Their whole body language shifts. People look up, they lean in, their body language starts subtly responding to what's going on in the story, maybe showing signs of fear, disgust or distress. We see this in person, we see it when people are reading books, magazines or on their phones but it is under fMRI scanners that we can really see the phenomenal effects of stories upon our brains.

Stories stick in our minds

Firstly, when a story is being told, a mirroring starts to occur between the brain of the person telling the story and the person (or people) listening to the story. Uri Hasson from Princeton University calls this a neural coupling. Their brains start lighting up in such similar ways, you could almost overlap their two brain scans and see they were identical. When lots of people are listening to the same story, the effect is multiplied. It creates an incredible connection between people in the room.

Secondly, when sensory and motor actions are described in a story, the parts of our brain that deal with sensory and motor actions start lighting up. So, as I described the smell of antiseptic, the part of your brain that deals with smell might have lit up. As I described holding the twins in the palm of your hand, the part of your brain that deals with holding might have lit up. It's like we're there in the room, experiencing what the protagonist in the story is experiencing, seeing what they see, hearing what they hear, feeling what they feel. Our senses are activated and put on alert.

But, thirdly, when we listen to stories, two powerful neurotransmitters are released in our brain: oxytocin and cortisol.

Connect!

Oxytocin is the connection neurotransmitter. It makes us feel warm and cosy. It's the neurotransmitter that's released when we're holding hands, making love or when someone is telling us a good story. Cortisol is the stress neurotransmitter. It makes us focus and pay attention.

Paul Zak has carried out a number of studies into the power of story. He'll tell people stories and then ask them if they would give money to one of the other participants in the study. He'll check people's blood for oxytocin and cortisol before and after telling them the story. The oxytocin and cortisol levels indicate how engaging the stories have been, how deeply they've connected. He can predict who will give money based on nothing more than their oxytocin and cortisol levels.

So, stories are not just entertaining and inspiring, they also get people to give you money! It's the 'Children in Need' effect: it explains why television charity appeals are so popular. You swear you won't donate and then, 20 minutes later, you're reaching for the phone, tears streaming down your cheeks, credit card in hand. You just can't resist.

Oxytocin and cortisol also ensure the story becomes imprinted on our memory. According to Jennifer Aker at Stanford, we are 22 times more likely to remember a story than a statistic, but I really don't know why I bothered telling you that, because if the statistic is right, you'll soon forget it, but you'll remember the story I told you about Alice.

Now, my story won't have worked on all of you. Not all of you will have experienced a shift in oxytocin and cortisol levels – some of you are almost bound to be a little psychopathic – but, in most contexts, the story does enough to tip the balance.

Statement and Story

We see the power of story again and again in all sorts of scenarios, in the boardroom, at conferences, at presentations. Someone may just have presented the most carefully prepared PowerPoint deck, full of rigorously collated facts and stats, jam-packed with rich thought-through insight and analysis, and then someone puts their hand up and says, 'That's all very well, but the other week I spoke to someone at our branch in Rotherham and you won't believe what they said to me . . .' And BOOM. From that point on, the whole conversation is guided by the story. It's like the invisible hand in the conversation, imperceptibly directing people a certain way, and all those meticulously collated facts and stats count for nothing.

Stories provide one of the most powerful proof points, but of course they are not scientific proofs. A story doesn't establish something is true in the way that science does. Science can say for certain that water is two parts hydrogen to one part of oxygen: a story is only ever a perspective. And different stories can provide very different perspectives on the same issue.

Different stories, different perspectives

Take the issue of whether children should be allowed on social media. This is a contentious issue in which there is no absolute right or wrong, but it's an issue which policy makers and parents around the world are currently trying to navigate, especially post-coronavirus, with social media having provided one of the few reliable ways in which children can connect. It's a thorny issue. Different stories can swiftly lead people to reach dramatically different views.

Connect!

In my last book, *You Are Not Human: How Words Kill,* I told the tragic tale of Katelyn Davis. Katelyn was a twelve-year-old schoolgirl from Georgia, Atlanta. She did not have an easy start in life. She grew up poor in a chaotic household, but she found she developed a status on social media. With her own YouTube channel, as well as outlets on many other platforms, she regularly posted videos, sometimes several times a day. In some of these videos she would sing or share thoughts on spirituality or philosophy. In other videos, she could be seen arguing with her mother, alleging criminal acts. Sometimes she accused her stepfather of emotional, physical and sexual abuse. Sometimes she described being bullied at school.

Towards the end of December 2016, her videos started becoming more distressing. She'd discovered that someone had been catfishing her[5] online for several months, under the pretext they were in love with her when they just wanted to humiliate her. This had been her first experience of love, and the betrayal left her feeling distraught. On 30 December 2016, her followers watched online helplessly and with horror as, on a live-streamed video broadcast on Live.me, she put a rope around a tree in her backyard. 'I'm sorry I'm not pretty enough,' she said through tears. 'I'm sorry for everything. I'm really, truly sorry. But I can't do this.' And then, in full view of the camera, she tied the rope around her neck and hung herself.

A story like this would put anyone off allowing their own children on social media. And, indeed, that was the position

---

[5] Catfishing is when someone assumes a false identity or persona online in order to deceive or swindle someone else.

I took with my own daughters. But then my eldest daughter, Lottie, started pushing to be allowed her own TikTok account. She was twelve years old. I refused for months, but she kept pushing. *All my friends have got accounts. I'm being left out. This is SO UNFAIR.*

In the end, and especially with the isolation during lockdown, I felt I had no choice but to agree, but not without putting in place some protections. So, after a little research around privacy settings, posting privileges and so on, I gave her permission to have an account, but only on the basis that she would not be posting videos of her own. She could watch videos and she knew I would be monitoring the account. I also sat her down and had a big talk with her about all the hazards that lay online, from paedophiles to porn, bullying to bulimia, scams and addiction. She listened carefully, nodded her agreement and, after I'd finished, she hugged me and told me I was the best daddy ever. It was great. Job done. And, for a little while, I even felt like the best daddy ever.

But then, a couple of months later, I wandered into her bedroom to see her do the instantly recognisable slam-screen-shut of someone on a computer who's been looking at something they shouldn't. (We've all been there.) I demanded she show me her screen. She refused. After a little protesting, she relented. I saw she had been on TikTok, further examination revealed she'd not been on the account which I had set up for her, but a new TikTok account: an account she'd set up on her own, and an account to which I had no access. I saw she'd posted several videos from this new account. I was shocked. I took a sharp intake of breath.

Connect!

'I'm so sorry,' she pleaded. 'You can take away my phone for a week . . . a month!' I didn't answer at first. I was furious. Then I started scrolling through the videos she'd posted, one by one. Her videos were all short – 30 seconds or so, some less – but they all had a common theme: female empowerment. They were brilliantly creative, dealing with issues of misogyny, sexual abuse and harassment, showing Suffragettes, female footballers and speeches by Emma Watson, Malala Yousafzai and Oprah Winfrey – speeches that I had shown her and got her to study when we were home-schooling. One of the videos showed Ursula in Disney's *The Little Mermaid*, a movie we'd watched when she was a toddler, saying 'A woman doesn't know how powerful her voice is until it gets taken away.'

As I went through the videos, I felt such mixed emotions. On the one hand, I felt so disappointed – she had clearly broken my trust. But also, I was seriously proud of her and impressed with the videos she'd created. My wife and I have both worked in communications our whole careers and this was great content, and she was getting a phenomenal number of views – hundreds of thousands in some cases. But I was also worried. There was no doubt she had been sucked into the big, bad world of social media with all that represented. Some people were being abusive, even swearing at her. This was not a safe space. My every instinct was to scoop her and protect her, but I was also proud of how she was expressing herself. I wanted her to be a positive, confident woman with a strong voice, but surely I needed to punish her as well? She'd disobeyed me.

Statement and Story

My moral compasses were pointing in all sorts of different directions. I didn't know what to do. Eventually, after turning it all over, I looked at her and confessed I'd got this wrong. I said it was right that she posts her own content, and she should be free to do so without censorship from me, but that, in future, she should think extra carefully about what she posted, and restrict her settings, so her posts were only visible to her friends. I also took her phone away for a month as punishment. I'm watching carefully and keeping it all under review. It seems to be going OK so far and before too long I may feel like the best daddy in the world again. But we'll see.

Did I do the right thing? You'll reach your own conclusions. As we explored in the previous chapter, we all possess different moral compasses. I'm sure some of you will believe I responded the right way, others will believe I handled it badly. It's all about perspective. But, by hearing my story, you have now seen the world through my eyes, so you're much more aware of my perspective, values and beliefs. That's what happens. Researchers at Ohio University found that after we listen to people's stories, we are more likely to follow their values and beliefs. That's why it's so important we share our story.

For many years now, Meghan Markle has shared her story about how she influenced Procter and Gamble to change their dishwashing liquid adverts. The first time I saw her speak was at the One Young World Summit in Dublin in October 2014. I had written a speech for one of the other keynote speakers and I saw that she was on a panel discussion. I watched her share her story. She stood out from the other panel members, largely because of that story. As Kate Robertson, the co-founder of One Young World, said afterwards, 'She was so eloquent, so erudite. It wasn't your average actress stepping up and talking about gender equality. It was the real deal – very forthright, very confident and very uncelebrity.'

Meghan was not necessarily born with an instinctive ability in storytelling. She had constantly worked and challenged herself to get better. And, in particular, she'd studied the work of other great storytellers and sought to learn from them.

She wrote on her blog, The Tig, how moved and inspired she'd been by Chimamanda Ngozi Adichie's brilliant TED talk – *The Danger Of A Single Story*. In her TED talk, Adichie, a Nigerian author, talked about how, as a child, she'd only heard stories that told of life from the perspective of rich, white English people. She had grown up believing these were the only stories that could be told, so all the early stories she wrote were also of characters who were white and blue-eyed, playing in the snow and eating apples, even though she had no direct experience of that world.

She then started writing stories which were truer to the world she came from, as the child of a middle-class family in Nigeria. She talked about how many of the stories that people told of Africa were stories of failure, whereas the stories she knew were stories of hope, resilience and courage. In her TED talk, Adichie urged more people to share their stories, saying 'when we realise there is never a single story about any place, we regain a kind of paradise'. Meghan wrote in her blog how impressed she was by Adichie's speech. Her blog was noticed by someone at the United Nations who contacted her and asked if she'd be interested in becoming a UN ambassador on female empowerment. Meghan replied and said she'd be delighted.

In September 2014, Meghan was invited by the United Nations to attend a conference they were hosting in New York, where actress Emma Watson would make a speech. Watson, who played Hermione Granger in the Harry Potter franchise, made an emotional speech about gender equality in which she talked about how 'I've seen my father's role as a parent being valued less by society, despite my needing his presence as a child as much as my mother's. I've seen young men suffering from mental illness, unable to ask for help for fear it would make them look less "macho". I've seen men made fragile and insecure by a distorted sense of what constitutes male success.' Watson argued that men were 'imprisoned' by these stereotypes. According to Sean Smith's biography of Markle, Meghan was impressed by the relatability of Watson's speech and used it to create a template for her own speeches.

Meghan had also been inspired by Sheryl Sandberg, Chief Operating Officer of Facebook. Sandberg's book, *Lean In: Women, Work and the Will to Lead*, urged women to share their stories and Sandberg practised what she preached. She was a prolific speaker and her speeches were stuffed to the brim with stories. Instead of simply asserting that women were being kept out of the top jobs, she made her points through amusing and frequently self-deprecating anecdotes, such as this story, told in her 2013 TED talk:

Connect!

'A couple of years ago, I was in New York pitching a deal in one of those fancy New York private equity offices. It's a three-hour meeting and two hours in, there needs to be a bio-break, and everyone stands up and the partner running the meeting starts looking really embarrassed. And I realised he doesn't know where the women's room is in his office. So I said, "Did you just move in?" And he said, "No, we've been here for about a year." And I said, "Are you telling me that I am the only woman to have pitched a deal in this office in a year?" And he looked at me, and he said, "Yeah. Or maybe you're the only one who had to go to the bathroom."'

Meghan had seen the power of Adichie, Watson and Sandberg's speeches. She used the knowledge she had gained from these when she delivered a blistering speech of her own at the United Nations in 2015. She also followed the MY STORY – OUR STORY – WHAT NEXT structure. She started her speech relating her story about Procter and Gamble (MY STORY). She then talked about how women were fighting for equality around the world, citing examples from countries such as Rwanda (OUR STORY). And then she ended her speech with her vision for the future (WHAT NEXT), in which she paraphrased her hero Eleanor Roosevelt: 'It isn't enough to simply talk about equality. One must believe in it. And it isn't enough to simply believe in it. One must work at it. Let us work at it. Together. Starting now.'

Stories like Meghan's have the power to create change. Cultures are little more than compilations of stories told and retold anyway. In any culture, when we change the stories, we change the culture. We've seen this occurring time and again, all over the world, especially in the last few years when it comes to gender equality.

The story of Jyoti Singh's horrific rape and murder in New Delhi in 2012 helped to shift attitudes towards women and sexual assault across India, leading to the introduction of a swathe of new laws, including a mandatory minimum sentence of 20 years for gang rape and new fast track courts to deal with rape cases.

When thousands of stories of sexual abuse and rape emerged from Hollywood as part of the #MeToo movement, behaviours began to change there, leading to a number of high-profile convictions.

Oprah Winfrey delivered an amazingly powerful speech at the Golden Globe awards in 2018 at the height of the #MeToo scandal. She also used the MY STORY – OUR STORY – WHAT NEXT structure. She began by recalling her own childhood. She moved on to commend the courage of those who had stepped forward to say 'me too'. And she ended, invoking the new dawn imagery we explored in Chapter 1: 'A new day is on the horizon! And when that day finally dawns, it will be because of a lot of magnificent women, many of whom are right here in this room tonight, and some pretty phenomenal men, fighting hard to make sure that they become the leaders who take us to the time when nobody ever has to say "me too" again.'

The #MeToo movement spread around the world. The Danish entertainment industry was shocked to the core in September 2020 when TV presenter Sofie Linde dropped a bombshell while presenting an award at the Zulu Comedy Gala. She told a story about how she had, as an 18-year-old trainee, been told by a high-profile presenter that if she didn't give him a blow job, he would ruin her career. She looked straight into the camera and addressed her attacker directly. 'I'm pretty sure you're watching. You know who you are very well.' The audience was shell-shocked, but her revelation encouraged many more people across Scandinavia to come out and share their stories.

Stories have an incredible power to create change. And we all have the power to create change with our stories. Sharing stories is something we all have the power to do. Telling stories is fundamental to what it means to be human; to be human is to tell stories. Sixty-five per cent of normal conversation is swapping stories and gossip. But what makes a great story? You might say a good story has a beginning, a middle and an end (more usually a beginning, a muddle and an end in corporate speeches). There are definitely three parts to a good story, but there are a few different perspectives we can take on what those three parts comprise.

Beginnings, middles and ends

Let's start by winding the clock back 2,500 years to Aristotle. In his book *Poetics*, still cited by many as the definitive guide to storytelling, he said that a great story requires three elements: pity, fear and catharsis. Pity is where the audience feels empathy with the protagonist. Fear comes as the protagonist encounters some kind of problem or dilemma. Catharsis occurs at the point that problem is resolved, at which point we are absolved of pity and fear.

This ties in with the movie-maker's perspective. Robert McKee is a professor at the University of Southern California who has, over the years, schooled 65 Academy Award winners, 200 Emmy Award winners and 100 Writers Guild award winners. He defines a good story as 'a strong protagonist overcoming the forces of antagonism to meet the object of their desire'. Again, you can see there are three elements to McKee's definition: a protagonist we feel pity for; forces of antagonism that generate fear; and the pursuit of a desire which will, upon resolution, generate catharsis.

And this also matches what we learn from neuroscience. Zak's research gives us the chemical formula for a great story. When we feel pity for a protagonist, it causes the release of oxytocin – which makes us feel warm, relaxed and sympathetic to the lead character. The fear of forces of antagonism causes the release of cortisol, making us feel stressed, focusing on the action. Then the pursuit of resolution activates our reward networks, causing the release of dopamine, making us feel good as the story heads to the end. And that's it. That's the structure of pretty much every story you've ever heard. Data scientist David Robinson analysed the plots of 112,000 stories and movies and found they all follow this basic structure: things get worse and worse and worse, until finally they get better.

So that's what makes a good story. But what stories can we tell? Where do we find our own stories? As a speechwriter, the question at the front of my mind from the second I start working with a client is: 'What's your story?' But possibly the worst way to find their stories would be to walk into their office and ask, 'What's your story?' That's like the photographer who thrusts a nine-inch lens into someone's face and tells them to relax and smile. It has the opposite effect to the one intended. It makes them freeze! Instead, I try to create an atmosphere where the stories fall out naturally. I might start by telling some stories of my own, reflecting on my own memories or connections with the company, the date or the local area. Or I might look around their room for any apparently meaningful mementos – photos, awards, paintings – which might have stories behind them, and then ask about them.

But, if they seem in the mood for some creative play, I might ask them to do the 'Desert Island Discs challenge'. *Desert Island Discs*, for those not familiar with it, is one of the longest running and most successful radio shows in the UK, broadcast on BBC Radio 4. The basic premise is that the guests must imagine they are ship-wrecked on a desert island, and they have to choose eight songs they can take with them to this island: eight songs that represent different moments in their life. I started doing this exercise because a few of my clients appeared on the actual programme and I was amazed at how it got them to open up publicly in a way they'd never been inclined to do so before.

Doing the 'Desert Island Discs challenge' tends to bring the stories out naturally. The power of music is such that just thinking about the song can instantly take them back in time, making their memories much more detailed and accurate. Over the years, I've heard incredible stories doing this exercise, many of which are still imprinted on my memory. Stories from doctors working in rural communities in India, dealing with the aftermath of rape, abortions and murder. Stories from engineers in the Deep South of America about helping families deal with bereavements after horrific industrial accidents. Stories from bankers in Southeast Asia about their experiences of harassment and discrimination. All of them powerful stories which would inspire you to agitate for change.

- So, what would your Desert Island Discs be?
- Say a little about your memories of the song.
- Try and make sure you find a song to accompany all the big moments in your life: first love, first jobs, first successes, first experiences of pain and loss.

It's quite a fun and thought-provoking exercise to do. I have a playlist on my iPhone called Desert Island Discs which I'm constantly updating as different songs assume more or less importance at different times in my life, but this is how my playlist looks right now, together with the connected memories:

Connect!

Song	Connected memory
'Seasons in the Sun', Terry Jacks	Happy early childhood. Growing up near Hyde Park. Dad left when I was a baby. Grew up in a one-bedroom flat without money but a loving, caring mum.
'Another Brick in the Wall', Pink Floyd	Went to an inner London Primary school where I was constantly mischief-making, agitating and giving the teachers backchat!
'Bohemian Rhapsody', Queen	Won a scholarship to a posh private school where I discovered a passion for music and language and I made it my mission to become a songwriter. I wrote a song a day for years.
'Unbelievable', EMF	My first job was playing piano in a restaurant, making me convinced I was on the road to stardom! I sent my songs to record companies and the response was a universal 'meh'.
'Hey Jude', The Beatles	Reconciled to the futility of trying to be a songwriter, I started writing speeches for politicians where the same techniques proved useful. Will never forget being at the Grand Hotel in Brighton on 9/11, leading half the Cabinet through a sing-along of 'Hey Jude' on the piano.

'Something', The Beatles	Met my wife Lucy who also worked in communication. Instant attraction! We met, we married, we travelled around the world. She encouraged me to have bigger ambitions for myself: encouraging me to get a masters degree and set up my business.
'Papa Loves Mambo', Perry Como	Becoming a father to my two gorgeous girls, Lottie and Alice, was incredible and changed my perspective on the world entirely. I've always tried to be a great dad to them both. . . .
'Another World', Joe Jackson	My job gives me a great opportunity to travel and, whenever it's possible, the family comes with me. We all love travelling and have been to dozens of countries together. We learn something new from every country we visit.

Take the time to prepare your own Desert Island Discs. Maybe do it with a friend or family member and talk through your choices. It can be quite enlightening and, as we explored in a previous chapter, talking about ourselves is inherently pleasurable anyway.

But it's also useful to think about how you might use your stories to inspire, influence and energise others. Which of your stories could you connect to the moral mission we talked about in the last chapter? Which of your stories could you connect to your top five morals? How could you connect your stories to some of these points, points that we frequently have to make in a professional, business or social context.

MOMENT 1	– we can change
MOMENT 2	– less is more
MOMENT 3	– put other people first
MOMENT 4	– we can achieve more together than alone
MOMENT 5	– make a plan
MOMENT 6	– make a big leap
MOMENT 7	– have a big dream
MOMENT 8	– stay true to yourself

I can see instantly how different stories from my life could be used to make these points, but what stories could you tell to make these points with power? You sometimes need to twist the story a little, bending it around a little to fit the point, but pretty much every story can be connected to pretty much every point in some way or other. And these stories make our points so much more powerfully because they come from our souls. These are our origin stories. If I tell any of those stories from my Desert Island Discs, I wouldn't be able to help my lip wobbling or eyes sparkling, which show I'm speaking from my heart. Audiences respect that and respond to that. We start from a point of authenticity and honesty. Even if it's all down-hill after that, at least we started well!

You may be reluctant to share your stories and in particular to disclose private details from your life, and that's fine, but the deeper you go, the deeper the connection you make.

Statement and Story

Researchers at the State University of New York at Stony Brook, the California Graduate School of Family Psychology, the University of California Santa Cruz and Arizona State University carried out an experiment in which they put students into pairs and got them to spend 45 minutes chatting with one another. The students were provided with questions which got progressively more personal. At one end, there were questions like, 'What was your favourite holiday?' At the other end, there were questions like, 'How do you feel about the relationship with your mother?' At the end of the experiment, those students who'd got deeper and more personal reported feeling much closer than those students who'd stuck to small talk.

Some people feel afraid of telling their stories. Some of us have things in our backgrounds that we think we should hide. Some are fearful that if we share our truths, people will exclude us, alienate us, ostracise us, or think us weak. In fact, the opposite is true. By revealing our vulnerabilities, we show ourselves to be strong. Sharing stories brings people together, instead of driving us apart. And when we share our stories, instead of judging us, most people tend to look at us and say, 'Wow! You too?'

If you're new to telling stories, I suggest starting small, perhaps sharing your stories with just one person at a time, and then slowly move up from there. The more you tell your story, the better it gets. Instinctively, you'll start making improvements in response to audience feedback. You'll start elaborating and exaggerating those sections where people appear most interested, and quickly speeding up or cutting out those bits when they're not.

Connect!

But the power of story, once harnessed, is quite extraordinary. Telling stories is the one thing that can instantly turn someone from a 1/10 communicator to a 9/10 communicator. Instead of leaving people bored, all of a sudden they discover they are engaging emotions, activating senses and generating an enormous energy. And once you become adept at using story, you can use that power to drive all sorts of ambitions: launching a business, starting a campaign or making the case for change at work.

Stories don't need to tug at the heartstrings to be effective. I wrote speeches for Richard Solomons when he was the CEO of InterContinental Hotels. He sometimes shared a relatively simple story from his childhood:

'I grew up in north London in the 1960s and 1970s. My dad ran a car rental company, which can be a tough business at the best of times: margins are low, risks are high and the competition is fierce. I remember one Saturday in the 1970s, we were just getting ready to go out when the phone rang. My dad answered it and turned around afterwards and explained we couldn't go out any more. 'Why?' I asked. He said a couple honeymooning in Scotland had just broken down in one of his cars. He needed to go up there and get them a replacement car right away. I protested, but my dad was absolutely clear, so we ended up travelling to Scotland together that weekend. Ever since then, I've never forgotten the importance of always putting customers first.'

It's a simple story that makes a simple point. Customers first. Richard could have simply said, 'I believe in putting customers first,' but by explaining why he believed in putting customers first, he connected people more deeply with his own values, beliefs and background.

Our stories don't need to be about big life events. They can be things that happened to us the other day, things we saw on TV, things our family said, things that happened at work, customers we spoke to, suppliers we visited. Actively observe what happens to you in your day: what moves you, surprises you, makes you think and makes you laugh. Keep a journal or open a notes file on your smartphone where you can write down interesting things that have happened to you. Dramatise them. Improve them. Having a selection of stories up your sleeves makes you a better friend, companion, leader or manager. It can also help you influence people, and maybe even create change.

Aline Santos is the Chief Marketing Officer at Unilever. Unilever owns many of the biggest brands in the world – Persil, Dove soap, Lynx, Marmite, Ben & Jerry's and Magnum's ice cream. They also have one of the biggest advertising budgets in the world: 8 billion dollars a year. Aline is a wonderful woman and a brilliant storyteller who is using her position to create change not just in Unilever but across the advertising sector. Unilever was one of the founder members of the UN Women sponsored Unstereotype Alliance, formed to 'break stereotypes' in advertising and make advertising a 'force for good'.

Aline has made dramatic changes to the way Unilever advertises its products over the last few years. Now, when they show doctors on screen discussing soap, they show female doctors, because that's what you get in the real world. When they show people cooking in the kitchen, they show men cooking as well as women, because that's what you get in the real world. She is also pushing the boundaries dramatically in some areas and in particular markets. For instance, she put transgender people in an advert for tea in India. Afterwards, an elderly couple wrote to her to say that the advert had inspired them to reconnect with their own transgender son, from whom they had been alienated for 20 years.

Aline knows all about the importance of role models, fictional or not. In a TEDx talk at Covent Garden, London, she described how boxed in she felt growing up as a young woman in Brazil, explaining that women were raised to believe they could only become a teacher or a housewife. Her turning point came when she saw Sigourney Weaver on screen in *Alien*. 'She was amazing. She was the opposite of all the stereotypes that I'd seen before in my life. It was like Sigourney was looking at me, talking to me and saying, "Hello! Wake up! You can be whatever you want to be!"'

The story of *Alien* inspired Aline to change. And now Aline is using that story to inspire others to change, as well as creating and promoting new stories that are inspiring change, particularly within the advertising industry and business.

Which brings us back to Meghan Markle, an early pioneer in shifting attitudes in advertising. Today, Meghan Markle is still using her stories to inspire change, and not just change within the world of the advertising industry, but much more widely. For centuries, people in Britain have grown up learning powerful stories about the Royal Family: stories about the courage of King Henry VIII, the longevity of Queen Victoria, the stoicism of Queen Elizabeth II. In recent decades, new stories have emerged about the Royal Family, which create a very different picture.

In 2021, Markle gave an interview to Oprah Winfrey in which she made a number of accusations against the Royal Family. She said they were silencing her. She said they'd ignored her cries for help when she was suicidal. She also said that, when she was pregnant, there were 'concerns and conversations about how dark [the baby's] skin might be . . .'.

Buckingham Palace issued a statement on behalf of the Queen in response to Meghan's accusations saying, 'Some recollections may vary . . .' And indeed, recollections almost certainly will vary. Stories only ever provide a perspective, no more. That's all they can ever do. But, as Chimamanda Ngozi Adichie has argued, we should beware the dangers of a single story. Everyone has a story. Everyone's story is valid. Meghan's story is being heard. Is yours?

Past and Present

Pets At Home is one of the biggest, newest and most successful retail chains in Britain. Formed in the early 1990s, they run 453 supermarket-sized pet stores across the country, selling everything from guinea pigs to geckos, hamster wheels to hairball remedies. In 2019, they decided to undertake a major transformation programme. For most people who work in business, simply hearing the words 'major transformation programme' is enough to trigger instant palpitations, conjuring up images of management consultants marching in, armed to the teeth with PowerPoint decks, flash suits and clipboards, ready to obliterate long-standing processes, routines and rituals, and firing people quicker than you can say, 'Where's Tom? Not seen him around for a few weeks.'

We've all been there, we all know the drill and we all know how these things go. After the change has been announced with huge fanfare, doubts emerge, resistance grows, until eventually the whole thing fizzles out with a whimper. John Kotter, Professor of Leadership at Harvard Business School, says that more than half of organisational change programmes fail. The trouble is that whenever a change programme is introduced, three powerful forces of resistance emerge: fear of change, fear of loss and fear of the unknown.

So how did the CEO of Pets at Home, Peter Pritchard, seek to overcome these fears? Well, for a start, instead of calling his undertaking a Major Transformation Programme, he called it 'Project Kylie'.

Kylie! Kylie . . . Hmm. Now, different people of different ages will have different memories of Kylie – she's been through a few major transformation programmes herself over the years – but all those memories will be pretty good. People in their forties will remember rushing home from school in time for eighties hit soap *Neighbours* to see 'girl-next-door-Kylie' wearing jean dungarees and fooling around with Jason Donovan. Others may remember 'sex-siren Kylie' of the noughties, spinning around the dance floor to a thumping house beat in butt-clenching golden hot-pants. Some may remember the 'grande dame Kylie' who in more recent years has graced chat-show sofas.

By calling his major transformation programme 'Project Kylie', Pritchard made a powerful connection. He connected something people would naturally be fearful of with something they couldn't help but adore. He took his major transformation programme and sprinkled glitter dust over it, and it didn't cost him a bean! And, what's more, by putting her name into the very title of the programme – *Project Kylie* – he made it impossible for anyone to talk about the change programme without thinking of Kylie, making criticism all but impossible. It was difficult to imagine, for instance, someone standing beside the tea point working themselves up into a real rage, barking, '*I can't flipping stand Kylie!*' '*That Kylie's a total nightmare!*' '*Kylie's going to be the death of me!*' The sentence sounds absurd, like ranting against kittens.

Of course, the Kylie connection wouldn't necessarily have worked for everyone – some people might have an allergic reaction to this kind of corporate messaging and others may have thought not of Kylie Minogue but Kylie Jenner – but it certainly seemed well judged for the context, the demographic and the message of reinvention he was seeking to project. As Pritchard said, 'We chose the name Kylie as she reflects our evolution – she's the fun Queen of Pop, she's got an amazing ability to reinvent herself, which is what we're trying to do, and everybody loves a bit of Kylie.'

His reference to Kylie gave everyone a blast from the past, and we all love a blast from the past. This is why shops, advertisers and radio stations carefully curate playlists to match their audience's demographic, knowing that a big chorus from our teen years can instantly evoke memories and feelings of adolescence, getting people spending. It's why TV stations serve up endless repeats of shows we've watched before, because people don't just watch television for novel entertainment, but for reminders of sweeter, easier times. It's why *Friends* is still the most watched show in the UK, a quarter of a century after it first aired. Likewise, it's why, on social media, photos of old-fashioned sweets, cassettes or vintage phones guarantee lots of likes as they induce a sense of nostalgia.

Past and Present

Seeing the past in the present

For all the talk about mindfulness and living in the moment, the truth is we spend a lot of our time in the past. While outwardly, our eyes might appear to be focused upon what's in our literal field of vision, in reality, we are frequently exploring the world through various layers and filters. We have the power to exist in several worlds simultaneously. As I'm writing this now, in my mind's eye, I can quickly conjure up images from pretty much any point in my past or my imagination. I can conjure up memories of my first history class at secondary school and see where all the desks are, the posters on the walls, which friends sat where, and can even vividly imagine the teacher angrily stomping towards me to grab my ear. I can instantly summon up memories from the weekend, going swimming with my daughters, diving into the deep end with them. I can instantly remember the lovely granary toast I had for breakfast this morning, with melted butter and honey dripping down the side. I can stir powerful emotions and instincts by conjuring up these memories from the past, and this is something we all have the capacity to do.

We have a particular propensity to turn back to the past when we are trying to make sense of something new and perhaps confusing in the present. We do this instinctively: it's a useful way to begin the process of reasoning and understanding. We've already explored how we'll quickly form views on people's trustworthiness by checking their face against other faces we've known in the past, looking for connections. We do the same when confronted with new situations. If we go to a football match, the first thing we do is check the teams' past form. *This game will be like that game.* If we're thinking about which stocks to invest in, we study graphs of past performance. *This curve looks like that curve. GET IN!* If we're about to embark on a new relationship, we'll reflect on past relationships. *This relationship feels a bit like that relationship. GET OUT!*

Our brains instinctively hunt out these connections. *This is like that. Now is like then. This situation is like that situation.* But the danger with this approach is that we can make a connection which is flawed. If someone thinks the major transformation programme will be like another major transformation programme that led to job losses, then it's not going to be very appealing. But we can make connections which might lead their thoughts another way. The connections that we make are a choice. And the point in the past we choose to connect to is vital to determining how people will then think, feel and act.

The Roman rhetorician Quintilian said that the first lesson in rhetoric should cover the telling of history. Aristotle also commented on how 'We predict the future in relation to the past.' Cicero also advised that orators should begin their speeches with a brief narrative history section coming straight after the exposition and this is still a standard way to begin a speech. But how do we know which points in history to turn to? When we connect a point in the present with a point in the past, the possibilities are literally infinite. Peter Pritchard called his change programme Project Kylie and that was great, but there was any number of other places he could have gone.

Past and Present

He could have called it 'Project Moon-shot', connecting Pets At Home with John F Kennedy and the Apollo mission, citing Kennedy's ambition to put a man on the moon by the end of the decade, 'not because it's easy but because it's hard'. This mission has now been invoked by so many leaders to motivate people for change that the term 'moon-shot' now appears in the dictionary as a noun for a challenging and innovative project or undertaking. Many leaders tell the story about JFK visiting the NASA space centre and meeting a janitor cleaning the floor who proudly told him, 'I'm helping to put a man on the moon'.

Alternatively, Pritchard could have called it 'Project Burning Platform', connecting Pets At Home with the courageous story of Andy Mochan, a superintendent who was on the Piper Alpha oil rig when a huge fire broke out on 6 July 1988. One hundred and sixty-six crew members and two rescuers died in that fire but Andy Mochan was the one crew member who survived because he took the courageous decision to jump 30 metres into freezing waters. As he said afterwards, 'It was fry or jump, so I jumped'. Many businesses now cite Andy's story to encourage people to 'make the leap' and the term 'Burning Platform' is now regularly used as shorthand for a company which will face dire consequences if it does not move fast.

Or he could have called it 'Project Winston', connecting Pets At Home with the persistence shown by Churchill during the Second World War. This reference would have led people to feel courageous, inspired and on the path to victory.

Connect!

Alternatively, he could have gone for a pop culture reference. He could have called it 'Project Sgt Pepper'. 'Project Yoda'. Or 'Project iPhone', alluding to other big moments.

I don't think any of these options are necessarily better than Project Kylie, but my point is that the moments in history we can connect to is infinite, it is a choice, and it is one we should make deliberately and carefully. The connection we make with the past determines how people will respond in the present, often in ways that even people themselves do not properly understand.

There was a famous experiment by Thomas Gilovich at Stanford in the early eighties. He asked a group of 42 international relations students to imagine they were high-ranking officials in the US State Department who needed to advise the Secretary of State on a foreign policy dilemma, the facts behind which were set out in a briefing paper. The briefing paper explained that a small democratic country was being threatened by an aggressive totalitarian neighbour. The students were asked to advise how the US should respond, using a scale that ranged from hands-off/appeasement at one end, right through to highly interventionist and military deployment at the other.

The students were split into two groups. Each group's briefing paper contained slightly different, seemingly trivial pieces of information. One group was given information which subtly put them in mind of the Second World War. They were told, for instance, that the briefing took place in the 'Winston Churchill Hall'; that the current US president was from New York (the same state as Franklin D Roosevelt, who was

US president during World War II); and that the impending invasion would be a 'Blitzkrieg' style of assault. The other group was given allusions to Vietnam: they were told that the briefing was held in the 'Dean Rusk Hall', that the current US president was from Texas (the same state as president at the outbreak of the Vietnam war, Lyndon B Johnson) and the impending invasion was referred to as a 'quick-strike'.

Afterwards, when they presented their recommendations, those who had been primed with World War II allusions were far more likely to favour a strong interventionist stance than those who were put in mind of Vietnam. Not only were the students massively influenced by the analogy, they didn't acknowledge afterwards that those details had influenced them.

The past governs the present

This research was carried out in 1980 but it seemed particularly prescient in the run up to the Iraq War in 2003 when hawkish leaders on both sides of the Atlantic were seeing and making direct connections between events in the Middle East and the Second World War. On the evening of 9/11, President George W Bush dictated in his diary that the 9/11 attack was 'The Pearl Harbor of the twenty-first century'. Similar connections were being made across the Atlantic in the UK where prime minister Tony Blair made direct comparisons between Iraq and World War II, especially in his parliamentary speeches. In one conversation with a civil servant about Iraq, Blair said, 'What you don't understand is that, in this scenario, I am Churchill and you are Chamberlain.' It's hard to argue with a British prime minister who says something like that.

Even if Bush and Blair hadn't been actively connecting Iraq with Nazi Germany, members of the public may have made that connection anyway. The Second World War is a regular reference point and there are prominent reminders of World War II at the heart of both country's political capitals.

At the time of the Iraq War, I worked in Whitehall as the speechwriter to Patricia Hewitt, who was then the Secretary of State for Trade and Industry and minister for Women and Equality. In the two minutes it took to walk from her office at 1 Victoria Street to the House of Commons, there were at least four extremely prominent images of Churchill on sight. Immediately outside her office there was a photograph of young Winston Churchill, a former president of the Board of Trade. Then, you go past Westminster Abbey, where Churchill is entombed, with a memorial stone bearing the legend, REMEMBER WINSTON CHURCHILL. Then, as you walk through Parliament Square, you see a huge 12-foot bronze statue of Winston Churchill. Finally, in the Members Lobby inside the Palace of Westminster there stands another huge bronze statue of Churchill.

A large majority of parliamentarians voted in favour of the Iraq War but it's intriguing to imagine whether things might have been different if the symbols around the House of Commons had been different. What if there was a statue of John and Yoko singing 'Give Peace a Chance' in Parliament Square? What if there had been signs of more peaceful protestors around Westminster? Mahatma Gandhi, Bertrand Russell,

Mirabehn? What if the slogan REMEMBER GANDHI was written above the entrance to the House of Commons? Might parliamentarians have been minded to vote differently?

Writing now, at the beginning of 2022, there is once again a lot of talk about the Second World War, as parliamentarians around the world consider what action they should take in response to the Russian invasion of Ukraine. When President Zelensky addressed the UK House of Commons on 8 March 2022, he actively invoked Churchill's 'we will fight on the beaches' speech:

'I remind you of the words that the United Kingdom has already heard because they are important again. We will not give up and we will not lose. We will fight until the end at sea and in the air. We will continue fighting for our land, whatever the cost. We will fight in the forests, in the fields, on the shores and in the streets. We will fight on the banks of our rivers, like the Dnipro.'

One can only imagine how deeply these words will have resonated with parliamentarians, surrounded as they are by images of Churchill. That's why these symbols really do matter and they do influence the way we think, even on a subliminal level. This might explain why politicians so frequently turn to the language of war to talk about all sorts of things: a war on obesity, a war on drugs, a war on litter. The analogy can be unhelpful in all sorts of ways: it can repel many people and lead them to feel disempowered and under attack. But in other ways it can prove helpful because it grabs attention, establishes authority and the press loves it. One study found that 17 per cent, almost one in five, of articles in *Time* magazine between 1982 and 2000 contained a war metaphor.

Most recently, the Second World War became the analogy of choice as the world came to terms with the novel threat of coronavirus. It was interesting to observe how the war analogy developed, as our comprehension of the threat evolved. In the early days and weeks of the virus, there was very little war language, especially in the UK. A search of *Hansard* in January and February 2020 reveals zero references to war in the context of coronavirus from the government; instead, the language was all about journeys, with politicians talking about 'taking steps', having a 'four step' plan and this being 'a marathon, not a sprint'.

It was at the beginning of March 2020 when leaders around the world started actively making connections between coronavirus and war. They spoke excitedly about convening 'war rooms', drawing up 'battle plans' and talking about the 'arsenal' of 'weapons' they had at their disposal to 'defeat' and 'overcome' this 'invisible enemy'. Donald Trump described himself as a 'wartime president'. Boris Johnson said his was a 'wartime government'. Emmanuel Macron made a major speech around the simple refrain, *'nous sommes en guerre'*: *We are at war.*

Of course, we were not really at war. No shots were fired. No battles ensued. But the press caught on. In March 2020, there was a more than ten-fold increase in the number of articles in the British press that used war references,[6] up from 1,457 articles in February to 16,549 articles in March. At first, the connection with war proved controversial. Simon Jenkins argued in the *Guardian* on 6 March 2020 that the phrase a 'war against coronavirus' 'should be banned', making the rather extreme argument that 'never, ever, should a government use war as a metaphor in a time of peace'. But the metaphor captured attention and prevailed (much like Boris's 'cake') and now it is almost impossible to think or talk about coronavirus without using the language of war, so strong is the connection.

The connection with war undoubtedly brought benefits for many. It provided the media with a ready supply of attention-grabbing headlines, forcing people to focus on the issue. It connected with clinicians, who tend to speak about health-care through the metaphor of war anyway (e.g., they regularly

---

[6] That is, an article that included one or more of the words 'battle', 'war', 'frontline', 'troops', 'bomb', 'blitz', 'surrender', 'invisible enemy', 'killer' and 'siege'.

Connect!

speak for instance about *battling* cancer, *fighting* obesity, *combating* flu). It also helped politicians, providing a ready frame of reference in which the public could understand and back the taking of emergency powers, as well as unprecedented removals of basic civil liberties.

Most people accepted the connection between coronavirus and the war and could see the similarities, and the analogy started developing in all sorts of ways. Public interest focused on a 99-year-old retired Second World War veteran, Captain Tom Moore, who raised millions of pounds for the National Health Service by walking in circles around his garden. Pictured in full military regalia, Captain Tom Moore became a symbol of the national war effort.

Even Queen Elizabeth II helped deepen the connection between coronavirus and the Second World War in the public's minds. The Queen is not known for her oratory – indeed, if she has become known for anything as a speaker in her 70 years as monarch, it is being able to speak for long periods of time without saying anything at all – but she surprised everyone on 5 April 2020 when she delivered an incredibly powerful and emotive broadcast, every word of which seemed carefully crafted to strengthen this connection in people's minds between coronavirus and World War II.

She started off paying tribute to the doctors and nurses who were serving 'on the front line'. Then she recalled making her first ever broadcast to the world together with her sister from Windsor Castle during the Second World War, to reassure children who had been evacuated. She ended with a glorious three-part repetitive list which actively evoked that war-time spirit by combining the rhetorical style of Winston Churchill with the lyrics of Dame Vera Lynn.

'We will be with our friends again
We will be with our families again,
We will meet again.'

The broadcast was less than five minutes long but, as the *LA Times* put it afterwards, 'the Queen nailed it'. Similar plaudits flowed in from around the world.

The analogy with the war was powerful and it genuinely made a difference in the fight against the virus. In 2021, Professor Jonathan Charteris Black carried out a study to check the impact the analogy might have had on public behaviour. He gave people different pieces of text about coronavirus – like the Gilovich research on WWII/Vietnam we looked at earlier – and then he asked people how they would respond, based on a number of options ranging from carry on as usual through to putting their whole household into quarantine. One group of people was given literal text (i.e., no metaphors); the other half was given text that included words like 'war', 'hit', 'broke out', 'marches', 'attack', 'deploying', 'frontline', 'Blitz'. The group that were given the war metaphors were more than twice as likely to take the most extreme option, and say they would put their whole household in quarantine. So the war metaphor might have played a big role in making people stay home and stay safe.

After a time, there was little dispute that the war analogy was appropriate for coronavirus. Even Simon Jenkins, reversing his previous position, started writing articles about the 'political battleground' of coronavirus. However, there were other aspects of coronavirus where the correct analogy was not so easy to find, and it became a source of contention.

For instance, when coronavirus first emerged, no one could quite be sure what it was. The best way scientists could, at first, make sense of it was by finding something from the past it was similar to. But different scientists connected to different points in history. Some said coronavirus was like the Spanish flu of 1918. With that in mind, they instantly saw the need for governments to impose extreme measures, anticipating a once-in-a-century global catastrophe, potentially resulting in millions of deaths. Many Asian countries, on the other hand, saw coronavirus as another version of SARS, which they were only just recovering from, so they were swift to introduce tough restrictions. Others viewed coronavirus as being not much different to seasonal flu, i.e., nothing scary here, business as usual, which was the line taken by the UK government in the early days.

When it came to the introduction of the vaccine, again, different people made different connections. Those who were instinctively in favour of the vaccine connected it with the fantastically successful smallpox and typhoid vaccines, which had represented enormous steps forward for civilisation, saving millions of lives. Sceptics, on the other hand, feared the vaccine might be more like the 1976 swine flu vaccine, which was quickly developed and rushed out pre-election by Gerald Ford in the United States, but which was later linked with hundreds of cases of Guillain-Barré syndrome, which can cause paralysis, respiratory arrest and death. Or the infamous 1955 Cutter polio vaccine in which hundreds of thousands of children were inadvertently injected with live polio, causing 40,000 to develop abortive poliomyelitis.

All of these analogies are tendentious and arguably misleading, and also, to some extent, self-serving and political. In actual fact, every situation is unique, and different to anything that has happened before. But reaching for analogies is not necessarily a bad thing. Considering and eliminating different analogies can be a very helpful way to solve problems, even for some of the brightest brains on the planet.

One study analysed the way that scientists discussed the problems with the rovers on Mars. As the scientists pondered and probed the issues, they worked their way through a whopping 94 different analogies. The researchers found that there was a clear correlation between the levels of uncertainty expressed in the conversation (measured by use of hesitant terms like 'I guess', 'I think' and 'maybe') and the use of analogy. This does suggest that the more doubtful we are about something, the more likely we are to reach for an analogy.

Likewise, when the Iraq War was debated in Congress, an astonishing 72 different analogies were used. Another study of the press reporting of global disasters – including the 9/11 attacks on the Twin Towers, the terrorist attack on the Taj Mahal Palace Hotel in India and the anti-Mubarak demonstrations in Egypt in 2011 – found 881 different historical analogies. Almost every article contained a new analogy. That's an awful lot of analogies.

Connect!

Some people object to the use of analogies, like Elon Musk who has argued we should take care to 'reason from first principles rather than by analogy. The normal way we conduct our lives is we reason by analogy. We are doing this because it's like something else that was done. Or it is like what other people are doing.' He argues we should boil things down to the most fundamental truths and then reason up from there. That can work, but we do naturally reason through analogy, and when you find an analogy that works, it can provide a critical breakthrough on difficult problems.

For example, take this medical dilemma:

Suppose you are a doctor faced with a patient who has a malignant tumour in his stomach. It is impossible to operate on the patient, but unless the tumour is destroyed the patient will die. There is a kind of ray that can be used to destroy the tumour. If the rays reach the tumour all at once at a sufficiently high intensity, the tumour will be destroyed. Unfortunately, at this intensity the healthy tissue that the rays pass through on the way to the tumour will also be destroyed. At lower intensities the rays are harmless to healthy tissue, but they will not affect the tumour. What type of procedure might be used to destroy the tumour with the rays, and at the same time avoid destroying the healthy tissue?

When the dilemma is presented like that, it's hard to find a solution. In fact, when Mary L Gick and Keith J Holyoak put it to the test, just 8 per cent of students could find a solution. But then the students were provided with an analogy:

Past and Present

A general wishes to capture a fortress in the centre of a country. There are a number of roads radiating outwards from the fortress. All have been mined so that while small groups of men can pass over the roads safely, any large force will detonate the mines. A full-scale direct attack is therefore impossible. The general's solution is to divide his army into small groups and then converge simultaneously on the fortress.

They were told that this story could provide a solution to the radiation problem. After being presented with the attack dispersion story, 92 per cent of people were able to find a solution to the problem.

That's the power of making connections. Through making connections between one thing and another thing we can change how people think and make something which is otherwise incomprehensible, comprehensible. But we can also change how people feel. Like with Project Kylie, we can make something scary into something sexy.

Power over the past is power over the present

And the beauty is that we can connect anything with anything else. We can connect the most desperately dull processes and programmes with the most glamorous and greatest sports stars, movie stars, scientists, doctors, revolutionaries, writers, artists, entrepreneurs, inventors and explorers in history. A sales team outperforming sales targets might be like Muhammad Ali knocking down George Foreman in the Rumble in the Jungle, Simone Biles winning a string of gold medals at the 2016 Olympics, or Lady Gaga performing at Joe Biden's inauguration. Completing the annual report might be like climbing Everest, touching the moon, colonising Mars. And the most desperately dull teams could become like BTS, the Suffragettes or gangsters in Capone's Chicago. It's all about finding connections which suit the moods we wish to convey and having the courage to make them.

As we've seen already, Steve Jobs often made connections between Apple and the Beatles, and he used this in many ways. He played Beatles songs during Apple launches. When Jobs appeared on a panel with Bill Gates, he characterised their relationship by quoting from the Beatles song 'Two of Us'.[7] Some of the sounds on the computer were based on connections with the Beatles (the big chord that sounds as the Mac starts up was based on the famous final chord at the end of the song 'A Day in the Life'). And sometimes Jobs would tell people stories about the Beatles.

The Walter Isaacson biography of Jobs records one occasion when he played bootlegs of the Beatles' demo recordings of 'Strawberry Fields Forever' to explain how their work as a band had influenced the creative process at Apple, commentating as the recordings played, 'They were such perfectionists. They kept going and going. This made a big impression on me when I was in my thirties. They did a bundle of work between each recording. They kept sending it back to make it closer to perfect. The way we build stuff at Apple is often this way. It's a lot of work, but in the end it

---

[7] Bill Gates, touched by what Jobs said, made 'Two of Us' one of his Desert Island Discs when he appeared on the show in 2016.

just gets better and soon it's like, "Wow! How did they do that?! Where are the screws?'"

Dream dinner party

The Beatles was an authentic connection point for Steve Jobs to make, because he was a huge Beatles fan. But what connections can you make?

I have a little exercise that I run through with my clients to help identify potential connection points which are meaningful to them. You've probably done something similar before, for fun. I ask them to write out their list of their dream dinner party. They have eight seats around the table. They can invite anyone at all, living or dead. Who would they invite? Why don't you give it a try? Who would come to your dream dinner party?

I've never had a client who didn't really enjoy doing this exercise. They will merrily start scribbling on a napkin in a restaurant or tapping on their phone as we travel. It provides an invariably welcome opportunity for reflection.

It's interesting seeing my clients work through the exercise. They take it very seriously and seem keen to check off all their different interests, marking off the different parts of their identity. Sometimes, they come up with quite obscure people – eighteenth-century Romantic painters, nineteenth-century philanthropists, or twentieth-century ice-hockey players I've never heard of, meaning I then have to order in a stack of biographies. I always try to encourage them to come up with the most diverse list possible, drawing in people from different fields, backgrounds and cultures. Sometimes they come up with more surprising names, perhaps calling out a revolutionary or a gangster rapper, which is exciting, because it says something I didn't know about them before, and that's kind of the point. These connections can help us see people and situations afresh.

I keep my own dream dinner party as a notes file on my phone and update it from time to time. It's only ever a snapshot, a moment in time but right here and now this is who I'd have at my dream dinner party:

John Lennon
The Queen
George Orwell
Malala Yousafzai
Meghan Markle
George Lucas
Steve Jobs
Muhammad Ali

They're all there for different reasons. Some I am huge fans of, others I'm more curious about and would want to interrogate. I'm forever amending and adjusting mine. But these are some of my regular go-tos.

The dinner party list provides a ready source of connections. As with our Desert Island Discs challenge, you can instantly see how you could make random connections between my heroes and all sorts of points we must often make in a business context about the need for innovation, collaboration, purpose, trust, focus, diversity, sustainability and so on.

Past and Present

We can make these connections in a number of ways.

We could simply refer to our heroes. We might say that someone with entrepreneurial traits is the new Steve Jobs, a fledgling campaign group might be compared with the Suffragettes, or an up-and-coming politician might be compared with Barack Obama.

Such a connection can work wonders for a person's self-esteem, but it can also change the way others perceive them, even experts. Thomas Gilovich, the researcher behind the Second World War/Vietnam study we looked at earlier, also did experiments on how connections like these work in relation to sports stars. He got a group of sports journalists to rate the prospects of unknown college football players, based on brief profiles of those players. The researchers then manipulated those players' profiles. Some of the players were actively connected to brilliant players from the past (for instance highlighting they shared a birth date or the home town of a brilliant player) while others were not. All of the sports journalists who took part in the study gave higher ratings to the players who shared these connections, even though of course rationally it would not make any difference at all to their potential as a player.

One of the other ways in which we can make connections with our dream dinner party guests is by quoting them. Quoting great people is like bringing back witnesses from the past to support our case. It's like having Walt Disney, Margaret Thatcher or Steve Jobs stand alongside you saying, 'This dude knows what he's talking about.' It's really powerful. The more obscure quotes are sometimes the more intriguing. Everyone knows about George Lucas's incredible work on *Star Wars* but his thoughts on innovation are less well known, but are no less intriguing.

One thing that can work well is when we tell stories from the lives of people on our dream dinner party list. We've already explored the amazing power of story. Stories from history can prove very compelling, because when we are sharing stories about people we really admire, our eyes will light up and we'll speak with a passion that might not necessarily be there if we're speaking about business process re-engineering.

One top businessman I've worked with is Roberto Funari, who has worked at a number of big companies over the years. I remember when I first met him, I noticed he had a signed Pelé shirt on his office wall. During our meeting, we were talking about the marketing strategy he was launching, but I couldn't take my eyes off that Pelé shirt. In the end, we decided to open his speech by referencing it.

'Last Christmas, my mother got me the best Christmas present that any Brazilian could ever hope to receive – a signed Pelé shirt. I remember growing up as a kid on the streets of Rio watching Pelé score amazing goals like this [show video]. You see what is going on there? He has the opposing team running at him, his own teammates are calling at him, trying to catch his eye, but not once does he take his eye off the ball. Ladies and gentlemen, this is our problem. In the last few years, we've taken our eye off the ball. The ball is the customer and I'm here to make sure we get our eye back on the ball and that is why I'm launching this strategy today.'

He then ran through the eleven points in the strategy, showing the numbers on football shirts, before rounding off the speech with a Pelé quote: 'Success is no accident. It is hard work, perseverance, learning, studying, sacrifice and, most of all, love of what you are doing or learning to do.'

BOOM! The connection was made. The neurons fired together; the neurons wired together. While the 'eye on the ball' metaphor was hardly original, sharing this story in this way meant that, from that point on, whenever the marketing strategy was mentioned, straight away everyone was thinking of Pelé, with all the glamour and excitement that involved. The audience loved it, so did Funari.

In 2019, he became the CEO of Alpargatas, which makes Havaianas shoes, selling 250 million pairs a year. Havaianas is studied as a textbook case on how to turn a mass-market brand into an aspirational one. On his appointment, Funari gave an interview with *Forbes India* in which he described Havaianas as the most iconic Brazilian brand after Pelé.

Funari's use of video was especially effective in his speech because we live in an age where everyone's used to rapidly consuming captivating content on TikTok or YouTube. Replicating that pace and excitement in a presentation keeps people engaged. So, keep an eye out for little clips that you can use to support business points like resilience, collaboration or evolution. They can really make a point land well in people's minds, with imagery that sticks forever.

I remember once writing a speech for a CEO whose colleagues were fearful the company was slipping back. We found a video of Australian ice-skater Steven Bradbury's stunning 1,000-metre win at the Winter Olympics 2002 and told his story. Bradbury was never a favourite to win gold. He hadn't even expected to be in the finals. He only made it through because so many people had fallen out or been disqualified along the way. Everyone expected Apollo Ono from America to win and indeed Apollo Ono had been leading right through the race. Then, on the final lap, literally just yards from the finish line, skaters representing China, South Korea and Canada smashed into Apollo Ono and Steven Bradbury went flying through to seize gold. The video is amazing to watch and it makes an important point about the power of persistence and patience. It also makes people feel excited and confident.

It's not just sporting stories that work well. Sometimes there are stories from the news that can be used to make powerful points. There was an incredible incident in London in 2015 when a circus unicyclist, Anthony Shields (also known as Wonder Nose), was run over by a bus and was trapped underneath it, severely injured. Incredibly, dozens of commuters stepped forward and lifted the 10-ton bus, helping him out. The video is breath-taking and of course this also makes an important point, about what we can all achieve when we do the heavy lifting together.

Connections can be made with all sorts of things. Little clips from nature programmes, history programmes, travel programmes and so on can all be used to land big points in a memorable way, and this can be a good alternative for those who are more uncomfortable with the personal story. So, keep an eye out for inspiring clips when you're scanning social media. You never know when they could come in handy.

Analogies do not need to be too far-fetched to be effective. Sometimes, it can be more effective to reach for an analogy which is more closely related to the issue in time.

For instance, going back to Pets At Home, Pete Pritchard might well have drawn an analogy between how Pets At Home needed to innovate and how energy companies had innovated in recent years. Or he might have asked 'What would Elon Musk do if he ran Pets at Home?' Or he might have drawn analogies with HMV's failure as a retailer because they failed to innovate and the dangers of Pets At Home failing to innovate. But, to get people really excited about change, I still think there could scarcely be any better option than Kylie and her butt-clenching golden hot-pants.

This and That

& Juliet is one of the most successful musicals to have opened in London's West End in recent years. Combining Shakespeare's *Romeo and Juliet* with the songs of Swedish pop maestro Max Martin, songwriter/producer for the likes of Taylor Swift, Katy Perry, Britney Spears, Justin Timberlake and the Backstreet Boys, the musical transports us back in time four hundred years to see William Shakespeare tussling over the plot of *Romeo and Juliet* with Anne Hathaway, his wife. Hathaway doesn't like Shakespeare's story and thinks it's all a bit too dull and depressing. She would prefer it be a more uplifting story so she suggests that, instead of killing Juliet off at the end, Juliet should come back to life, break free from her terrible family and find her own voice and place in the world. William Shakespeare demands to know why, to which Hathaway replies with the lyrics from the Backstreet Boys' Martin-written smash record, because 'I Want it That Way'.

Max Martin and William Shakespeare make a surprisingly good combination. They both target their words at popular audiences, both make extensive use of the same rhetorical devices such as antithesis, anaphora, asyndeton, anadiplosis, alliteration and aposiopesis (we'll cover rhetorical devices in a later chapter) and, in particular, they both use many of the same metaphors.

In particular, Shakespeare famously depicted young Juliet as the sun in Romeo's extended soliloquy, in a passage which will be instantly familiar to anyone who studied GCSE English.

What light through yonder window breaks?
It is the East and Juliet is the sun . . .
The brightness of her cheek would shame those stars
As daylight doth a lamp. Her eye in heaven
Would through the airy region stream so bright
That birds would sing and think it were not night.

The same fiery metaphor runs through Max Martin's big hit, 'I Want it That Way', the song which features at the beginning and the end of *& Juliet*, in which the protagonist sings to the object of his affection that she is his fire, his one desire.

Love as fire is a commonly understood metaphor. Many everyday phrases arise from the connection point between love and fire. *I held a torch for her. She lit a spark. She kindled my interest. He's ignited my passion. He's super hot. My loins are raging. It got a bit steamy. The sex was smoking. We set the bedroom on fire. Our relationship fizzled out. She went cool. The flame's gone out. I got my fingers burnt.*

Connect!

Of course, none of this talk is literal – our house isn't literally on fire when we are having great sex (or at least we should hope it isn't), it is metaphorical. When we use metaphor, we are describing something as something which it is not. So the formula for a metaphor is x=y. In this case, x is love and y is fire. A metaphor is a substitution. When we use metaphor, we substitute one thing with another thing, replacing this with that. But, by so doing, we are also connecting this and that, linking them together in people's minds. When we use metaphor, we are connecting two worlds: in this case, love and fire.

We are not saying love is *like* fire. That would be a simile. When we use simile, we are effectively inviting people to consider the connections between x and y. This makes it rather more likely that they might object to our connection, or develop an alternative simile. *Love's not like fire. Love's like poison.* We might propose all sorts of alternatives. In his TEDx talk, Al Vernacchio proposed a new simile that love's like a pizza – and everyone should get a slice. One could certainly see a market in *Oven Ready Loving* . . .

Metaphors have greater natural authority than similes. When we use metaphor, we are not inviting people to consider whether there is a connection between x and y, we are simply asserting that there is one. This makes it less likely that people will object and more likely that they will simply nod along with us.

The metaphor of love as fire makes sense anyway because, although love and fire are fundamentally different, they do share some important qualities in common. We've already explored how warmth is a metaphor for social relations, with Modi's cup of chai. When we are cuddling someone we love, our body temperature literally rises, creating a similar feeling to a lovely warm fire, so there is a connection there. Fire is started by rubbing sticks together, creating friction, and a similar process might get us warmed up for some hot sex. And, while the heat of fire is attractive, alluring and comforting, it also possesses dangers because we all understand that, left uncontrolled, fire can quickly spread, potentially overwhelming us. Our house on fire is the stuff of nightmares so this provides a warning that, left to get out of control, our love could destroy us, a message that was certainly apt in the case of Juliet.

We see many fire metaphors through pop music. The Trammps sang about how the heat was on in their hit, 'Disco Inferno'. Peggy Lee sang in 'Fever' about how Romeo charmed Juliet saying, 'Julie baby you're my flame'. And, more recently, Adele opened her Grammy-winning song, 'Rolling in the Deep' singing about the fire starting in her heart.

But the metaphor of love as fire was not only the metaphor of choice for Shakespeare in 1595, the Trammps in 1976 or Adele in 2011, it dates back literally thousands of years. The same metaphor also appears in the Old Testament, written in about the tenth century BCE. The Book of Solomon describes love as 'flashes of fire, a raging flame'.

Bishop Michael Curry quoted the Book of Solomon in his sermon at the wedding of Prince Harry and Meghan Markle in May 2018. The idea of love as fire provided the theme for his whole speech. His 1,500-word sermon featured 20 references to fire, from the beginning, middle and right through his rousing peroration. It's worth checking out the whole of his speech on YouTube just to see the extent to which he explores, explains and examines the metaphor, conjuring up different thoughts, moods and feelings. Sometimes it feels less like a sermon about love than it does a speech about fire.

That's the mysterious way metaphors work. By connecting one world (love) to another world (fire), it grabs our attention and gets our brain firing, especially when the idea comes from a charismatic and physical speaker like Bishop Michael Curry. He electrified St George's Chapel with his evangelical delivery that day. You can practically see the energy shooting around the pews of the chapel. He even caused the Queen to shuffle at one point. No question, Bishop Curry stole the show.

I went to a wedding in the Lake District in the summer of 2021 which didn't quite reach the grandiose levels of a royal wedding (we were in a tepee!) but still the vicar used the same metaphor of love as fire, albeit in a different way. He talked about love in a marriage as a pilot light in an old gas boiler; you could turn the flame up, you could turn the flame down, but you could always rely on the pilot light to keep on burning. My eco-minded brother-in-law Matt and his wife Lucy don't own a gas boiler, but they got the point.

The idea of love as fire is conceptually a metaphor we can all buy into but it is by no means the only one. As with analogy, it's just one possible connection point, from a field of possibilities which is literally infinite. Love can be anything we want it to be. Let me demonstrate what I mean by simply taking the first random things I see and trying them out as metaphors for love. So love can be a tree which has roots but branches out and changes with the seasons. Love can be a vehicle that transports us, keeps us safe and takes us places. Love can be a window which shows us the beauty in the world. Now, as I look to the objects on my desk, I see three more possibilities. Maybe love is a mask that hides us away from our friends. Or is it a cup of coffee that energises us and gives us a boost? Or is it a computer: exciting, but also dangerous, full of distractions? We can connect anything with anything. Obviously, some work better than others, but the possibilities are infinite.

The history of pop music can almost be seen as an endless quest to find new metaphors for love. Is love a losing game as Amy Winehouse saw it, or is it a drug, as it was to Roxy Music? Is it a stranger as it was for Annie Lennox or is it Pat Benatar's battlefield? Different artists in different contexts have different perspectives. One study found that Mariah Carey alone used no less than 17 different metaphors for love across her catalogue, ranging from love is a dream, love is a captive animal and love is a physical force through to love is a machine, love is war and even love is torture! Some can seem more apposite than others, but this depends on our experiences, moods and perspectives.

Some great songwriters alight on metaphorical themes which they use time and again throughout their career. Abba, for instance, frequently wrote about love as gambling – 'Take a Chance on Me', 'The Winner Takes it All', 'Money, Money, Money'. It's not surprising to learn that Benny was known to enjoy a spot of gambling when he was away from the stage . . . George Michael regularly wrote about love as religion – from

Connect!

'Faith' to 'Father Figure', 'Jesus to a Child' and 'Cowboys and Angels', 'Heaven Help Me', 'Praying for Time' and 'The Edge of Heaven' – again, perhaps not surprising, given the many nights he spent frequenting the legendary gay London nightclub Heaven. Freddie Mercury seemed keen on war metaphors for love/sex, with his talk about gunpowder, gelatine and dynamite ('Killer Queen') or being ready to reload, like an atom bomb, about to oh-oh-oh-oh-oh explode ('Don't Stop Me Now'). The idea of sex as war wasn't unique to Freddie – many people speak about the penis as a weapon, a gun or a pistol and we might bang away until shooting our load (or, alternatively, we might be said to be firing blanks). It's a very penis-centric view of the world, but one can imagine that Freddie Mercury's view of the world probably was quite penis-centric.

Once you've figured out that Freddie Mercury's metaphor for sex is war, those early verses of 'Bohemian Rhapsody', which may once have seemed nonsensical, suddenly take on a clearer meaning. If the penis is a weapon and ejaculation is shooting, maybe the bit about putting a gun against his head, pulling his trigger now he's dead was a confession of gay infidelity to his then girlfriend, Mary Austin (together with the expression of remorse that he might have thrown the life they were building all away?).

After Freddie Mercury's death, his former lover, Jim Hutton, confirmed the theory about 'Bohemian Rhapsody'. 'Freddie was never going to admit it publicly, of course, because he always had to carry on the charade about being straight for his family. But we did discuss it on a number of occasions. "Bohemian Rhapsody" WAS Freddie's confessional.'

This and That

Other songwriters play around with metaphors until they find one that works. My friend, Ian Dench, is an Ivor Novello Award-winning songwriter who has co-written hit songs for the likes of Beyoncé, Shakira and The Prodigy. He says the songwriting process is often like throwing something at a wall until finally something sticks. He loves using big metaphors in his choruses, because, 'metaphors can be interpreted in so many different ways, allowing people to read what they want into it'.

He describes writing the song 'Red', a hit for Australian singer Daniel Merriweather. At this time, he and his song-writing partners loved picking random words to create song titles, which they'd done with the global hit 'Tattoo' for Jordin Sparks. With 'Red', to start off with, they had the bones of a great song, with a story and a great idea, but the song had no hook and no title. Inspired by the success of Coldplay's song, 'Yellow', they decided to reimagine the song around the colour red. Instantly, the song came together, delivering with just one word both the hook and the title.

Red has multiple meanings symbolically, and could be interpreted in a variety of ways, which is one of the beautiful things about metaphor. But, in this context, and against the backdrop of verses that told the story of a pained and strained relationship, it seems to me that red means anger.

Metaphors can elevate an idea to a whole new level. As the rapper Nas says, 'Metaphors are brain busters. When you can come up with a great metaphor that can change everything in a positive way.'

Connect!

Aristotle said that to be a master of metaphor was a sign of genius and when you look back through the course of history, you can see that he may well be right, and I'm not just talking about Benny, Bjorn and Nas.

Mastery of metaphor is genius

Adam Smith was probably the most influential economist in the history of economics. His metaphor of the 'invisible hand of the market', which first appeared in his 1759 book *The Theory of Moral Sentiments*, suggested that the market was a person. This metaphor leads us to assume the market would be capable of thinking, feeling and behaving like a human being, endowed with morality, empathy and sympathy. By using this metaphor, he was able to defuse the biggest criticism of free-market economics, which is that markets may be efficient but they are incapable of morality, and can inadvertently lead to inhumane treatment of people.

And Adam Smith would not have arrived at the metaphor of the invisible hand by accident. As well as being an economist, Adam Smith was a gifted rhetorician. He delivered many lectures on rhetoric. In 1749, when he was just 26 years old, he gave a lecture on rhetoric at Glasgow University in which he talked specifically about the power of metaphors, and how they could give an argument strength.

Winston Churchill was one of the most influential statesmen of the twentieth century and he was also a master of metaphor. When he spoke about an 'iron curtain' descending on the continent of Europe in his 1948 speech in Fulton, Missouri, he was speaking through a metaphor that could be

178

interpreted on multiple levels. The iron subconsciously evoked the idea of the Soviets as hard, cold and unfeeling. The curtain suggested morality: the role of curtains is fundamentally to keep light out; and light is a common metaphor for moral purity (hence the baddies in movies can always be found sitting in darkness). And then the whole phrase 'the iron curtain' would have been understood, certainly at the time Churchill delivered his speech, to mean the fire safety curtain you get in a theatre, which connects into another metaphor, the idea of global politics as theatre. There is a broader and widely understood metaphor of politics as theatre in which we have actors on the global stage, following their cues and reading lines. As Shakespeare said, 'all the world's a stage' . . .

Churchill, like Smith and Shakespeare, also studied rhetoric when he was young. When Churchill was just 22, he wrote a brilliant essay called *The Scaffolding of Rhetoric* in which he described analogy as 'among the most formidable weapons of the rhetorician', referring to its power to connect the known and the unknown, the abstract and the concrete and the finite and the infinite. He described its effect upon an audience as 'electrical', saying it enabled audiences to 'decide the problems that have baffled his powers of reason by the standard of nursery and the heart.'

And Churchill practised what he preached. His speeches were frequently infused with metaphor. Throughout the Second World War, his speeches painted a metaphorical narrative that went from darkness to light. He spoke about how bombed out London would 'burn and glow through the gloom of Europe [and] become the veritable beacon of its salvation'. General Charles de Gaulle, the leader of the French resistance, used similar language in his talk about '*la flamme de la résistance*' – the flame of French resistance. They were making the flames of war attractive and using them to give people hope.

Metaphors may reduce problems to the 'standard of the nursery', as Churchill said, but that doesn't stop them completely dominating debate in some of the most elevated areas of human thought, from economics and philosophy to science.

James Watson and Francis Crick depicted DNA as the 'building blocks' of life, giving rise to a language of genetic engineering and blueprints that continues today. Giacomo Rizzolatti coined the idea of 'mirror neurons', which has shaped how many of us think about behavioural science. I'm using the metaphor of connections and electricity throughout this book. *Connect. Generate power. Create energy. Get people fired up.* This is the same metaphor that Churchill used in his essay but it also taps in to a deeper metaphor of the brain as a machine, a metaphor that actually dates all the way back to the seventeenth century when Danish anatomist Nicolas Steno addressed a small group of thinkers at Issy on the southern outskirts of Paris and argued that the brain should be seen as a machine saying, 'The brain being a machine . . . we must dismantle it piece by piece and consider what these pieces can do separately and together'. The renowned zoologist Matthew Cobb argued in his book *The Idea of The Brain* that Steno's vision has dominated the way we perceive brains ever since, for better and for worse.

This and That

Metaphors play a critical role in scientific and technological development. As technologies change, and our perspective on those technologies change, so too do the metaphors we use to describe them. Take the way we speak about the worldwide web.

To start off with, when the worldwide web was invented by Tim Berners-Lee in 1989 it was perceived as just that: a web. Intriguingly, Berners-Lee's initial proposal for funding actually called it the 'mesh'. A mesh is a different image to a web but it still possesses many of the same properties, involving a grid-like shape, much the same image which is also present in the idea of an interNET. That idea matched his perspective on what he was creating: he wanted something that would enable people to connect with one another freely.

Then the politicians stepped in. They had a different metaphor because they had a different perspective. They wanted to exercise control over this new worldwide web. It was Vice President Al Gore in 1993 who first coined the idea of an 'information superhighway'. When I first started writing speeches for British government ministers in the late nineties, this phrase could be heard everywhere. The image of a highway was perfect for governments who wanted to control the web, because we all instinctively understand that highways need strict rules about who goes on there, what they do, where they go. With that imagery in mind, you would instinctively feel that laws and regulations were not merely desirable but essential for the safe operation of this new worldwide web.

Connect!

Rhetorically, however, you can imagine that the information superhighway metaphor would not have been too attractive for the folks in Silicon Valley. They didn't want to be bossed around by government, burdened with red tape and regulation. They wanted freedom to explore uncharted territory, to expand the frontiers of knowledge, to boldly go where no man had gone before. So, they had a different perspective and that manifested in a new language around . . . CYBERSPACE!

The language of cyberspace is now ubiquitous in the way we talk and think about our interactions with the internet. We 'launch' our *explorer*, 'fire up' our search 'engines', click on 'hyper'-links, 'land' on sites, sometimes they 'crash' and only the intrepid would dare venture into the 'dark' web. If someone interrupts us while we're tapping away online, we may well say, 'Sorry, I was in another world'. We subconsciously perceive it, think about it and often speak about internet exploration as space travel.

We all instinctively perceive the internet is *up there*. Maybe you'll put a video *up* on YouTube? Maybe people will *down*load it. Maybe you'll put a photo *up* on Facebook . . . Try saying to people that you're putting photos *down* on Facebook and they will look at you as if you're crazy, Maybe you'll store your photos in a *cloud* . . . But it's a myth. Our photos aren't really stored in fluffy white masses of condensation, but in huge data banks dotted around in far-flung parts of the planet. The idea of space travel is actively promoted by Silicon Valley in their branding and product interfaces. Of course, we have 'Android' or 'Galaxy' phones. Google says they deliberately designed their search pages to replicate the feel of being on the bridge of the Starship *Enterprise*.

In October 2021, Mark Zuckerberg launched 'The Metaverse', his vision for how cyberspace might look in the future. His demonstration started with him instantly teleporting (his word) us straight into a spaceship in outer space where his friends were waiting for him in a gravity free environment:

'Hi. What's up, Mark?'

'Whoa! We're floating in space? Who made this place? It's awesome!'

'Right! It's from a Creator I met in LA.'

I wrote in my last book, *You Are Not Human*, about the danger that the cyberspace metaphor could promote disconnection from the real world. The launch of Metaverse, with its promise to transport us even deeper into cyberspace, seemed particularly untimely, coming as it did just days before world leaders met in Glasgow for COP26 to discuss climate change.

Climate change metaphors are something different entirely. Just as technology metaphors have shifted over time, so too have metaphors for climate change. As perspectives have changed, so too have the metaphors.

Different metaphors, different perspectives

To start with, for many years, carbon emissions were depicted in terms of a 'carbon footprint'. It's ironic that, while we regularly use apocalyptic metaphors to talk about all sorts of mundane things, such as a football team's defeat, a fall in profits or a bad speech, when we are considering something as literally apocalyptic as climate change, we use the timid imagery of a footprint. Footprints are not harmful. They do not suggest lasting damage. We all know that footprints, whether they are on a drive, a carpet or even a sofa, are temporary and can be easily cleaned up. So that's hardly likely to inspire people to feel fear.

In recent years, that metaphor has developed. Many businesses now talk about being on a 'journey' to reducing carbon. They talk about being on a 'path' to sustainability, on the 'road' to carbon zero, 'driving' change, taking 'steps', overcoming 'obstacles', and staying on 'track'. This metaphor suggests motion, but it still doesn't really create an intense pressure to act. Journeys are largely passive. We can sit back, relax, the driver will take us there.

Those who felt a little bit more pressure talked about climate change as a 'race'. This was a bit different. With a race there was a clear impetus. The clock was ticking. There was a motive to move quickly. We were 'falling behind'. We were 'losing'. In the run up to COP26, the United Nations launched a massive initiative to bring together businesses, regions and investors to tackle climate change and they billed this as *The Race to Zero*. Many world leaders picked up this rhetoric. For instance, the prime minister of Singapore made a speech saying, 'We are all in a collective race, not against each other, but against time to overcome the challenge of climate change . . .and save the only planet we have'.

When the actual COP26 meeting got underway, a new metaphor emerged. Prince Charles called for nations to go on a '*war*-like footing', putting together 'a vast *military* style campaign.' Boris Johnson continued the military metaphor in his own characteristically outlandish way, with an extended riff about how James Bond invariably ends his movies, 'strapped to a doomsday device desperately trying to work out which coloured wire to pull to turn it off while a red digital clock ticks down remorselessly to a detonation that will end human life as we know it. We are in roughly the same position, my fellow global leaders, as James Bond today except that the tragedy is that this is not a movie and the doomsday device is real. We may not feel much like James Bond, not all of us necessarily look like James Bond, but we have the duty to defuse that bomb and to begin the fightback against climate change.'

The difference between a race metaphor and a war metaphor might seem arbitrary, simply stylistic, but that is to completely underestimate the true power of metaphor. Metaphors can be absolutely fundamental to the substance of the debate, having a huge impact on how people perceive the issue, shifting how they think, feel and act.

In 2018, Stephen Flusberg, Associate Professor of Psychology at Purchase College, carried out a study to check the power of different climate change metaphors. He got 3,000 people to read an article about climate change. One thousand people were given an article that referred to it as a war, another thousand people were given an article that referred to it as a race and one thousand people were given an article that used no metaphor at all. The articles looked like this:

<u>THE WAR AGAINST CLIMATE CHANGE</u>
When will Americans start to combat excessive energy use and kill the problems related to air pollution and

the destruction of natural resources? The entire country should be recruited to fight this deadly battle. The United States is joining the campaign to reduce its carbon footprint in the next few decades. This is a war we can't afford to lose!

THE RACE AGAINST CLIMATE CHANGE

When will Americans go after excessive energy use and surge ahead on problems related to air pollution and the destruction of natural resources? The entire country needs to step up to the line and get in front of this challenging problem. The United States is joining the race to reduce its carbon footprint in the next few decades . . . This is a race we can't afford to lose!

THE ISSUE OF CLIMATE CHANGE

When will Americans start to address excessive energy use and resolve the problems related to air pollution and the use of natural resources? The entire country needs to direct their efforts to address this important issue. The United States is joining the effort to reduce its carbon footprint in the next few decades. This is a situation we can't afford to ignore!

Flusberg found that the war metaphor made people perceive more risk and urgency around climate change, and also led people to report a greater willingness to change their behaviour to tackle climate change, for instance by decreasing their use of air conditioning or by paying more to offset carbon. The study is clearly important, and suggested the United Nations might have missed a trick by billing the run up to COP26 as a Race to Zero, but Flusberg's 2018 study only compared the race and war metaphors. Later that same year, someone else came along with a new metaphor that was set to completely change the discourse about climate change right around the world.

Greta Thunberg first heard about climate change in 2011 when she was eight years old. She was so depressed about it, she stopped talking and eating properly. She couldn't understand why no one was doing anything to tackle climate change so, eventually, she decided to do something herself. On 20 August 2018, she walked out of school and started a school strike for climate outside the Swedish Parliament. At the same time, her parents had just published their book, *Our House is On Fire* and those five words became Greta's rallying cry to the world: *Our House is On Fire.*

On 25 January 2019, she gave a landmark speech to world leaders at Davos saying, 'I don't want you to be hopeful. I want you to panic. I want you to feel the fear I feel every day. And then I want you to act. I want you to act as you would in a crisis. I want you to act as if our house is on fire.'

The phrase immediately caught on. The facts hadn't changed but the discourse was transformed. The new metaphor had changed something abstract and distant into something immediate, dangerous and in all our homes. Also, it created a pressure for each of us to act instantly; after all, if your house is on fire, you don't sit around and wait for others to act (as you might in a war), there is an absolute imperative

for you to take immediate action yourself, right away. This is a bona fide emergency. But also the idea of the house spoke to another metaphorical idea: that of the world as a family, with shared interests and a shared responsibility to act. These were the underlying messages which flowed from Thunberg's metaphor, and they had the desired effect, causing people to act.

In May 2019, the UK Parliament declared an environment and climate change emergency. In November 2019, the European Parliament declared a climate emergency. Greta's metaphor (a Gretaphor?) had really got under people's skin. I remember seeing an Extinction Rebellion march going down Whitehall in October 2019 with several people carrying effigies of a burning House of Commons made from cardboard boxes. *Our house is on fire.* The metaphor had completely changed the way people perceived climate change, and created a sense of urgency. Research by Oxford

English Dictionary found that the use of the term 'climate emergency' increased by a whopping 76-fold between 2018 and 2020.

There was no ambiguity in Thunberg's fire metaphor. It was designed to instil fear and that's exactly what it did. It spoke directly to our instinctive brains and demanded an instant response. Vicky Lai, a cognitive neuroscientist at the University of Arizona who has carried out extensive research into the effects of metaphors on the brain, says that we have a bias towards negative metaphors. To protect ourselves, we process danger-related inputs faster and remember them longer.

Change the metaphor, change the response

This is the power of metaphor. Studies have shown how changing nothing more than the metaphor in a piece of text can lead people to fundamentally different reactions on topics ranging from whether people will support policies, invest in companies and even back foreign wars. There's no doubt about it, metaphor is potentially the nuclear bomb of communication.

A 2011 study by Lera Boroditsky and Paul Thibodeau showed describing crime as a 'beast' preying on communities led people to support more punitive 'tough on crime' policies (a 'lock 'em up and throw away the key' perspective, the kind of view you might see extolled in the *Daily Mail*), whereas describing it as a virus led people towards a more preventative 'tough on the causes of crime' view of the world (a view you might see in the *Guardian*).

Different politicians can activate these different metaphors as they feel appropriate. When Theresa May was prime minister in Britain from 2016 to 2019, her Home Secretary, Sajid Javid, made several well-reported speeches arguing that crime should be treated like a virus. He was establishing a perspective that would lead people to invest in youth centres etc. Then, when Boris Johnson was appointed prime minister, one of the first things he did with his new Home Secretary, Priti Patel, was announce he wanted to 'cut the head off the snake' of organised crime in Britain. It is through such subtle shifts in metaphor that public attitudes can be changed.

Since 1999, the Frameworks Institute has carried out research into a wide range of social issues to find the best metaphors for achieving change. I've worked alongside their UK arm, Frameworks UK, and seen at close hand how they have helped transform discourse around a range of vital issues.

For instance, they recently helped poverty campaigners, the Joseph Rowntree Foundation, to improve the discourse around poverty. For many years, people had spoken about poverty as a war. *We must fight poverty. We must eradicate poverty. We must tackle poverty.* Frameworks UK surveyed 20,000 people to find what metaphors would work better. They found that using the metaphor that poverty was a trap made people a) far more likely to accept that there was a problem and b) far more likely to want to do something about it. So, to invoke this imagery, you might talk about how people are *locked in* poverty, how poverty 'holds people back' and 'restricts their choices'. The Frameworks Institute have created a toolkit, which is available online, to show people how they can weave this imagery into their everyday language.

They also looked at ways to encourage people to take ocean health and marine conservation more seriously. They found that describing the ocean as a living being makes it easier for people to understand the challenges facing the oceans. So they use words like 'injuring', 'inflicting' and 'infecting' to depict the damage being done to the ocean. This helps rouse sympathy. And they talk about 'healing', 'reviving' and 'curing' to talk about solutions. This helps build confidence. Communicators can highlight 'symptoms', 'conditions', 'syndromes', 'ailments' and report on the 'diagnosis', the 'prognosis' and the 'treatment' required. This is brilliant. It instantly conjures images and activates emotions. There's a Pixar movie waiting to be made there. *It's An Ocean's Life.*

Even though metaphors are incredibly powerful and a sign of genius, we all have the capacity to use them and we all do use them in everyday speech. There are a number of conceptual metaphors we all slip into every day without much thinking about their meaning or consequences. We might talk about being at a cross-roads (life = journey), feeling under attack (argument = war) or feeling blue (emotion = colour). We use metaphor on average once every 16 words, so it is hard to speak for long without reaching for a metaphor (metaphor = physical being), and metaphors are very loaded (metaphor = gun) and metaphors plant ideas in our mind (metaphor = seed).

By listening to people's metaphors, we can understand much more about their world view. Do they view life as a journey or a war? Do they view their employer as a family or a prison? Is their mood bright or dark? Knowledge of someone's metaphorical perspective is essential for creating rapport and showing empathy. Once you understand someone's world view you can speak within that world view. If you don't understand it, the danger is that you'll speak in a metaphor that conflicts with their world view.

Metaphor reveals perspective

Quite often, when you see people arguing, their disagreement is based less on disputed facts than it is upon diverging metaphorical perspectives which are deeply imprinted in their subconscious minds. Some people will speak through one metaphor, others through another. Earlier, we looked at the issue of social media and whether children should or should not have access. Those who are in favour might depict social media as a lifeline, a friend or a window to the world. Those who view it more negatively might depict it as an addictive drug, a poison, or toxic.

Analysing people's metaphors gives you a deep insight into their view of the world. You can even, to an extent, gauge their political views. People on the left in politics tend to use more war metaphors than those on the right, so at left-wing rallies you might hear lots of talk about 'fighting' for our rights, 'battles' ahead, vital services being 'under attack' while people on the right tend to use more nature and personification metaphors: the 'heart' of our nation, our 'DNA', planting 'seeds'.

As a speechwriter, I always examine my clients' metaphors carefully to ensure I can write to their world view. The results are often intriguing. People who love music might instinctively reach for music metaphors (people need to be in 'harmony', in 'concert', singing from the same 'hymn sheet'). People who love sport might instinctively reach for sporting metaphors (you 'smashed it out of the park'!). People who love science might instinctively reach for chemical metaphors (getting the 'elements' in place). But one of the problems I frequently encounter, especially within large organisations, is that different people in different parts of the company have completely different perspectives on what that company is metaphorically, and therefore speak using completely different metaphors.

The founder of the company might speak about the company as a person. This is not surprising because they view it as their baby. So they might talk about its 'outlook', making it 'stronger', improving its 'relationships'. Alternatively, they might talk about how it has 'lost its way', got 'flabby' or been subjected to some 'savage cuts' over the last few years. Speaking of something as a person is a natural way of expressing affection. When we love things, we naturally speak of them as people. For instance, people who love their houses might speak of the kitchen as the 'heart of the house', or people who love their cars might give them names. I have a VW camper van. *Her name is Poppy. She's part of the family. We could never part with her.*

But people who work in HR or Strategy can't stand the metaphor of personification. That's because they want to control the company and we all understand that people are fundamentally uncontrollable. So they use a different metaphor. They prefer to view the company as a car, because cars are easy to control. They might talk about 'driving' change, 'accelerating' reform or having a 'change of gear'. If there is a problem they want staff to address, they will issue staff with a 'tool-kit'. This metaphor is very attractive for people who want to be in control because it suggests that directing a company is as easy as driving a car, as if all we have to do to take a company in a new direction is flick on the indicator, put our foot on the pedal and off we go. If only business were that easy! It's an absurd fantasy, but they love it.

However, people who work in sales can't stand that metaphor. It makes them feel cold, trapped, dehumanised. If the company is a machine, then that makes them nuts and bolts: not there to innovate or create, just there to fulfil a function, no more no less, and as soon as they fail to fulfil that function, oomph, they're taken out and replaced. They'll resist this metaphor. They might respond by saying the strategists haven't got a clue what it's like on the 'front-line'. So they have a different metaphor. To them, competition is a 'battleground'! *It's war out there. Totally brutal! We're getting killed!*

Other people might have different perspectives still – the business might be a sport, a garden, a family, a spaceship, or a cake. The difficulty is that if you then put all of these different metaphors together, you wind up with the classic business bullshit that is squeezed out of the bowels of every large organisation every day of the week.

We're 'unlocking the value within our core markets by taking a clear view of destination, taking a sharper focus on where we play, identifying our must-win battles that will drive growth, building opportunities, planting seeds, deploying new resources and raising the bar in our core capabilities.'

This and That

Most of the time, I suspect the cause of mixed metaphors is 'drafting by committee': different people with different perspectives work together on the same text and instead of resolving their different perspectives they try to let them co-exist, ending up with text which is a dog's breakfast, a car crash, a weak foundation and a slippery slope to the worst kind of corporate bullshit.

It reminds me of the story of Samuel Johnson, the great English writer, who was walking around the streets of London one day with his biographer, James Boswell, when they saw two women standing on their doorsteps, arguing fiercely with one another, waving broomsticks. Johnson said to Boswell, 'Those two women will never agree, for they are arguing from different premises.'

Instead of standing on your own doorsteps shouting at one another, a better strategy is to walk into the other person's house. By speaking within people's existing metaphorical perspectives, we show that we see the world the same as they do, which is a great starting point for influence.

Let me give an example. If I'm trying to persuade someone about the power of metaphors, first I would try to identify their metaphor for communication.

If they said that they needed more firepower when they speak, I might assume that their underlying metaphor was communication=war, in which case the best way to depict metaphors might be as weapons. So I might say metaphors are very 'loaded', they'll help you 'shoot someone's argument down', they'll 'blow your opponent's objections out of the water', 'smash them into smithereens', they're an 'important weapon in your arsenal'.

Connect!

If, however, they said that they needed to plant thoughts in people's minds, that might suggest an underlying metaphor of communication as gardening. I might say that metaphors can become 'embedded' and take 'root' quickly and stay 'planted' in people's minds forever.

One of my favourite movies is the Peter Sellers film *Being There*. In the movie, Sellers plays a not very bright gardener who manages to get to the top of American politics by sharing his thoughts about gardening. Everyone assumes he is speaking metaphorically and sharing profound insights but he's not. He's literally just speaking about gardening.

Midway through the film, there is a moment when the president asks Sellers' character (erroneously known as Chauncey Gardiner) for his views about how to stimulate growth in the economy. By using the frame 'stimulate growth', the president has shown he views the economy through a gardening frame (a common metaphor in economics).

Chauncey Gardiner replies, 'As long as the roots are not severed, all is well and all will be well in the garden. First come spring and summer. But then come fall and winter. And then come spring and summer again.'

Sellers is speaking literally but the president believes he is speaking metaphorically, and he has shared some profound wisdom. From then on, he quotes Sellers' character in his speeches. The metaphor proves powerful enough to shift his perspective on economic management and changes his approach to policy. The force of nature metaphor suggests you should leave well alone, guiding you towards a laissez-faire approach – which is why politicians on the right wing of politics tend to use nature metaphors more than politicians on the left. It is consistent with their economic principles.

By the end of the film, Sellers' character is being tipped to become the next president. It must be said it wouldn't be the first time someone was powered to the White House by a good metaphor. *It's morning in America. Drain the swamp. The battle for the soul of America.*

Great communicators, instinctively or not, speak in metaphors that connect with an audience's instincts and values. There's a great example in another movie, *The Blind Side*. This 2009 film tells the true story of Michael Oher, an American footballer who overcame an impoverished upbringing to become a huge football star, with the support of his adoptive parents, Sean and Leigh Anne Tuohy. There is a key moment in the movie when Leigh Anne (played by Sandra Bullock – who won an Oscar for the role), uses metaphor to improve Michael's performance.

His playing has not been brilliant in the session. The coach is getting fed up with him, so are the rest of the team. He keeps missing shots and wasting opportunities.

Usually, when sports coaches are motivating people about sport, they use the metaphor of war. This is effective because it turns something ultimately trivial into a matter of life and death. That's the approach Al Pacino takes in his speech in the movie *Any Given Sunday*, when he fires up his team saying, 'Three minutes to the biggest battle of our professional lives', urging them to go out there and 'fight and die'.

But Leigh Anne doesn't think the war metaphor will connect with young Michael, who is a gentle soul. Instead, she

thinks that she can connect to something with deeper resonance. She knows that Michael is blessed with exceptionally strong defensive instincts: the school said that he is in
the 98th percentile when it comes to 'protective instincts'. His
whole life has been shaped by a need to protect people and he
has demonstrated extraordinary acts of courage to protect his
new family.

So, Leigh Anne walks across the pitch towards Michael
and says:

'This team is your family, Michael. You have to protect
them from those guys. OK? This is your quarterback. When
you look at him, you think of me and how you have my back.
OK? This is your tailback. When you look at him, you think
of SJ and you don't need anything or anyone to hurt him,
all right?'

She ends by asking him, 'Are you going to protect the
family, Michael?'

'Yes ma'am.' He nods.

Leigh Anne has taken something fundamentally trivial
(football) and connected it with something incredibly important to Michael (family). By so doing, she's drawn energy
from the thing he's passionate about (family) and directed it
towards the thing he's not so passionate about (football). She's
tapping directly into his most powerful instincts. Family is
something which our every instinct, anthropologically, directs
us to protect.

Many great employers do what Sandra Bullock's character did here and use family metaphors. Richard Branson has
always personified Virgin and says he has always seen his

company as a family. This kind of language, used repeatedly at all levels in an organisation, can shape the way that people feel and create a deep moral bond.

In 2018, Costa – one of the UK's most loved chains of coffee stores – was taken over by Coca-Cola. Now this was a takeover that could have been regarded with hostility. When Kraft Foods took over the chocolate manufacturers Cadbury in 2009, it was depicted as a foreign invader stealing a national treasure. The metaphorical language in this instance could have been similar. But Alison Brittain, the CEO of Whitbread, which owned Costa, depicted the sale as a marriage. She explained the sale to journalists, saying. 'Other suitors weren't wearing the right suit or driving the right car. It's Coke we decided to go up the aisle with, with a very large ring on our finger.'

Connecting the takeover with marriage was genius because we all know that no one can poo-poo a wedding, no matter how unsuitable we might consider the pairing. That would be completely socially unacceptable. The marriage reference inescapably guides us in one way, just as a reference to divorce may nudge us in another direction.

I did a study on the power of the family metaphor in 2018, while the Brexit negotiations were reaching their height. I asked 100 people how much they thought Britain should pay to the EU as part of the final settlement. Asked like that, 11 per cent said Britain should pay the EU nothing. I then asked another 100 people, but this time I introduced a family metaphor. I asked how much Britain should pay to the EU as part of the *divorce* settlement. Simply introducing that single word *divorce* doubled the amount of people who believed the UK should pay nothing to the EU up from 11 per cent to 22 per cent. That's the power of metaphor.

You can understand why a divorce reference would activate a desire in people to hold on to everything they have. And you can also understand why the family metaphor would lead people to feel a loyalty and commitment they might not otherwise feel. Metaphors have the power to arouse some of our deepest instincts.

These kinds of metaphors can be used in all sorts of ways. One of my favourite scientists is the Malaysian soil expert, Dr Lulie Melling: a world-renowned expert in soil management. She often has to speak to farmers in Southeast Asia about the best way to manage their peatland and keep it productive. She needs to teach them how to squeeze the peat soil and determine its strength, how to check its moisture content, how to interpret the colour of its liquid and how to check the peat's purity. The farmers she is communicating with are not always literate or very well educated, and she needs to find a way to engage them. So how does she do it? She connects the science of soil – something they may not find interesting – with something which is bound to penetrate their attention and make them prick up their ears.

She explains to them, 'Peat soil is actually very sexy. It's always soft and wet. Treat the peatland like your wives. If you love her but leave her high and dry, you will have unwittingly set off a ticking time bomb of contempt. Beneath her calm surface of grassland is a dried-up layer of angry debris – just waiting to be ignited into a raging fury where there's a spark of fire.' She's also organised conferences for farmers titled, 'I'll show you how to use the hole' and 'Big Hole, Small Hole and KY Jelly'.

Research shows our brains often struggle to differentiate between literal and metaphorical representations. fMRI studies have shown that when we hear people speaking metaphorically about motor actions, for instance, 'chewing over an idea', 'bending the rules' or 'getting a grip', the parts of our brains which actually deal with those actions will light up. So, beneath the laughter, Melling may be creating a physical response. Whatever, her messages are definitely getting through. Her unique approach has led to an increase in the yield of palm oil estates on tropical peatland.

The crucial thing is understanding the instincts and values of the people you're trying to connect with. In *The Wolf of Wall Street*, Jordan Belfort (played by Leonardo DiCaprio) gives a powerful speech to his aggressive young buck traders as he tries to excite them about picking up the phones and selling stock in Steve Madden's shoe company, which is just being floated. He uses the metaphor of war. He tells them that their telephone is a 'loaded M16', and says, 'It's up to you, each and every one of you, my highly trained killers. My killers who'll not take no for an answer. My fucking warriors who'll not hang up the phone until their client either buys or fucking dies . . . You'll be ferocious. You'll be relentless. You'll be telephone fucking terrorists.'

I met someone who was actually in the room when the real-life Jordan Belfort gave that speech. He said it was exactly as it was depicted in the movie (except the real-life Belfort wasn't quite as good-looking). Whatever your views on his ethics, Jordan Belfort certainly knew how to rouse a crowd. So too did President Donald J Trump, who was also a master of metaphor. Like Belfort, Trump also liked war metaphors.

When Trump launched his campaign to become president of the United States on 16 June 2015 from the lobby of Trump Tower in New York, his opening words were built around an extended war metaphor:

'Our country is in serious trouble. We don't have victories any more. We used to have victories, but we don't have them. When was the last time anybody saw us beating, let's say, China in a trade deal? They kill us. I beat China all the time. All the time. When did we beat Japan at anything? They send their cars over by the millions and what do we do? When was the last time you saw a Chevrolet in Tokyo? It doesn't exist, folks. They beat us all the time. When do we beat Mexico at the border? They're laughing at us, at our stupidity. And now they are beating us economically. They are not our friend, believe me. But they're killing us economically.'

This passage is just 125 words but within that there are six uses of the word 'beat', two uses of the word 'victory 'and two uses of the word 'kill'. He used metaphor once every twelve words on average and, by so doing, he was able to paint a clear picture of a country in mortal peril, speaking to people's deepest instincts. We were not in New York but on the battlefield. Our lives were in danger. Trump used fighting metaphors throughout his presidency, which might explain why his rallies were such charged affairs, sometimes breaking out into violence.

Trump came under fire for his speech at the Capitol Building on 6 January 2021, with its relentless fighting talk and war metaphors. But he wasn't the only candidate to use this kind of rhetoric in that election. Joe Biden also spoke repeatedly about his election campaign as a *battle for the soul of America*. During his campaign, he spoke about 'The battle to control the virus. The battle to build prosperity. The battle to secure your family's healthcare. The battle to achieve racial justice and root out systemic racism. The battle to save the climate. The battle to restore decency, defend democracy and give everyone a fair shot.'

Also, when Kamala Harris issued her challenge to become a presidential candidate in a speech at Oakland, California she used the word fight 23 times, with fighting providing the dominant theme throughout (her speech also followed a MY STORY – OUR STORY – WHAT NEXT structure).

Harris's speech took us through a range of different stories, but all of them revolved around a central theme of fighting. She spoke about her mum's work fighting infectious disease as a doctor. She depicted her own role as a lawyer involving fighting, saying she fought transnational gangs, fought the big banks, fought to hold the administration accountable, fought for a fairer criminal justice system, fought for healthcare. And then, as she looked to the future, she talked about how she would fight for truth, fight for justice, fight for equality. Her speech also revolved around a quote from Bob Marley: 'Get up, stand up, don't give up the fight.'

Become a master of metaphor

Visionary leaders speak through clear, consistent metaphors. But how do we find metaphors? This is something I spend a lot of time doing with my clients. It's fun, it's playful. Like many of the points in this book, it's a case of playing around creatively until we find a connection that works. Throwing things at the wall until something sticks. But there are a few ways we can approach it.

Sometimes I will explore whether the metaphor of personification helps articulate the company's message. It's a good starting point to bring a company to life. It's a bit like the Pixar strategy, you can draw some eyes and a smiley face on anything – a clock, a candlestick, a cat – and instantly make it more loveable and approachable.

LET THERE BE LIFE!

So, why not give it a try! Think about your company, your community or country as a person. And answer these questions . . .

- Draw your company as a person. What do they look like? Are they male or female? Old or young? Rich or poor? What kind of car do they drive? What kind of newspaper do they read? What clothes do they wear, what food do they eat, what's their favourite movie? Draw them.

- What's their purpose? Where are they trying to get to? What is their intention? Are they trying to climb a mountain/land on the moon/get out of a burning house?
- What are the obstacles that stand in their way? What do these represent? Which are the major and minor threats? Who is their nemesis?
- Who are their friends? Do they have a network of family and friends? Who is their soul mate/the love of their life?
- What is the climate like? Is it stormy, wet and windy? Or is there a new dawn on the horizon and the prospect of brighter days ahead?
- What is the terrain like? Rough? Rocky? Are we in a swamp? Or are we gliding downhill?
- Are there any crossroads ahead where we need to take major decisions?

Once you've answered these questions, you should be able to draw a picture. It's literally a doodle on a bit of paper, but congratulations, you have the beginnings of a consistent metaphorical narrative which you can speak to.

DREAMS AND NIGHTMARES
Alternatively, if we want to approach it a bit more strategically and systematically, we follow this simple three-step approach.

Step 1. What mood are you trying to create?

How do you want people to think, feel and act? Do you want to activate particular moral codes (e.g., responsibility, loyalty,

Connect!

compassion)? Do you want to stimulate particular emotions (e.g., disgust, love, fear, hope, pride, shame)? Do you want to encourage a particular behaviour (e.g., stay at home, go to restaurants, etc.)?

Step 2. What metaphors might stimulate these moods?

There are certain metaphors which speak to our instincts in particular ways. They are the stuff of nightmares and the stuff of dreams. By connecting with these fields, we can make something inherently attractive or inherently repulsive. This might be a handy reference.

The stuff of nightmares	The stuff of dreams
Darkness	Light
Death	People
Disease	Health
Hunger	Food
Dirt	Water
Danger	Security
Vermin	Plants
Dungeon	Freedom
Cold	Warmth
Paralysis	Motion
Emptiness	Culture
Loneliness	Games
Alienation	Friends/Family

This and That

Sometimes, it can be interesting to brainstorm and see what works. If the company was a food, what food would you be? If your relationship with your customers was a marriage, what would your wedding vows be? If your competitors were animals, what animals would they be? When I ask my clients questions like this, it gives the conversation a fresh energy. Other times, I might show them a series of images – of war, sport, travel, adventure, food, disease – and see which, if any, resonate in the context of their corporate challenges, and then ask them to elaborate.

Step 3. How can you tell this story?

Once you've got the idea, build a story around it. A story should have the same elements we discussed on page 133: Robert McKee's definition of a strong protagonist overcoming the forces of antagonism to reach the object of their desire.

Start by creating desire for your metaphor, maybe by highlighting its absence. So, if you're depicting a future deal as 'food', perhaps talk about how we've been 'starved', 'hungry', 'craving' this for a long time. If your metaphor is that corruption is 'dirt', maybe start by saying how the system is filled with 'dirty' money and it's time for a 'clean-up'. If your metaphor is that truth is 'light', talk about how we are emerging from 'dark' times and that a new 'dawn' is on the 'horizon'. If we've got a 'fighting' metaphor we might have a narrative about how we've been 'battered' and 'bruised' over the last few years but now we're getting 'back on our feet', 'recovering our strength', 'building up our stamina' and we're ready to 'come back fighting'. If we've got a 'sailing' metaphor, we might tell a story about how the 'dark clouds swept in' a few years ago, and since then, we've been 'navigating stormy waters' and had to keep a steady 'hand on the tiller, not rock the boat, maintain our course' and now we can see there are 'safer shores ahead, brighter days', and if we just keep on going we'll 'reach our destination'.

If we're going for a 'sickness' metaphor then we might tell a story about how we've had a tough few years, we've not been at peak performance and now we face a choice about whether we emerge 'stronger' from the experience, or 'weakened'.

This is how metaphors work best. Think like a theatrical impresario constructing a dramatic narrative on the stage, and this is your storyboard, like you're William Shakespeare . . . Or Anne Hathaway. You have the power to create whatever narrative you want.

Greta Thunberg gets this. That might be why she's now one of the most influential people on the planet. She comes from a theatrical family. Her mother is a famous Swedish singer, and her father was an actor, and Greta herself spent much of her childhood travelling around the world accompanying them to performances so she is well schooled in the art of theatre. Both her mother and father have appeared in major public performances of *Romeo and Juliet*. One of her mother's big hits, and Greta's favourite songs as a child, was, 'L'amour est un oiseau rebelle' – *Love is a rebellious bird*. Greta knows better than most that the world is a stage.

In a speech in July 2021, titled 'The Show is Over', she exposed the whole global debate about climate change as nothing more than a show, a façade, a performance. She condemned global leaders as nothing more than actors, 'acting as saviours', 'pretending to care'. She challenged them: 'Perhaps role-playing helps you to sleep at night? Saying things for the sake of it because the words are in your script. But while you are busy working the stage, you seem to forget that the climate crisis is not something distant in the future, it is already taking so much from the most affected people in the most affected areas.' She ended by saying, 'The audience is weary. The show is over.'

It's more than four hundred years ago that Shakespeare came up with the line that Juliet was the sun. But today it is Greta who is shining bright, illuminating the debate, showing us the way forward. Forget Juliet – maybe Greta is the sun.

ENERGISE!

Your brain may already be sparking with ideas. Maybe you have already got ideas for some stories you can tell, which you can weave together to create a powerful MY STORY – OUR STORY – WHAT NEXT speech. That's brilliant if you do, but if you really want to create change, you're going to have to deliver your message in a way that really gets people fired up. And that's what we're going to cover next.

What is it about the way some people put their words together that means they really stick, and get under your skin, so you remember what they've said later by heart? How is it that some people are able to project their ideas in a way that lights up the room, while others leave us in the dark? Why is it that some people fill us with joy, so we smile at the simple thought of them, while others fill us with dread?

That's what we're looking at in this part of the book and we're going to start by looking at the connection between rhythm and reasoning.

Rhythm and Reasoning

Have you ever had a song stuck in your mind? A chorus or refrain that slips in and, no matter what you do, you can't shake it out? Mine usually come to me late at night, in those twilight moments before sleep when, with no other sound to disturb me other than the rhythm of my breath and the beating of my heart, they pass in undetected and go around and around my head, sometimes for days.

One slogan that has been going around my mind lately is that old Gillette advert: 'Gillette – the best a man can get'. This slogan, which premiered during the 1989 Superbowl to launch Gillette's new Sensor range, features images of a man succeeding in every aspect of life: in work, sport and relationships.

Gillette has invested over a billion dollars in promoting this slogan over the last 30 years so the chances are you've heard it before. It's probably also likely that you can, like me, instantly recall the images that accompanied it, of a super-successful, super-smiley man with his super-perfect family. It's a great campaign. The best a brand can get, you might say.

Connect!

But what is it about that slogan and campaign which made it succeed where others failed? Well, for a start, it is stuffed with ancient rhetorical devices. Back in Ancient Rome, schools would teach students heaps of different rhetorical devices: ways of structuring sentences to achieve different effects, from anadiplosis to anastrophe, catachresis to chiasmus, hyperbaton to hyperbole. I've refrained from using the ancient terms for rhetorical devices in this chapter because I think they can make rhetoric seem harder and less accessible than it really is, but if you want to get into all that, I recommend Richard A Lanham's *A Handlist of Rhetorical Terms*. Copywriters, speechwriters, poets, playwrights and editors still actively deploy many of those same rhetorical techniques today to make sentences sound more credible, compelling and convincing. *Snap, Crackle and Pop. Just do it. Up Yours Delors.* You start with your message, apply a few appropriate rhetorical devices and then, Bob's your uncle, you have a slogan. In this way, you're connecting reasoning with rhythm, meaning with music, purpose with poetry. Just like that.

Let's see how it's done. Let's look closely at that simple slogan: *Gillette – the best a man can get.* It's only seven words long but there's a lot going on.

Firstly, it follows what's known as an iambic beat. This is a poetic device, where the stress is placed on alternate beats. Da <u>Dum</u>, Da <u>Dum</u>, Da <u>Dum</u>, Da <u>Dum.</u> Gillette – the <u>best</u> a <u>man</u> can <u>get</u>. Many literary geniuses have deployed this device over the centuries. From William Shakespeare – 'My <u>horse</u>! My <u>horse</u>! My <u>Kingdom</u> <u>For</u> a <u>Horse</u>!' to Dr Seuss – 'I <u>will</u> not <u>eat</u> them <u>Sam</u> I <u>am</u>!'

Rhythm and Reasoning

There's a reason why this Da Dum, Da Dum sound is so irresistible to the ear. This _is_ the rhythm of our life. (That one comes from nineties dance group, Corona). It's the ultimate sound of comfort: the sound we heard in our mother's womb; the sound we hear when we rest our head upon a loved one's chest; the sound we hear from deep inside our soul when we're lying in bed going to sleep at night. It's the key to our very existence, the sound of our beating heart. There could be no more familiar or reassuring sound in the world. So, when speech follows that rhythm, it's already under our skin before the words have even been spoken.

The rhythm of life

Shakespeare was a big fan of iambic verse and many of his most famous lines were written to that da dum beat.

'If music be the food of love, play on.'
'Now is the winter of our discontent.'
'I come to bury Caesar, not to praise him.'

But Shakespeare frequently went one step further as well, using a technique called iambic _pentameter_, which is when you have five Da Dums in a row. Why five? With an average heartbeat of around 70 beats per minute and an average respiratory rate of around 12 beats per minute, we get about five heartbeats to each breath. So iambic pentameter connects not just with our heartbeat but with our breathing as well. So sentences which are written in this form connect subconsciously with the rhythm we live by

Connect!

from the moment we're born until the second we die. This <u>is</u> the <u>rhyth</u>m <u>of</u> our <u>life</u>.

But that's not all there is to be said about the Gillette slogan. The second half, 'The <u>best</u> a <u>man</u> can <u>get</u>', contains a magical three iambic beats. There's something about those three beats together that sounds marvellous, memorable and magical.

There is a magic in the rule of three. The Romans used to call the rule of three *tricolon*, which sounds like part of your digestive system, but which is simply the rhetorical device of putting your arguments into threes. As Julius Caesar said, *Omne Trium Perfectum*. Perfection comes in threes. Many of the greatest soundbites in history have been based around three-part lists. *Veni. Vidi. Vici. Government of the people, by the people, for the people. Liberté, égalité, fraternité. Duty, Honour Country. Beans Meanz Heinz.*

The rule of three may be an ancient rhetorical device but it remains just as powerful today. A study by Georgetown University and the University of California in 2013 checked the power of three-point arguments against four-point arguments. They carried out tests in a range of settings, from product copywriting through to in-store advertising and political claims and each time they got the same result: three claims good; four claims bad. They called their research 'three charms, four alarms'. It's sound advice. So, if you want to persuade people to buy your product, make it 'cleaner, greener and cheaper' *not* 'cleaner, greener, better and cheaper'.

It feels counter-intuitive to cut down the number of points we make. We imagine that the more evidence we pile on, the more convincing our argument becomes but the opposite is true. The more we pile on to our argument, the less convincing it becomes. There's something uniquely credible, compelling and convincing about an argument which comes in threes. So keep it simple. Bish, bash, bosh. In and out. Just like that.

There are all sorts of theories for why the rule of three works. It may be because we're naturally used to thinking in threes. When we follow a major premise to a minor premise and a conclusion, we're thinking in threes. *All dogs have four legs. This is a dog. Therefore this has four legs.* When we're splitting the difference, i.e., taking the midpoint between two extreme positions to find a moderate position – on the one hand this, on the other hand that, therefore I think the other – (also known as triangulating in political terms), we're thinking in threes. It's the Goldilocks principle. *Not too hot, not too cold, this is just right.*

Connect!

Also, studies have shown that when we're looking for patterns, three tends to be the magic point at which we discern a pattern has been established. For instance, if a team wins three games in a row, that's the point we'll deduce that they're on a winning streak. Likewise, if a team loses three games in a row, that's when we'll deduce they're on a losing streak. We make the same decisions when it comes to detecting price trends on investments. Three days of continual rises represents the point at which we see the pattern. It cannot be reliably deduced before then.

Photographers, designers, artists, architects and even plastic surgeons all talk about the rule of three. There's something in the brain that just loves threes. *'Ready. Aim. Fire!' 'On Your Marks. Get Set. Go!' 'Look Left. Look Right. Cross!'* Many of the greatest advertising campaigns in history have been based around the rule of three, from the *'Mm! Mm! Good'* of Campbell's Soup through to the *'See it. Say it. Sorted.'* ads we've seen in railway stations for many years now. In 2021, Greta Thunberg accused world leaders of 'Blah, Blah, Blah'. Leaders responded to her, saying they were taking action, action, action. Cynics might respond with, *'Yeah. Yeah. Yeah.'*

Much of the public health messaging on coronavirus was based around the rule of three. Dr Tedros Adhanom Ghebreyesus, the head of the World Health Organization, urged all countries around the world to *'Test! Test! Test!'* from the very beginning of the pandemic. In the UK, in the early days of the pandemic, the slogan was, *'Catch it. Bin it. Kill it'*. Then, during the first lockdown, the slogan was *'Stay home. Save lives. Protect the NHS.'* Then, as we were urged to go out again, but exercising caution around handwashing, social distancing and mask wearing, the message was, '*Hands, Face, Space.*'

The rule of three is such a simple rhetorical device to use and yet it makes your appeal more powerful in so many different contexts. The rule of three is especially effective in big set-piece speeches. Professor Max Atkinson did some famous research in the early eighties to discover what makes people applaud at party conference speeches. He found three-part lists generated applause so frequently he called it a 'clap trap'. But it's interesting, and not coincidental, that both of the studies I have cited concerning the rule of three, one by UK researchers and the other by US researchers, both use rhymes to present their findings: 'clap trap' and 'three charms, four alarms'.

They're making the case for the rule of three but they're doing so using rhymes. As well they might, because there's separate research which shows people are also more likely to believe something is true if it rhymes. People find the phrase 'What sobriety conceals, alcohol reveals' to be more believable than 'What sobriety conceals, alcohol unmasks'. Likewise, the phrase 'Woes unite foes' seemed more believable than 'Woes unite enemies'.

So that's another aspect of the Gillette slogan that increases its attractiveness. 'Gillette – the best a man can get.' It rhymes. It chimes. It's ridiculous to think we might be so easily misled and convinced by a simple rhyme but it's what linguists talk about as the processing fluency of language: how easy is a sentence for the brain to process. Giving someone a long sentence with long words is like giving them a long pepperoni baguette and asking them to swallow it whole, whereas giving them a rhyme is like asking them to take a sip of fruit juice. It slides down a treat. Rhyme is sublime.

It's the 'rhyme as reason' effect. The sentence sounds simple so the underlying thought seems simple. Shakespeare knew all about this. Shakespeare had his smartest characters speak in rhyme. When he wanted to indicate a speaker was slightly unhinged, as with King Lear or Hamlet, he had them shift from poetry to prose, thereby subtly indicating to the audience that all was not well.

Why do rhymes still have so much power? Partly, it may be learned. We all grow up with rhymes. Many of our earliest and most important life lessons are delivered in rhyme: we learn the letters of the alphabet in rhyme, we learn how many days there are in a month in rhyme and we learn many other pieces of life wisdom in rhyme. Still to this day, whenever I need to work out whether I want to head east or west on a motorway, I mutter to myself, 'Never Eat Shredded Wheat' before flicking the indicator, reminding myself of the points of a compass.

You can see that all these learning experiences built up over time could lead us to instinctively connect truth with rhyme. But even as adults, we still frequently pass on wisdom through rhyme. Sayings like 'Red sky at night, shepherd's delight' exist in dozens of languages around the world. Many aphorisms rhyme. They're not necessarily true – a friend in need is not necessarily a friend indeed, they might be a bloody nuisance – but they sound true. Nietzsche said rhyming was the language of the gods. Many religious texts, especially the Koran, are filled with rhymes. Rhyme is also, however, very much the language of the advertising agencies: 'Gillette – the best a man can get'.

As well as rhyming, there is another point of interest to the Gillette slogan. It follows a puzzle–solution formula. The first part of the sentence establishes a puzzle which is resolved in the second half of the sentence. Puzzle–solution is another one of Max Atkinson's clap traps. It gives the sentence a feel of two halves: starting with the question and ending with resolution. It feels beautifully balanced.

Balance is inherently appealing to us. One of the most important skills for being human is an appreciation of the importance of balance in the body. As babies, we quickly learn: breath comes in, breath goes out; food goes in, food goes out; emotions come, emotions go. As a toddler, one of our vital first lessons in life is walking, which requires a careful balance between left and right. As adults, we understand the importance of balanced thought, balanced lives and balanced minds.

But we also understand that our natural world operates in balance. There is night and day, dark and light, cold and warmth. We also understand that society works in balance. The golden rule: 'do unto others as we would have them do unto us'. Balance appears to us to be fundamental to the natural order of the world. The world seems to have been created in a balanced way, and balanced is the voice of our creator.

Many religious texts communicate messages using this balanced structure. St Francis's peace prayer bounces along in balancing sentences, 'Where there is discord, may we bring harmony. Where there is error, may we bring truth. Where there is doubt, may we bring faith. And where there is despair, may we bring hope.'

Buddha frequently spoke in such balanced sentences as well.

'When watching after yourself, you watch after others. When watching after others, you watch after yourself.'

'There is nothing so disobedient as an undisciplined mind, and there is nothing so obedient as a disciplined mind.'

'He who loves 50 people has 50 woes. He who loves no one has no woes.'

We also get this kind of rhetoric in more modern religions and cults. Personally, I'm a big fan of Yoda, whose most famous quote is probably 'Do or do not. There is no try.' Great wisdom for life. And indeed, the Jedi philosophy has attracted a surprising share of followers, with more and more people identifying as Jedi in national censuses around the world, from Canada to the Czech Republic, Australia to Ireland, New Zealand to the UK. Many were almost certainly putting it as a joke, but in the 2001 England and Wales Census, 390,127 (0.8 per cent) of the population stated their religion as Jedi, making it the fourth largest religion, ahead of Sikhism, Judaism and Buddhism. The Office for National Statistics announced this in possibly the best-titled press release ever: '390,000 Jedi there are.'

Many advertising agencies revel in this kind of balanced rhetoric. Gerald Zaltman and Lindsay Zaltman argue in their brilliant book, *Marketing Metaphoria: What Deep Metaphors Reveal About the Minds of Consumers,* that balance is one of the seven most powerful metaphorical appeals you can make to consumers. And of course this balancing structure is frequently found in advertising slogans: *'Melt in your mouth, not in your hands'* (Minstrels). *'For mash, get Smash!'* (Smash). *'Tide's in. Dirt's out'* (Tide). *'American by birth. Rebel by choice'* (Harley-Davidson). *'Save money. Live Better'* (Walmart). *'Your vision. Our future'* (Olympus).

Simon Sinek is an ex-adman who's now a popular thought leader and writer on leadership. He started his career working in top New York ad agencies including Ogilvy & Mather and today he uses his superb sloganeering skills to convey complex leadership ideas in bite-size nuggets of wisdom.

'People don't buy what you do, they buy why you do it.'
  'Working hard for something we don't care about is called stress. Working hard for something we love is called passion.'
  'When you compete against everyone else, no one wants to help you. When you compete against yourself, everyone wants to help you.'

The balanced structure in the sentences suggests underlying balance in thought. It's Business Buddhism. Sinek uses the same sentence structure in many of his LinkedIn posts, which read like pieces of religious wisdom. See three random posts:

'Complaining begets more complaints. Anger begets more anger. Optimism begets more optimism.' (27,000 likes)

Connect!

'The selfish fear change. The selfless lead it.' (22,000 likes).
'When we win, we must remember that the next time we could lose. When we lose, we must remember that next time we can win.' (45,000 likes)

Of course, much great political rhetoric is based around these kinds of sentence structures as well, from Benjamin Franklin's 'If you fail to plan, you are planning to fail' to John F Kennedy's 'Ask not what your country can do for you, ask what you can do for your country' and Barack Obama's 'You stood up for America, now America must stand up for you.'

These balancing statements can take many forms. They can be opposites (I work to live, I don't live to work), comparisons (naughty, but nice) or phrase reversals (all you need is love, love is all you need).

There's just one further device to explore from this slogan, and that is exaggeration. Gillette is saying it's the best a man can get. I'm not sure that that is necessarily true or scientifically proven. Certainly by some measures it could be true but, also, just maybe, this might be hyperbole.

So, 'Gillette – the best a man can get'. It's just seven words long, but it contains at least five different rhetorical devices (one for every blade in the Sensor).

- Iambic pentameter
- The rule of three
- Rhyme
- Balance
- Exaggeration

Sticky slogans

The next time you need to create a powerful message, either to get yourself to do something, or to support your friends and family members to get something done, why don't you try creating a sticky slogan using those same techniques. First, boil down your message to the very essence of what you have to say and then keep adding on the different rhetorical devices until you've come up with something great. Give it a go. You never know! You might just wind up with a Times Square quality slogan but without the Madison Avenue bill.

Now we've looked at how you can use these devices to create slogans, we're going to look at how you can use a combination of them in sequence so you can very quickly create a super-powerful speech. This is the structure I set out in my 2016 TEDx Verona talk which you can see on YouTube. It has six steps. You can all use this technique yourself to create your own powerful speech. Treat it like an IKEA self-assembly kit. Don't insert your own steps. Don't muddle them up. Just trust the structure and follow the steps one by one.

Snappy sentences

OK. Step one. Let's start with three super-short sentences:
Stop! Look! Listen!
Look left. Look right. Look centre.
OK! Got it? Just like that.
How do you feel? Anxious? Nervous?
Super-short sentences like this mimic the sound of hyper-ventilating. They create a sense of urgency. They speak directly

Connect!

to your instinctive brain and they say danger. Stop! Look! Listen! It's the authentic sound of fear.

The Ancient Romans used this rhetorical technique all the time. It's called asyndeton and it's still used by leaders today. Donald Trump used it: *'Look at China! Mexico! Laughing at us!'* Business-people use it too: *'Profits down. Markets in turmoil. Competitors on the move.'* And also, campaigners: *'Floods in Asia. Droughts in Africa. Hurricanes in America.'*

Contrast these super-short, super-powerful sentences with the longer style of sentence which is invariably preferred by the most excruciatingly dull lecturer to be found in illustrious academic institutions. 'I am sure you will all be inescapably inclined to agree that, regardless of your undoubtedly divergent and disparate pre-existing views and beliefs, the short and pithy sentences which I have illustrated in the brief aforementioned examples sit in stark contrast with the more uncertain, complex and ambiguous language that is favoured by those who occupy certain, lofty academic institutions where sentences will invariably be dramatically extended to the absolute maximum point until they are drifting around in all manner of directions, occasionally rising, occasionally falling, then meandering into another parenthesis, before finally faltering and petering out.'

This kind of text explains why so many people literally fall asleep in lectures. It's the total opposite of the 'Right! OK! Let's go!' type of speaker. The breathless sentences scream, 'Wake up!' while the long-winded sentences whisper in your ear. 'Sleep . . . Sleep . . .' Of course, sometimes it can actually be the intention of speakers to send their audiences to sleep: that possibility can't be ignored. Some people actively want to avoid attention and scrutiny. Harold Wilson once said that you should never underestimate the power of being boring. I swear that many management consultants deliberately shroud their conclusions in impenetrable jargon and dense text to avoid being held to account. And if that's what you want to achieve, fine. If, however, you want urgency, go for super-short sentences.

And if you want the sentences super punchy, make them sentences of one word long. On becoming Leader of the Labour Party, Tony Blair said his priorities were 'Education! Education! Education!' John Major, the Conservative prime minister at the time, responded that his priorities were the same, only in a different order. *Ha ha ha.*

So that's the first technique, thinking about the breath that you need to rest your message upon – short (to wake people up!), long (to send them to sleep) or somewhere in the middle, as with iambic pentameter (indicating all is well). For the purposes of our super-short, super-powerful speech, we're going for the super-short, super-powerful sentences.

Repetition

The second device is three repetitive sentences. Now, this will feel like an anathema for many writers who are used to being told that any repetition in communication is bad. It's wasted words, wasted time, wasted effort. But repetition can be a powerful way to communicate emotion. When we're emotional about something, we fixate on it, and this then manifests in our speech, so repetition is the authentic sound of emotion.

This is what Churchill did with his legendary '*We shall fight on the beaches, we shall fight on the landing grounds, we shall fight in the fields and in the streets . . .'* He could have said this much faster, and indeed a ruthless editor may well have got the red pen out and cut that down to 'We shall fight on the beaches, the landing grounds, the fields and the streets'. Indeed John Colville, who was Churchill's Private Secretary, complained in his diary that Churchill's rhetoric was full of hot air, but of course Churchill knew what he was doing. He wanted to show he was emotionally fixated on the fight and the rhetorical repetition helped him convey that feeling.

Many of the greatest speakers in history have used repetition to incredible effect. In his extraordinary 'I have a dream' speech, Martin Luther King Jr. began no less than nine separate sentences with the words 'I have a dream'. In the same speech, eight separate sentences began with the words, 'Let freedom ring'. He could certainly have made his point more quickly, but would it have proved as powerful? Probably not.

Repetition can be used in a number of ways. You might fire off a series of three rhetorical questions, building anger and indignation:

'Is it right that the richest 50 people on the planet have the same wealth as the poorest 50 per cent of people on the planet? Is it right that every year more than a million children die under the age of five because of a lack of access to clean water and sanitation facilities? Is it right than one in ten people on the planet must survive on less than two dollars a day?'

Or it can be used to build a more positive energy:

'Our strategy team is brilliant. Our HR team is brilliant. Our sales team is brilliant.'

Repetition looks a bit lame on the page – like something out of a book for pre-schoolers. I always feel like I'm cheating when I write it into a speech, pumping up the word count to little effect, yet I never cease to be amazed by its power when you hear it spoken. The effect is remarkable. It generates such an energy in a crowd.

Balancing statements

The third device is three balancing statements. We've already explored the thinking behind balancing statements, so I won't go over all of that again. Suffice to say that this is the bit when you sound balanced, as if you're weighing things up. It makes you sound logical, rational and calm.

The three balancing statements might be opposites. *This is about rich and poor, black and white, old and young. While other businesses are cutting costs, we're investing. While other businesses are standing still, we're innovating. While other businesses are looking inward, we're reaching out. We're looking to the future, not the past; working together, not against one another; thinking about what we can do, not what we can't.* You might strengthen the sentence by adding alliteration. *What we're doing is not just about profit, but passion. Not just money, but meaning. Not cash, but compassion.* It feels vaguely hypnotic, like a pendulum swinging back and forth.

Metaphor

The fourth device is metaphor. We looked at metaphor previously: when we're using metaphor we're saying something is something it isn't. If we want to attract people towards something, we might use attractive images, metaphors of light, warmth, food, love or family. If we're wanting to make people recoil, we might use disgusting images, metaphors of dirt, disease, death, darkness or danger. But don't get carried away with metaphor. If you can taste sick in your mouth while you're saying it, you've gone too far. And you need to save some room for the fifth step.

Exaggeration

The fifth step is exaggeration. When we are emotional, our perspective naturally distorts, so exaggeration is an authentic signifier of emotion. Exaggeration has had a bad rap since that 'very stable genius' Donald Trump massively overused it, but it's part and parcel of everyday conversation. We all exaggerate, and always have, since the dawn of time. Prehistoric cave drawings found in France show exaggeration has been around for tens of thousands of years. Animals were depicted with tusks that were much larger than they could possibly be in real life, presumably to spark an emotional reaction. FEAR. People were depicted with enlarged breasts and genitals in order to generate another emotional reaction. LUST.

When we exaggerate, not only does it articulate our emotion, it also has the power to elicit emotion in others. This happens in art and in speech. Much ordinary speech contains exaggerative statements. *'I've been waiting forever for you!' 'I couldn't sleep at all last night!' 'I'm going to give this my heart and soul.'* When we use exaggeration, it is a bit like highlighting and underlining what we're saying, setting off fireworks and generating energy. It helps prepare everyone for the final device.

Rhyme

The final device is rhyme. A rhyme doesn't cost a dime. As we've explored already, rhymes are sublime. End with rhyme, works every time. 379 of the 821 scenes in Shakespeare's plays end in rhymes.

So that's the structure:

1. 3 breathless sentences
2. 3 repetitive sentences
3. 3 contrasts
4. Metaphor
5. 3 exaggerative statements
6. Rhyme.

Soapbox speeches

Give it a try. Have some fun. Why not write a little speech about something you really care about? What do you get on your soap box about? What's your regular rant? Maybe it's personal: persuading your partner to move house? Maybe it's political: like climate change, coronavirus or culture wars? Maybe it's professional: we must invest more in training, we need to put in place a serious strategy, or perhaps you want to argue that it's time to introduce a major transformation programme?

You can use this formula quickly to prepare a decent outline for all sorts of speeches. The political speech, the motivational speech, the business speech. This is speechwriting by numbers, but it can be a very effective way to quickly marshal thoughts and test arguments, if that's what you need. Even if you don't ever actually perform the whole speech verbatim, it is bound to generate some powerful lines of argument, as well as some knockout soundbites.

The more you practise these techniques, the more familiar you'll become with them, until eventually you'll start to internalise them and they'll become an authentic part of your everyday speech. At this stage, you will start using them naturally, instinctively aware of the different effects different device achieve. I need this to sound urgent – *breathless sentences*. I need this to sound passionate – *repetition*. I need this to sound considered – *balanced sentences*. I need this to capture the imagination – *metaphor*. I need this to hype them up – *hyperbole*. I need this bit to really stick – *rhyme*. When you're at this stage, people might say you've got the gift of the gab, you're a natural. It's practise, practise, practise.

People who have been in public life and making speeches for a long time tend to use all these devices instinctively. Narendra Modi, Joe Biden, Jacinda Ardern and Boris Johnson are the big election winners globally in recent years and it's interesting to note that, although they all come from extremely different backgrounds and political traditions, they all use the same rhetorical devices liberally in their big speeches.

Joe Biden

Joe Biden's biggest speech in the run up to the 2020 US Election was his speech to the Democratic National Convention. He opened that speech with a number of breathless sentences to create a sense of urgency:

'Economic injustice. Racial injustice. Environmental injustice.'
'Too much anger. Too much fear. Too much division.'
'I will defend us from every attack. Seen. And unseen. Always. Without exception. Every time.'

He used repetition to build up passion on a number of occasions:

'We will never get our economy back on track.'
'We will never get our kids safely back to school.'
'We will never have our lives back.'

'Remember seeing those neo-Nazis and Klansmen and white supremacists coming out of the fields with lighted torches?'
'Remember the violent clash that ensued between those spreading hate and those with the courage to stand against it?'
'Remember what the president said?'

Occasionally, he combined repetition with balance:

'Winning it for the generous among us, not the selfish.'
'Winning it for the workers who keep this country going, not just the privileged few at the top.'
'Winning it for those communities who have known the injustice of the "knee on the neck".'

And also:

'We will choose hope over fear, facts over fiction, fairness over privilege.'

Connect!

'I will draw on the best of us, not the worst. I will be an ally of the light, not of the darkness.'

His metaphor was simple and consistent. He introduced his metaphor with a quote from civil rights campaigner Ella Baker: *'Give people light and they will find a way.'* That metaphorical theme – Trump = darkness, Biden = light – ran through the whole of the speech.

'America's history tells us that it has been in our darkest moments that we've made our greatest progress. That we've found the light. And in this dark moment, I believe we are poised to make great progress again. That we can find the light once more.'

The Trump = darkness metaphor perfectly prepared the ground for his 'new dawn' rhetoric of his inauguration which we explored in the opening chapter.

And he closed the speech with the same metaphor he began with. *'May history be able to say that the end of this chapter of American darkness began here tonight as love and hope and light joined in the battle for the soul of the nation.'*

He used exaggeration throughout the speech, especially in his denunciation of Trump, who he said, *'takes no responsibility, refuses to lead, blames others, cosies up to dictators and fans the flames of hate and division.'*

And he ended with a rhyme from Seamus Heaney, a line from 'The Cure of Troy', rhyming both grave and wave and time and rhyme.

Rhythm and Reasoning

Joe Biden won 81,268,924 votes in the 2020 presidential election, more than any other candidate in any other election in the history of America.

Narendra Modi

Over in India, as we've already seen, Narendra Modi has won more votes than any other single person in the history of the planet. He won the 2019 Indian election with a whopping 229 million votes, more votes than any other candidate ever in a single election. Even his opponents say he is the 'finest speaker [they] have ever heard', describing him as 'mesmerising'. When he makes speeches in London, he can fill Wembley Stadium. He usually speaks in Hindi, but his speeches are translated into English. Let's look at the speech he delivered at the Bharatiya Janata Party's Delhi headquarters after the vote count in the 2019 election.

He uses the three breathless sentences, quoting his supporters' cry of 'Modi! Modi! Modi!'

He makes ample use of repetition:

'We haven't left our politeness,
We haven't left our wisdom.
We haven't left our values.
We haven't left our culture.'

At times, his repetitive refrains are reminiscent of Martin Luther King or Barack Obama:

'This is a victory for the young man who is dreaming of the twenty-first century.

Connect!

This is a victory for that mother who, with all her self-respect and dignity, is desperate for a toilet.

This is a victory for that sick man who waited 4 or 5 years for treatment and gets it today.

This is a victory for the farmers who sweat it out, who starve their stomach to feed our country.'

He uses rhetorical contrast on the same theme:

'This is not a victory for Modi. This is a victory for the aspirations of every citizen of this country craving for honesty.'

And more balancing repetitive statements:

'If there is a winner today, it is India.
If there is a winner today, it is democracy.
If there is a winner today, it is the people.'

He uses a clear and consistent journey metaphor throughout his speech. He talks about *walking shoulder to shoulder* with winners from all parties towards a brighter future as they undertake the *journey* to development.

There is lots of exaggeration. *'I won't do anything just for myself. . . . Every second of my time and every cell of my body is dedicated solely to the citizens of this country.'*

And, as for rhyme, Hindi is a very lyrical language and a Hindi-speaking friend advises me that Modi throws a rhyme approximately once every two minutes in this speech.

Rhythm and Reasoning

Jacinda Ardern

Let's now skip to New Zealand, where Jacinda Ardern won the 2020 election with a landslide win and an unprecedented majority for the Labour Party. Aged just 36 when she first became prime minister, she is much younger than Modi and Biden, but she still uses of a lot of the same rhetorical devices. Look at how she launched her campaign in August 2020.

She used breathless sentences to highlight Labour's achievements. *'Fewer children living in poverty. More homes are being built.'*

She used repetition in groups of three.

'That does not mean there aren't ideas to be debated, policies to be released, manifestos to be discussed . . .'

'This election is about the future. It's about leadership. And it's about values.'

'We have been strong, we have been empathetic and we have been kind.'

She used rhetorical contrasts to highlight the choice on offer for voters.

'It's about whether we stop and we change to another team or whether we keep those we know and trust.

It's about whether we build a few roads or whether we rebuild New Zealand.

It's about whether we stop and start again or whether we keep up the momentum we already have.'

Connect!

Like Modi, she also used a journey metaphor to support her overall campaign message of 'Let's Keep Moving.' She talked about *'grabbing hold of the opportunities that lie in front of us'*.

A sprinkle of exaggeration. *'Now is the time, more than ever, to keep going, to keep working . . .'*.

And she ends with a gentle three-part rhyme that bounces along beautifully: *'Let's keep going. Let's keep rebuilding. And let's keep moving.'*

Boris Johnson

And finally to the UK. In 2019, Boris Johnson won a landslide victory for the Conservative Party, slashing the Labour vote from the 12.9 million they'd won in 2017 to 10.3 million.

Johnson started his victory speech with breathless sentences.
'We did it! We did it! We pulled it off!'
Then three repetitive sentences.
'We broke the deadlock, we ended the gridlock, we smashed the roadblock.'
Then the contrasting sentences, spiced up with alliteration.
'From Woking to Workington; from Kensington to Clwyd South; from Surrey Heath to Sedgefield; from Wimbledon to Wolverhampton . . .'.
Then, he had religious metaphor running through. He talked about the NHS 'that performs *miracles*', 'a *sacred* trust for me, for every newly elected Conservative MP, for everyone

in this room and everyone in this party'. And he talked about making it his *'mission* to work night and day', which takes us on to the next bit.

Exaggeration. *'I will never take your support for granted. I will make it my mission to work night and day, to work flat out to prove you right in voting for me this time, and to earn your support in the future.'*

There were rhymes throughout. He said the case for Brexit was now *'irresistible, irrefutable, unarguable.'* He said he wanted to make this country *'the cleanest, greenest on earth'*. And he ended with, *'Let's get Brexit done. But first, my friends, let's get breakfast done.'*

Of course, Boris Johnson knows all of these devices. And not only does he know how they work in practice, he even knows the actual ancient rhetorical terms for them. I remember seeing him speak once about Winston Churchill's 'We will fight them on the beaches' speech, when he highlighted Churchill's use of *anaphora* and *tricolon* in this passage, recognising not only the rhetorical devices Churchill was using, but even knowing the ancient terms for what might be better known in plain English as repetition and the rule of three.

Perhaps seeing all of these world leaders speak using the same rhetorical devices has left you feeling rather cynical about this generation of politicians? Maybe it's time for a new generation? Maybe you might enter politics yourself? In which case, perhaps you might make a speech arguing that you would be different from the rest? Something like this perhaps . . .

Connect!

A new generation of politicians

Biden. Johnson. Ardern and Modi.
They think the same.
They act the same.
They even bloody talk the same.
They're more concerned with rhetoric, than reality
With soundbites instead of substance.
With making headlines instead of helping people in their day-to-day lives.
The time has come for us to fight back.
To seize control.
To claim back what is rightfully ours.
We need to get rid of this small clique of self-serving politicians.
And have some normal people in power.
People who speak normal English
Without rhetorical flourish.
Ladies and gentlemen, this is our hour
For normal people to take back power.

The truth is that any speaker can thrive using these same set of techniques. While they can appear contrived (especially when analysed in the cold light of a book), the reason these techniques work is because they are all natural manifestations of physiological conditions that derive from different emotional states. If a speaker feels a sense of urgency, they naturally become breathless. If a speaker feels obsessed with an issue, they naturally become repetitive. So, even speakers without any schooling in rhetoric will find themselves naturally using these devices.

Check out Malala's use of the rule of three, repetition and contrast in her fantastic Nobel Prize Acceptance speech, delivered when she was just 16 years old. 'This award is not just for me. It is for those forgotten children who want an education. It is for those frightened children who want peace. It is for those voiceless children who want change.'

Check out the way that Volodymyr Zelensky used these devices in his appeal to the Russian people delivered in spring 2022. 'Who is going to suffer from this most? The people. Who doesn't want this more than anyone? The people. Who can prevent all this from happening? The people.'

While some may scorn these rhetorical techniques, the truth is that they've been tried and tested over thousands of years. When they're used well and you have a strong argument, they can really help land a message. Equally, when persuaders fail to use these techniques, they can find their message does not land in quite the way they wanted.

In 2019, Gillette celebrated the thirtieth anniversary of their original 'The best a man can get' advert with a new campaign. Times had changed a lot since their first advert. With masculinity increasingly seen as toxic against a backdrop of multiple accusations of rape and sexual assault in the #MeToo movement, Gillette decided to reposition themselves as pioneers for a new kind of masculinity. They rewrote their slogan, changing it from 'Gillette: the best a man can get' to 'We believe: the best men can be'.

Connect!

They launched 'We believe: the best men can be' with a video. The video began with harrowing scenes of men belittling women on television and in the boardroom, their aggressive and violent behaviour going unchallenged, as a narrator asked:

'Is this the best a man can get? Is it? We can't hide from it. It's been going on far too long. We can't laugh it off, making the same old excuses.'

The video then showed men beginning to step up, speak out and challenge the behaviour.

'Bro! Not cool! Not cool!' one character intervened.

The narrator continued.

'But something finally changed. And there will be no going back. Because we believe in the best in men. To say the right thing. To act the right way. Some already are, in ways big and small. But some is not enough. Because the boys watching today will be the men of tomorrow.'

It was an admirable moral stance. The video certainly got attention, and was watched millions of times within hours of its release. But it's fair to say that the reaction was not universally positive. Within two days, dislikes outpolled likes on YouTube by 10 to 1, #BoycottGillette started trending on Twitter and the company was accused of woke-ism, virtue-signalling and hypocrisy. Within a week, Gillette's online mentions had swung from 85 per cent positive to 54.8 per cent negative.

However, the company showed no regrets. Procter and Gamble Chief Brand Officer, Marc Pritchard responded saying, 'This sparked an important worldwide conversation.'

Pankaj Bhalla, Gillette's North America brand director said, 'We expected debate' while Gillette president Gary Coombes defended their decision to 'publicly assert our beliefs while celebrating men doing things right.'

They were doing what they believed to be the right thing and surely that is to be commended. But was their slogan truly the best Gillette could get? Despite working on this chapter for the best part of a year, not once has 'We believe: the best men can be' got under my skin and gone around my head at night. It's not hard to see why it's failed. It's not iambic, it doesn't rhyme, it's not hyperbolic, it doesn't chime, it's not a triptych, it's a waste of time.

Personally, I'd have gone for 'Gillette: The Best *We All Can Get*.' A line we won't forget.

Serious and Silly

When Texan lawyer Rod Ponton attended an online hearing of the 394th Judicial District Court with Judge Roy Ferguson on 9 February 2021, he could scarcely have imagined that by the end of the day he would become an internet sensation. While he was fully prepared for his legal deposition, what he didn't realise was that his children had changed the Zoom settings on his computer. The Judge watched bemused as Ponton's strained voice came from behind a cat filter.

'I don't know how to remove it,' Ponton pleaded. 'I have an assistant here. I'm here live,' he insisted. 'I'm not a cat.' The cat's eyes darted hilariously from left to right, as Ponton tried to remove the filter. It was pure comedy. Within days, the video had been viewed millions of times around the world and been shared by hundreds of celebrities, usually with laughing emojis. Novelist Margaret Atwood tweeted the video saying, 'I on the other hand am a cat. How do I get this human filter off?'

It's probably no coincidence that this video went viral around the first anniversary of the coronavirus pandemic. At this time, many people were processing complex emotions: grief, anxiety and fatigue at the relentless tide of bad news. In the midst of such seriousness, the brief bout of silliness provided welcome and essential relief. After all, as they say, you've got to laugh. And you really have. *You have got to laugh.*

You've got to laugh

Sigmund Freud said laughter was an essential process for our body to deal with built-up tension in our minds and bodies. It's a way of processing trauma and releasing pent-up psychological and physiological energy. Just watch someone laugh and you'll see the incredible energy that is generated. And it's totally instinctive. As neuroscientist Sophie Scott has pointed out, when we laugh, we look and sound a little like chimpanzees, experiencing spasms and emitting sounds that would be more at home in the jungle.

Laughter is one of our most primitive needs. We speak of laughter as cathartic, and there are some clues to its true purpose within the origin of that word. The word catharsis derives from the old Greek term for cleansing ourselves of the bad stuff, typically in the context of defecation and menstruation, so it's always been seen as a vital way of getting rid of the bad emotional stuff that builds up inside us. And it's important we get the chance to do it regularly and effectively; if we don't, we can become unwell.

Whenever there's a big national or global tragedy, you can count the minutes before the first inappropriate jokes start circulating, usually accompanied with the obligatory, 'Too soon?' Of course, the truth is it's never too soon, which is why so many people's first reaction to receiving bad news is frequently to burst out laughing.

So Rod Ponton was providing an essential service by giving us a laugh during this difficult period. And he was not alone. Thousands of TikTok and YouTube videos circulated during the coronavirus pandemic, often attracting millions of views, and usually providing a much healthier alternative to the evening news. We had the lady who gave a news interview from her home office with a huge dildo standing proud on the bookshelf behind her. We had the cats, dogs, children, boyfriends and girlfriends who accidentally (or not) bumped their way into camera shot and behaved badly. We also had the many people who inadvertently left their cameras on while performing all sorts of acts which are best kept private, in full view of their hysterical colleagues.

These viral sensations uncovered and exposed, in an amusing light, a phenomenon many of us were grappling with at the time: the blurring, blending and occasional collision between our personal and professional lives. All of us who were working from home were grappling with the challenge of how to maintain our professional personas within our personal spaces. These videos exposed the inherent tensions, complexities and, ultimately, the absurdity of it all.

Now there are many theories of humour and types of humour we could explore in this chapter – irony, sarcasm, one-liners, shaggy dogs, slapstick, rhymes, riddles, limericks and many more – but, in keeping with the theme of this book, I'm going to focus on just one type of humour: the connection point between the serious and the silly. I'm going to explore how actively identifying and exploiting that connection point can generate an incredible energy that can deliberately be used to reduce tension, bring people together and create good feelings. To paraphrase Francis of Assisi, where there is gravity, may we bring levity; where there is pomp, may we bring play; where there is seriousness, may we be silly. And there really has been a lot of seriousness we've needed relief from in the last few years.

Serious times

As well as coronavirus, there's also been fraught political debate in many countries around the world. The 2020 US presidential election was the most divisive in living memory. With riots on the streets and allegations of insurrection, it felt at times like America could be on the brink of a civil war. It all came to a climax in 6 January 2021, with the storming of the Capitol building, Trump's removal from social media and Biden's heavily policed inauguration. It was clear this was far from normal. Inaugurations are normally joyful events where all sides come together after the election and unite again. That was not the case in this election. In a break with precedent, Trump refused to show up to the ceremony. In a further break with precedent, Joe Biden's speech directed hostile language towards Trump's supporters. Both sides called foul play. The election offered little resolution and the country still seemed hopelessly divided. It was all looking very serious.

But something silly instantly emerged to give everyone relief and it came in the shape of a photo of former potential Democratic presidential nominee Bernie Sanders, sitting

Connect!

alone at the inauguration wearing a mask, a grey parka coat
and a pair of hand-knitted woollen mittens. He looked cold,
grumpy and fed up. His appearance was so at odds with the
pomp, grandeur and celebration of the occasion that it was
delightful in its incongruence, seeming to capture the feelings
of many of us that day as we also watched on as passive
observers, feeling the chill.

Bernie in his mittens became the defining image of the day.
Biden's speech may not have trended, but #BerniesMittens
certainly did. It didn't take long before the PhotoShoppers were
out in force manipulating that Bernie image and, before long,
Bernie in mittens could be seen alongside Neil Armstrong on
the moon landing, at the fall of the Berlin Wall and alongside
Roosevelt and Churchill at the Potsdam Summit. He could
be seen dancing Gangnam Style with Psy, on the couch in
Central Perk with the cast from *Friends* and he even appeared
upon Sharon Stone's body in the infamous interrogation scene
in *Basic Instinct*. He could even be seen in post office queues,
on public transport and in train stations. Someone even created
a website so you could drop and capture your very own Bernie
in mittens to right outside your own front door, using Google
Street View. An incredible ten million people did just that.

The more absurd the backdrop, the greater the laughs. Key
to the humour was the incongruent overlapping of worlds.
Seeing Bernie on the *Friends*' couch brings together two
worlds that we have never previously connected. We were
connecting the deadly serious world of a democracy in crisis
with the fun and flirtatious world of Ross, Rachel, Phoebe,
Joey, Monica and Chandler. The connection between two

unrelated worlds surprises us, confounding our expectations, shifting our perceptions and exciting our brains as we delight in the incongruity.

The 'incongruity theory' has long been seen as an important element of comedy. Depicting serious people in silly ways has always made people laugh, from the ancient satirists of Ancient Rome to today's political cartoonists, Twitter memes and, of course, those brilliant improvisation nights at The Comedy Store.

Moral philosopher Francis Hutcheson was part of the Scottish Enlightenment and a teacher of Adam Smith. He wrote in his 1725 book, *Reflections on Laughter*, that he saw laughter as a response to the perception of incongruity. We see our world is disordered, and our brain tries to process the incongruity but can't quite cope. We're left surprised, bewildered and all we can do is laugh. *You've got to laugh.*

German philosopher Arthur Schopenhauer argued in his eighteenth-century book *The World as Will* that these incongruent connections work because they challenge our flawed perceptions of the world. We spend much of our time constructing an illusion that the world is serious, orderly and stable while all the time knowing deep down that it's chaotic, volatile and unpredictable. The world makes no sense. The incongruence confirms this. It's quite a relief to have that illusion confirmed and see everything for the silliness it really is.

Fast forward two hundred years from Schopenhauer and comic writers still practise that kind of approach. Dan O'Shannon has been the writer/producer of some of the biggest hit TV sitcoms of the last few years, including *Cheers*, *Frasier* and, more recently, *Modern Family*. He also sees incongruity, the collision between two worlds, as critical to comedy. He describes in his book, *What Are You Laughing At? A Comprehensive Guide to the Comedic Effect*, how incongruity arises from the 'overlay of two concepts as we understand them', creating 'disharmony or unexpected conceptual hybrid'.

And that's what we got in the Rod Ponton video: a collision between the serious world of law and the silly world of children, kittens and facial filters. The collision between the two worlds was surprising and made us laugh. Likewise in the Bernie meme, we saw an amusing collision between the serious world of politics, and the silly world of being in a grump on a cold day, seeking refuge in warm mittens.

So we're exploring the connection between the serious and the silly. Because, on the one hand, we do have lots of serious things to contend with: coronavirus, climate change and culture wars. It is possible to feel weighed down with all sorts of deep, dark thoughts and memories. And then, on the other hand, we have ducks. Now, no disrespect intended to any readers who are fans of ducks, but there can be no doubt that ducks are very silly. They look silly, sound silly and even their very name is silly. *Duck*. Sausages are pretty silly as well. So are bananas. And so are silly smiley faces, squeaky high voices and centipedes. So, there are our two worlds. A serious world and a silly world.

Connecting the serious and the silly

So how can we connect that serious world to that silly world to create some relief? Well, it's easier than you might imagine. Let me demonstrate.

Serious and Silly

Think of the last person who said something really mean to you, who insulted you, who said something to you that really upset you and left you feeling hurt. Maybe they didn't mean to upset you, but they did. And now, as you think back to that person, and what they said, it's probably fair to assume that you're feeling a bit serious, a bit stern. You're probably not smiling.

Now try something. Hold your hand out in front of you, as if it's in a sock puppet. Remember that person saying what they said, say it, and mouth those words with your hand. Now, gradually make that voice higher and higher, and squeakier and squeakier, as if that person has sucked air from a helium balloon so they sound even more stupid and ridiculous. Keep mouthing out what that person said, but make their voice increasingly more stupid and more ridiculous, exaggerating it more and more until you're smiling. Then when you're smiling, go further still. Make the voice even more ridiculous until you're actually laughing. That's it! Job done. It's fair to say you've found some relief. That's catharsis. That's also the power of connecting the serious and the silly. Now think what a gift you can give to other people if you can achieve the same effect with the serious stuff that is going on in their life. It really is as simple as that.

One person I worked for who was great at creating funny connections between the serious and the silly was Labour minister Alan Johnson. I remember well Alan's first appearance at the dispatch box in the House of Commons, when he had just been appointed a Parliamentary Under Secretary of State for

Connect!

Employment Relations in Summer 1999 – the most junior rank on the ministerial ladder. He was arguing back and forth with his opposite numbers on the Conservative benches, debating the rights and wrongs of employment protection rights and then, seemingly out of nowhere, he said, 'Trying to explain social justice to the Conservative Party is like trying to explain origami to a penguin.'

The image was so silly, so ridiculous and so surprising that everyone in the House instantly burst out laughing. It was such a huge conceptual leap, from the world of parliament, law and employment rights to the world of zoos, penguins and origami. Brains leapt to life as people recognised and struggled to process the incongruity. It was a revelation in people's minds. It's fair to say that this is not a connection anyone had made before.

The greater the conceptual distance that you travel, potentially the better the reaction you generate. There's less

252

cognitive work involved in processing an image which is only mildly incongruent.

So, for instance, instead of talking about teaching penguins to do origami, Alan Johnson could have said, 'Trying to explain social justice to the Conservative Party is like trying to explain origami to pensioners.' There's less of a conceptual distance there – many Conservative MPs literally are pensioners, so less cognitive processing is required. It doesn't engage the brain so much. It's not as funny, plus it's rude and patronising. Also, the image of pensioners learning origami is not as absurd as the idea of a penguin learning origami. Pensioners might well want to learn origami, so again it's not such a leap. Equally, it wouldn't have been as funny if he'd said, 'Trying to explain social justice to the Conservative Party is like trying to explain walking to penguins.' Penguins do walk and humans can train penguins. Alan's imagery was a uniquely absurd connection, it was silly, impossible to reconcile, so it gave everyone a laugh and provided some temporary respite from the dull, serious world of employment rights.

The thing is, the world is so serious, we sometimes need relief from it. Not all the time, and it's not always appropriate, but there can frequently be a great pleasure and relief from seeing serious people reveal their silly side, especially when they don't intend to. It allows us to feel temporarily superior. These are the things that really get attention and quickly go viral. We love it, for instance, when politicians trip up walking down Downing Street, or they inadvertently shut themselves into a cupboard, or they unwittingly walk down a red carpet with a piece of toilet paper stuck to their shoe.

Connect!

We also love it when they mis-speak, as so many do. One of my favourite malapropisms of recent years was when Australian prime minister, Tony Abbott, told a gathering of Conservative Party supporters that, 'No one, however smart, however well educated, however experienced, is the suppository of all wisdom.' This was a wonderful leap from one world to another: from the world of pompous politics to the world of arseholes. But while it is a big leap, the other element that makes it funny is that we do frequently see a connection between these two worlds: many people speak of politicians as arseholes, constantly speaking shit. I remember when left-wing politician Dennis Skinner described Tony Blair and Gordon Brown as 'two cheeks of the same arse'.

Or there was the time when former British prime minister David Cameron appeared on ITV's *This Morning* programme after the Brexit referendum and was asked how he felt when the referendum result came in. Momentarily uncertain whether he wanted to say that he spat at the television or shouted at the television, he blurted out, 'I shat at the television.' Maybe another portmanteau for Brexit could have been Britshit?

I remember once seeing a trade unionist giving a barnstorming speech at the Trade Unions Congress where he was talking about some wrangle he was in with his employers and he meant to say it was a catch-22 situation, a reference to Joseph Heller's fictional war satire. But instead of saying catch-22, he kept saying it was a catch-69. '*It's a bloody catch-69!*'

This is all good fun. I'm pretty sure these were genuine mistakes, that Abbott and Cameron inadvertently mis-spoke. But, as Cicero pointed out in his great book on oratory, *Rhetorica ad Herennium*, 'Things that sound stupid when they slip out accidentally are thought charming when we feign them.'

Searching for silly

As mentioned in Chapter 1, Boris Johnson appears to deliberately use double entendres to comic effect, selecting and leaning on particular words like 'prick' and 'stick it in' for the laugh and then feigning innocence when people react. His double entendres are so common it's hard to believe they're not intended. Former Foreign Minister Alan Duncan described in his diary one occasion when Boris Johnson, then foreign secretary, was chairing a meeting of the British government about Russia, and Johnson said the trouble with Putin was that he expected everyone to come and kiss his ring. Everyone in the meeting started giggling. Johnson looked baffled until his junior minister intervened and said, 'Foreign Secretary. Ten per cent of people here will think Pope. Ninety per cent will think anus.'

Boris deliberately plays the clown. He ruffles his hair, pulls out his shirt, shuffles around and winks at people off camera as if we're all in on some big joke. He sinks in rivers, gets stuck on zip-wires, breaks umbrellas at memorial services, does rugby tackles in football games and brings young children crashing to the ground during fun rugby games. We all recognise the archetype of the clown and there's something very endearing about that. The clown reminds us all of our inner silliness, that we are all just moments away from slipping over and becoming a laughing stock. Obviously to some it can be infuriating, but there is no doubt that it has been a major part in his ascendancy to the upper echelons of power.

It's not just in the UK that people have used humour to propel themselves to the top. Donald Trump hammed up his role as the larger-than-life billionaire on dozens of comedy programmes and movies. His rhetorical style and manner of delivery is that of the New York stand-up comic, owing more to Lenny Bruce than to Lincoln.

The largest party in Italy today – the Five Star movement – was originally started by comedian Beppe Grillo who first moved into politics by jokingly proposing a national 'Fuck You Day' (V-Day – the V stood for *Vaffanculo*).

The current president of Ukraine, Volodymyr Zelensky, also made his name as a very successful comedian and comedy producer before turning to politics. His rise to office started in 2015 after he created a popular TV show *Servant of the People*, which told a story about a history teacher who becomes president after railing against the elite with cries of, 'Fuck the motorcades! Fuck the perks! Fuck the weekend chalets!' The show literally started as a joke but Zelensky ended up winning the election in 2019 with 73.2 per cent of the vote in the second round. Zelensky was largely seen as a joke figure until Russia invaded Ukraine in March 2022. He was widely heralded for rising to the occasion and was invited to address parliaments around the world. The possibility of Ukraine even joining the European Union became stronger than at any time in its country's history.

It's quite bizarre. On both sides of the European Union, you have extraordinary geopolitical changes being brought about by two people who are like mirror images of each other. Johnson and Zelensky both started their careers on television, playing puffed-up comic versions of themselves. Both won elections with massive majorities with a big cry of 'fuck the elite!' And both are, in their different ways, redrawing the map of the European Union: Johnson, by taking the UK out of the European Union; Zelensky, in seeking to bring Ukraine in. It's funny what comedy can do . . . isn't it?

This reminds us of another aspect of the clown's archetypal role, as we've seen through the ages, from the Ancient Roman satirists to the clowns in Shakespeare plays to the stand-ups in comedy bars. The clown is not just there for laughs. The clown has power. The clown is subversive. The clown can create change. It is by subverting our perception of society that clowns gain the power to guide us to change society. If the serious world is not so serious, who cares?

Humour can create change in politics, but it can do so in business as well. Jennifer Aaker and Naomi Bagdonas at Stanford Business School have spent the last six years researching the role of humour, interviewing people across 166 countries. They said that 'At every turn, our findings challenged the false dichotomy between gravity and levity and uncovered the profound benefits of a life fuelled by levity. If there's one thing our research makes clear, it's that we don't need to take ourselves so seriously in order to grapple with serious things.'

Great leaders often seize any opportunity to crack through the seriousness and promote the silly. Richard Branson frequently pulls the most outrageous stunts, confounding expectations in any way imaginable, dressing up in drag, picking people up and lifting them above his head, setting off rockets. On the other side of the planet, Branson's protégée Tony Fernandez, the CEO/founder of AirAsia, the biggest airline in Southeast Asia, behaves in a similarly outrageous fashion.

But no one tops Steve Ballmer, the legendary former CEO of Microsoft, for silliness. Sometimes he'd come on stage roaring and fist-beating out a primal battlecry. He once roared so loud, his vocal cords required surgical repair. His antics were absurdly over the top – watch some of the 'crazy Steve Ballmer' videos on YouTube to see what I mean – but it's beyond doubt that he generated incredible energy and affection throughout the company.

More and more serious people are now embracing opportunities to publicly reveal their inner silliness. Appearing on reality TV programmes such as *Strictly Come Dancing/I'm A Celebrity . . ./The Masked Singer* provides a fast track to the public's hearts. Their displays of silliness make them far more relatable and even adorable as we see them as fools like us.

A willingness to show that you see the silly side of life can prove an attractive quality. This is why every president accepts with relish the opportunity to appear at the annual White House Correspondents' Dinner, because it's an opportunity to show the silly side of being president and unleash a whole load of self-deprecating jokes. Barack Obama was brilliant at these but even Donald Trump was prepared to mock himself. *'Nobody does self-deprecating humour better than I do. Nobody! It's not even close.'*

It's the same reason why many speakers keep a couple of self-deprecatory gags up their sleeve to open their speeches, so they can slide from the serious to the silly. It breaks the tension between the speaker and the audience at the beginning – a bit like cracking an egg open. The comedian, Bob Monkhouse, was the master of this – *'Everybody laughed when I said I wanted to be a comedian. Ha! They're not laughing now, are they?'* But there's also the old gag often used by businessmen: *'This morning I said to my wife, "Did you ever in your wildest dreams imagine that one day I'd be running one of the biggest companies in the world?" She looked me in the eye and replied, "Darling, you never featured in any of my wildest dreams."'* Or the person who, at a ninetieth birthday party in their honour, starts their speech by saying, *'Let me just say that, at this age, you're simply grateful that your bowels still work.'*

It's good to have a gag up your sleeve, carefully prepared and rehearsed. They're great to begin with, and generate an instant energy. The rest of your speech will feel like sliding downhill after that. When people laugh, the most extraordinary chemical reaction takes place. Dopamine, oxytocin and endorphin levels rise while cortisol levels fall. Cicero was a big fan of opening with a joke. He explained in his book on oratory that it made people instinctively side with you and admire you.

You don't even need to worry too much about whether the joke is that funny. Most of the time, it's a bit of a ritual, and we laugh more to fulfil a social function anyway. Robert Provine, a neuroscientist and psychologist at the University of Baltimore and author of the book *Laughter: An Investigation*, found we're 30 times more likely to laugh in company than we are on our own. That's why you can flick through a joke book at home without laughing out loud at all, whereas if a friend tells you those same jokes in a social setting, you'll be falling about the place laughing.

It's not just at the beginning of a speech that you might want to make a joke. Depending on the circumstances, as long as the audience is pre-disposed towards you (an important pre-condition!), I think it's a good idea to drop a little gag in every couple of minutes or so. They're like energy pills, helping people towards the finishing line.

Finding the funny

Sometimes it's just wise to find the funny and embrace the silliness whenever it emerges. If things go wrong in a speech, as they sometimes do, use it as an opportunity to show your fun side. A phone rings: *'That'll be my psychiatrist . . .'* Or, if the technology fails, you can resort to every man's ultimate fall-back line: *'I'm so sorry. This has never happened to me before.'* One very quick-witted speaker once tripped over a mic lead on the way to the podium and fell crash bang on the floor. Quick as a flash, he said, *'I will now take questions from the floor.'*

It's not just speeches that need lightening from time to time, so do meetings. This was especially true during the coronavirus pandemic when everyone was suffering a little from Zoom fatigue. Some unusual side industries emerged. A number of companies would bring donkeys along to your Zoom meetings for a few pounds. You didn't really need to go so far though. Just bringing your own cat or dog to the screen for a few minutes had a similar effect, giving people an opportunity to smile and relax, and also show your lighter side.

Having a sense of humour makes you more effective. A study by Wayne Decker of Salisbury University, Maryland, showed managers with a sense of humour were rated by subordinates as 23 per cent more respected, 25 per cent more pleasant to work with and 17 per cent friendlier.

Humour can also prove effective in negotiations. One study explored how humour can make you more likely to seal a deal. The line in the study was not even that funny – 'My final offer is X and I'll even throw in my pet frog.' The frog had nothing to do with the negotiations whatsoever and that was the point. It was completely incongruent and transformed the serious to the silly.

My favourite things

But how can you make connections? Well, it's a bit of a case of suck it and see. Sometimes a funny thought might just come to mind! Other times, you can try and force a random connection and see if anything magical occurs.

One exercise I do with my clients is 'My Favourite Things'. We rewrite the lyrics to the famous song from *The Sound of Music*, much as Ariana Grande did in '7 Rings', her 2019 reboot of the song, changing the original references to raindrops on roses and kittens and mittens to whatever things bring us most pleasure in the world.' We've already seen, in the Rod Ponton Zoom fail and the Bernie Sanders stories, the comic potential of whiskered kittens and woollen mittens.

Connect!

It was the combination between the serious worlds of law and politics and the silly worlds of kittens and mittens which proved so fruitful.

So write out a list of all your favourite things. Things that are guaranteed to make you smile! I've included a few prompts.

So it might look a little like this.

Favourite TV show
Favourite movie
Favourite song
Favourite meal
Favourite dessert
Favourite snack
Favourite animal
Favourite holiday
Favourite hobby
Favourite sport
Favourite board game

Now connect some of the serious things on your mind with things on your list. What if your profession was a board game? What board game would it be? If your company was a food, what food would it be?

Think of someone you work with now who's a bit too serious:

What if they were a TV character, what TV character would they be?

What if they were a food item, what food item would they be?

What if they were an animal, what animal would they be?
What if they were a foreign country, what country would they be?
What if they were a sport, what sport would they be?

Just give it a try and see what happens. If you find a connection that makes you smile, keep playing with it.

Jerry Seinfeld talks about the 'silly putty of the mind that enables you to reform what you see into what you want it to be', and that's exactly what we're doing here. We're connecting serious things we don't like with silly things we do like. Of course, we can't all be Jerry Seinfeld (or have his money), but we can all have some fun doing this. Sometimes it works, sometimes it doesn't. But if we play around enough, we're bound to stumble across something interesting, and if we craft and shape it a bit, we may just end up with a unique and original piece of humour that might entertain us and others. It might also introduce some fantastic new insights.

Don't be afraid to make big and ridiculous leaps: the more audacious the leap, the bigger the laughs. O'Shannon says he's learnt much in his 30 years as a comic but his main discovery was '*that incongruity was funny, just for the sake of incongruity. I didn't even need ideas to connect any more. The more incomprehensible the ideas were together, the more funny it was. If someone asked, "Why were you late today?" I might respond, "Because African elephants can weigh up to 330 pounds at birth." The incongruity is so bizarre you can't help but laugh. How else can you respond?*'

Connect!

Comic connections and change

But it's not just humour for the sake of it. These connections can fundamentally change the way people think and perceive something. In Chapter 1, we explored how Boris Johnson's absurd connection between Brexit and cake converted something complicated into something that would make us smile. Some CEOs can conjure up equally enticing imagery to make a corporate vision attractive, but then throw in a little comic twist at the end. I once saw one CEO tell this story:

'OK, I want you all to imagine that we are on holiday right now. We're somewhere gorgeous – tropical, lovely and warm. There are palm trees, blue skies, and you can feel the warmth of the sun on your skin. And there's a lovely, nice swimming pool. I suggest we all go for a swim. But then we get down to the swimming pool and, "Oh!" We all stand back a bit. "What's that?" We squint in the bright afternoon sun, look down in the pool and, oh dear . . . There are . . . three little poos floating in the swimming pool. I say, "It's OK! Go on! Jump in! They're only small! Have fun!" But . . . Do you really want to? So . . . I fish one of the poos out, so there are just two left. I say, "OK, look, you can jump in now, can't you?" But still . . . you hesitate . . . So, I fish the other poo out, leaving just one poo floating ominously in the swimming pool. Again, I say, "Come on! What are you waiting for?" You take my point? You need the swimming pool to be absolutely clean. This is why I have no room for people who don't believe in what we're doing here. You're spoiling it for everyone else. You're making the environment toxic.'

That's a big leap. With that story, we've been transported from an office to a luxury holiday resort. The poos in the pool are unexpected, incongruent and amusing, but they also make a powerful point to cynical or sceptical staff members. They're not just gripers; they're poos. We're laughing about it, it's silly, but in fact the point is deadly serious. If you mess with me, I'm scooping you out and you are gone.

Sometimes witty connections can change the way people perceive a product or service. Arnold Schwarzenegger is also a funny man. Arnie, like Boris, Trump et al, has also moved effortlessly between the worlds of comedy and politics. He has a natural gift for blending different worlds. He first rose to fame in the 1970s, in the documentary *Pumping Iron*. In the most memorable scene, Schwarzenegger said bodybuilding was 'as satisfying to me as cumming is, you know? As having sex with a woman and cumming. And so can you believe how much I am in heaven? I am like getting the feeling of cumming in a gym, I'm getting the feeling of cumming at home, I'm getting the feeling of cumming backstage when I pump up, when I pose in front of 5,000 people, I get the same feeling, so I am cumming day and night. I mean, it's terrific, right? So, you know, I am in heaven.'

Great connection. He connected an act which is mind-numbingly monotonous (lifting weights) with one of the most pleasurable acts imaginable (sex). By so doing, he helped transform perceptions of gyms and gym-goers. Many fitness professionals say the sector would never have taken off as it did in the eighties and nineties without Arnie. With his surprising connection, he grabbed people's attention, subverted their perceptions and changed their behaviours. This is the power of connection.

Arnie is a genius at what he does and he has often turned his talent for incongruent connections to help drive political change. At the time of the riots in the Capitol Building, he made a speech on social media in which he compared American democracy to the sword of Conan the Barbarian, going so far as to brandish the original sword at the camera at the climactic point of his speech! At the time of the Russian invasion of Ukraine, he released a speech on social media in which he compared Putin's duplicity behind the scenes of that invasion with the honour and integrity he found when he met the Russian weightlifter, Yuri Petrovich, backstage at a weightlifting competition in Vienna in the 1960s. These are far-fetched, incongruent connections, but they provide people with a new and surprising perspective on the world, and this can release in people the energy to do something new. Sometimes, the energy released can be much more powerful than even the comic anticipates.

In his Netflix show, *Jigsaw*, Scottish comedian Daniel Sloss connects the serious matter of relationships with the silly world of Sunday afternoon games, namely jigsaws. He rejects the common analogy that life is a jigsaw which is only complete when you meet someone who is a 'perfect fit', who 'brings everything together'. Instead, he argues romance is a *cancer*. While he's riffing on this theme, some members of the audience shuffle in their seats awkwardly. Sloss rubs salt in the wound. 'All I'm saying is if you're finding it hard to laugh at this routine, it's because deep down you don't love the person you're with. So, either start laughing or enjoy the awkward car ride home.'

The jigsaw metaphor is not dissimilar to the machine metaphor we looked at earlier. It's fundamentally restrictive, like a trap, a world in which you have no freedom to move. It's not an appealing way to think of a relationship. It represents physical confinement and makes you want to break free.

Within hours of completing his routine, Sloss received a message from an audience member, saying they had broken up with their partner after the show. Then he started receiving more and more messages from other couples who had been in the audience saying the same. Then his show went on Netflix and millions more watched it, and then the messages really came flooding in. By 2021, he claimed that his show had caused more than 120,000 break-ups, 350 cancelled engagements and 300 divorces. Sloss said he had no idea it was going to have that kind of impact. You've got to laugh.

And that's the point. You really have got to laugh. For all sorts of reasons. Because it's good for us, because it makes us better managers, better friends, better parents and better lovers. Yes, better lovers. Robert Levenson discovered in his 'Love Laboratory' in California that couples who were able to laugh together were more likely to stay in love together. So don't take yourself too seriously, search for the silliness wherever you can find it and, whatever you do, make sure you wear your cat filter (or human filter) with pride!

Stats and Symbols

On 2 November 2021, David Attenborough stepped up to the podium at the COP26 Summit in Glasgow to deliver a familiar warning about the threat of climate change. He was 95 years old and had been presenting nature programmes for the BBC since the early 1950s. His was one of the most trusted voices on the planet, the voice that had given so many of us our first lessons about life on earth. His speech was described as 'electrifying'. That's not surprising – Attenborough is one of the most phenomenal communicators in the world – but what was most remarkable to me, as a speechwriter, was that the whole of his speech was written around a number.

It's rare to see speeches built around a number. Normally, speeches are built around visions, stories or dilemmas. Martin Luther King Jr did not say, 'I have some data', he had a dream. Nor did Queen Elizabeth I 'have the statistics of a king,' she had the heart and stomach of a king. Normally, the numbers bit of a speech is the boring bit, the cue to the audience to nod off: like the section in the adverts when the cameras turn to the people in white coats to provide 'the science', its purpose purely to signify to the audience that some science does exist. But Attenborough's number was not a perfunctory add-on; it stood front, back and went right through the heart of his speech.

'It's easy to forget that ultimately the emergency comes down to a single number,' he began, 'the concentration of carbon in our atmosphere.' He then spent the bulk of his speech looking at how that number had moved over time, considering the implications. And he ended with a direct challenge to the audience: 'The generation to come will look at this conference and consider one thing: did that number stop rising and start to drop as a result of commitments made here?'

Numbers, on their own, don't usually get people excited on their own. If we really want people to get engaged with numbers, we need to make connections. And that's exactly what Attenborough did. He connected with a series of powerful symbols.

First, he connected that number with graphic imagery, so we could see how it had moved over time. On its own, 414 units of carbon per million is completely meaningless. No one has any idea if that's high or low, rising or falling, significant or insignificant, safe or dangerous. It only becomes meaningful when we can see its movement over time, and that's what he showed us, so we could visualise that number soaring and diving through history. He clearly showed it was an unprecedented high.

Second, he connected his number with story; and not just any story, the greatest story imaginable: the story of humanity. In his eight-minute presentation, he took us on a journey from the dawn of civilisation right up to the present day. He explained how, for hundreds of thousands of years, the amount of carbon in the atmosphere had fluctuated wildly, making temperature extremely volatile and the planet unpredictable. It was only when the number and the temperature stabilised that civilisation became possible. But in the last few decades, the number had shot up dramatically, causing instability and threatening human civilisation.

Third, he connected his number with imagery. As he talked through that history of the earth, he showed a series of emotive and dramatic wildlife images. The images changed in nature as the number rose and fall. As the number was low, so we saw images of nature at its most magnificent and majestic: the rice paddies of India; the Amazon in South America; the orangutans of Indonesia. As he depicted the number shooting higher, we saw images of fire, with fireworks going off, rockets taking off and forest fires. The symbolism of fire, connecting with Greta Thunberg's 'Our House is On Fire' metaphor, was everywhere. As the number peaked, he showed images of disasters: brutal hurricanes, savage storms, ice caps melting. As he contemplated the numbers rising higher, the images became progressively more apocalyptic. Then, as he considered the possibility the number might fall, the images became more tranquil.

Attenborough's speech was a case study in how to communicate numbers well. The human brain is said to process images 60,000 times faster than text. For all the current talk about how we love facts, stats and data, the truth is many people struggle to process numbers, even people who spend the whole day working with them, even some of the most powerful people on the planet.

Stats and Symbols

The problem with statistics

During the coronavirus pandemic, leaders were talking about numbers more than ever before, and this meant there were more gaffes about numbers than ever before. In his victory speech, President-elect Biden solemnly declared that 'two thirty million thousand Americans' had lost a loved one to coronavirus. It wasn't clear that such a number even existed and, if it does, it's not clear that that many Americans exist. On the other side of the pond, UK Home Secretary Priti Patel fared little better. She claimed at a Downing Street briefing, 'three hundred thousand and thirty-four, nine hundred and seventy-four thousand coronavirus tests have been carried out across the UK'. Again, does that number even exist?

And it wasn't just the politicians who were getting numbers wrong. The UK chief scientific adviser, Sir Patrick Vallance, inadvertently started a major panic about the vaccine's efficacy after he declared at a Downing Street briefing that '60 per cent of the people being admitted to hospital with coronavirus had been double vaccinated'. With only 60 per cent of the population then vaccinated, this suggested the vaccine offered next to no protection. It was not until three hours later that he issued a correction, saying he'd got it the wrong way around – 60 per cent of the people being admitted to hospital with coronavirus had *not* been properly vaccinated, a big difference. As they say, there are three kinds of people: those who are good with numbers, and those who aren't.

The experts, economists, statisticians and other people who are responsible for putting numbers together fare little better. When I was writing speeches in Whitehall, fact-checking speeches was often complicated by the fact that different economists would frequently profoundly disagree, on the most straightforward figures. I love the story about the mathematician, accountant and economist who all apply for the same job. The interviewer calls in the mathematician first and asks him, 'What does 2+2 equal?' The mathematician replies, '4. No doubt at all. Exactly.' Then the interviewer calls in the accountant and asks him the same question. 'What does 2+2 equal?' The accountant replies, 'On average, 4. Give or take 10 per cent either way. But, on average, 4.' Then the interviewer calls in the economist and poses the same question. 'What does 2+2 equal?' The economist gets up, locks the door, pulls the curtain, leans towards the interviewer, and says, 'What do you want it to equal?'

I don't mean to be mean. Some of my best friends are economists. But if economists struggle with numbers, the public don't fare much better. For many years now, pollster Ipsos MORI has published an annual global 'Perils of Perception' study which shows a huge disparity between public perception and reality on several vital issues. For instance, on the matter of climate change, only 1 in 25 people know that all the last six years were among the hottest on record. Most people think global poverty has been getting worse over the last 20 years, when in fact it has halved. On immigration, most people think around a quarter of their population is immigrant when the actual figure is less than half of that. Paradoxically, the more we talk about a topic, the more likely we are to misunderstand the scale of the issue. As Bobby Duffy, MD of Ipsos MORI

Stats and Symbols

Social Research Institute explains, 'This is partly because we over-estimate what we worry about.' It's that natural human capacity for exaggeration, which we explored in a previous chapter, both to others and to ourselves.

So, numbers are tricky, but it's essential that we can find ways to understand and communicate them effectively, because so much in our lives depends on them. This is true at home and in work, personally and professionally, whether we're sorting out our household budgets or trying to argue for funding at work. So how can we communicate numbers most effectively? The answer can be found by going back, [adopts David Attenborough voice] to the very origins of human civilisation, to understand the anthropological purpose that lies behind our capacity for processing numbers and scale and exploring how that capacity has evolved over time.

Stanislas Dehaene is a neuroscientist who has spent many years analysing how the brain processes numbers. As he's pointed out, we are all born with an innate instinct for processing numbers and scale. You can see this with newborn babies, even if only in a limited and rudimentary way. Researchers discovered that if babies are repeatedly shown a picture of three dots, before long, their brain activity levels start to reduce, signalling they recognise that the number remains the same. No new information is being received so they get bored and switch off. Then, if you show the baby a picture with four dots, their brain starts to become alert again. This suggests that even at just a few weeks old, a baby can recognise the difference between three and four dots. This same ability is also possessed by pigeons, racoons and rats.

Connect!

You can speculate why, from an evolutionary and an anthropological perspective, we might have an instinctive need to recognise differences in scale. This capacity is, in various ways, essential for our survival. It enables us to check we have enough food for our pack; to check all of our family or our wider pack is present; to quickly identify if a group of approaching predators is larger or smaller than us.

But our conception of scale is extremely limited. Our ability to glance at a group of things and quickly work out how many things are there (known as subitising) is limited in most people to around five. Any more than that and we start to struggle. With intense training, some people might be able to push their ability up slightly further, maybe to as high as 15. And then there are some other people with almost superhuman abilities to subitise, as demonstrated by Dustin Hoffman in the film *Rain Man* when, in a memorable scene in a restaurant, he was able to instantly say how many toothpicks had been dropped on the floor: 246. But, for most people, any more than five and we need to go to some form of mental calculation: either dividing them up mentally into little groups to simplify, or using some other technique, such as putting them into a grid-like shape. So, to make sense of bigger numbers, we move to a system of symbolism, connecting numbers with symbols.

Stats and symbols

How this begins is quite simple. The fingers provide a super-effective, instantly accessible form of calculator which lies literally at our fingertips. Most of us have already connected numbers to our fingers by the time we start school. The tips of our fingers are densely packed with nerve endings, so they are super sensitive, making memorisation incredibly easy, harnessing the powerful mind–body connection we explored earlier. Studies have shown a correlation between the sensitivity of a child's fingertips and their ability in maths.

The mind–body connection is really important to improving people's comprehension of mathematics. Studies have shown that when six-year-olds are trained to improve the sensitivity of their fingers, their mathematical ability also improves. It has long been known that there is a correlation between musical skill and mathematical ability and maybe this could also be a consequence of increased sensitivity.

Our whole basis of understanding numbers is fundamentally connected with our fingers. It's why in the Stone Age they developed tallies which count in fives (four sticks with one across seems a straightforward symbol for a hand). Later on, the Babylonians developed abacuses in tens. The Romans had a decimal system which matches the digits on both hands and, across most of the world, that is today the main system for money and most forms of measurement. Even the Munduruku, an Amazon tribe that Dehaene studied, only has words for numbers going up to five, and their word for 'five' literally means one hand. It all comes back to the tips of our fingers. It's intriguing to imagine how different the world might have been if we'd been born with eleven digits on our hands.

The connection between numbers and our fingers remains really strong throughout our lives. Researchers Ilaria Berteletti and James R Booth gave a group of eight- to thirteen-year-olds some complex subtraction problems. fMRI scanners showed that as they were making the calculations, the part of the students' brains that is dedicated to the perception and representation of fingers – the somatosensory finger area – still lit up, even though the students were not actually using their fingers to count. So, they were still thinking through their fingers, even though they were not using them.

Our fingers provide our introduction point, our learning point and our constant reference point for processing numbers, which makes it a little concerning that some schools are now discouraging children from counting with their fingers. Some teachers fear that using their fingers prevents children being able to use their mind, but the problem is the other way around. Without learning through their fingers in the early stages, they will not be able to use their mind properly as they get older. Neuroscientists like Brian Butterworth at University College London fear this could harm their ability to process numbers in later life. Butterworth warns that if children are not taught numbers through their fingers, there is a risk numbers will never have a normal representation in the brain.

One of the other ways in which we perceive the scale of numbers is through spatial representation. We connect numbers with points in space. Across the planet, we all share in common the idea that big numbers are high and small numbers are low. Every child who learns about the notion of infinity seems to do so in relation to outer space. It's that mind-boggling realisation you have as a child that things can go on and on endlessly.

Stats and Symbols

We also perceive scale through a left to right motion. Instinctively, we perceive small numbers being on our left and big numbers being on our right. When we add up, we instinctively visualise the number heading to the right. When we subtract, we instinctively visualise the quantity moving to the left. This direction also matches the direction of our writing, so the perception is reversed in cultures where writing moves from right to left, such as Arabic. Stanislas Dehaene speculates that this might be why travellers get disoriented when they enter Terminal 2 of Paris's Charles de Gaulle Airport, where small-numbered gates are on the right and large-numbered gates are on the left.

So, our instinctive capacity for processing numbers lies basically in being able to quickly recognise scale, space and symbolism. These instinctive mechanisms for perceiving numbers are worth keeping in mind if you're communicating numbers in any way, whether that's presenting figures at financial meetings, selling whelks on a stall in Camden Market or speaking about coronavirus. Bear in mind the brain's natural limitations. The key questions in most people's minds are these: is this big or is it small?; is it rising or is it falling?; and, last but not least: is this something that I really need to worry about, or not? These are the points that we must connect.

Making connections

Look at the way Johnny C Taylor, Jr, the CEO and president of the Society of Human Resource Management, did it in a speech in June 2020 when he wanted to emphasise the harm inflicted upon workers and the economy by coronavirus.

Connect!

He said, 'So far, $1.3 trillion in income has been lost by the US workforce. Let me put that into perspective. A stack of 1 million hundred-dollar bills would be 3.3 feet high – the height of a chair. A stack of 1 trillion? That would tower 631 miles high – 2.5 times higher than the International Space Station.'

Taylor's choice of connection made the number feel totally astronomical, way above our heads, unfathomably high.

He made a choice by comparing the size to the International Space Station. But he didn't have to pick that point. He could have compared it to anything. The building he was making the speech in, the Petronas Towers, or Mount Everest.

Equally, if he'd wanted to make $1.3 trillion appear small, he could have done that as well, making it so small we can hold it in our hands, visualising it with the tips of our fingers. He could have compared that figure to another figure that was much bigger, like GDP. He could have said that the sum lost to the economy was less than 6 per cent of GDP.

Through different connections we can either put a figure in outer space or we can put it on the tips of our fingers. The actual number has not changed but the symbolic point of connection has. The point of connection we choose to make is critical in determining how people will then think, feel and react to it.

Let's take another example. Let's go back to climate change and the amount of carbon which is released into the atmosphere by mankind every year. If you want to make that quantity appear a lot, you might follow the approach of Peter

Stats and Symbols

Tans, a senior scientist with the NOAA global monitoring laboratory, who says we are 'putting 40 billion metric tons of CO_2 pollution into the air every year. That is a mountain of carbon that we dig up out of the earth and release into the atmosphere as CO_2, year after year.'

A mountain is one of the biggest things we can possibly conceive, the highest land point we can see, so he is making the figure appear awesome. However, those who wanted to play down the threat might point out that just 5 per cent of global meteorological activity is shaped by human activity, putting that figure back on to the tips of our fingers.

You see how easily it is done. Numbers do not provide the safe haven from rhetoric we might imagine. As David Spiegelhalter, Professor at the Statistical Laboratory at Cambridge, has said repeatedly, 'Numbers do not speak for themselves. They can be made to look a number of ways – big, small, frightening, reassuring.' A point which was brilliantly demonstrated once by George Bernard Shaw, who wrote that, 'Statistics show that of those who contract the habit of eating, very few survive.'

Politicians are wise to these tricks and habitually present numbers either to look as big or as small as possible. For instance, when politicians talk about a rise in income tax, they invariably speak about it in terms of a penny in income tax, because that makes it sound like nothing. But if they're talking about cutting income tax, they'll talk about it in terms of saving you £1,343 a year, which makes it seem like a lot of money – that was the average family's annual heating bill in 2021. Likewise, if they are talking about jobs being lost, they'll announce it as a percentage: employment is down 0.05 per cent this month, which makes it appear minuscule. If they're talking about jobs being created, they'll talk about 30,000 new jobs, which makes it appear large – it's the population of Pontypridd.

The point of reference is everything. So, you see, we shouldn't necessarily accept the terms in which a figure is being presented. Sometimes, those presentational terms might be conspiring against us. Take the gender pay gap, for instance: the term used to describe the difference in average earnings between men and women. This difference is often described in terms of pence, i.e., the pay gap is 15 pence (in the pound). But describing it like this makes it sound like small change, coins down the back of the sofa, money that we can happily forget about and ignore. No biggie. If you wanted to make this appear large you could express it in terms of incomes over the course of a lifetime. Expressed that way, the average man earns £300,000 more over the course of a lifetime than an average woman. This is a whopping figure: more than the price of an average house.

We can connect anything to anything and, by so doing, instantly transform people's perceptions. So, let's give it a try ourselves and put this into practice.

Take a number you must talk about a lot:

- What point of connection could you use to make that number appear small?
- What point of connection could you use to make that number appear large?

Stats and Symbols

Maybe you could connect it to something on your fingertips to make it appear small? Maybe you could connect it to something unfathomably large to make it seem big? Maybe the biggest, most awesome mountain, skyscraper or natural wonder you have ever seen in your life?

In this way, you can transform numbers to speak to people's instincts.

Retail outlets are wise to the ways numbers can be presented to activate our emotions and instincts. For instance, because we are instinctively inclined to accumulate and amass food, they know offers should be presented in terms of giving people more of something, rather than less. One study showed shoppers had a 71 per cent preference for buying something that was labelled '50 per cent bonus pack' over something that was labelled '35 per cent discount', even though the latter offered better value. It's crazy, but it's all about the way we make sense of numbers through connections.

Another way that we can make sense of statistics is through connections to metaphorical symbols. When I bought my first flat in London, back in 1993, there was much talk about a 'bubble' in the London property market. The term was used to describe the large increases that had taken place in London property prices in previous years, amounting to around 10–15 per cent a year. But the term bubble was symbolic and suggestive. By invoking the idea of a bubble, the suggestion was being made that house prices were stretching beyond what was sustainable and would soon burst – because that's what bubbles do. A search of the British National Corpus shows that 'burst' is the second most frequent verb which precedes bubble, so it's little surprise that, with that connection in mind, I felt quite nervous when I bought my flat.

But, although the idea of the bubble was powerful and suggestive, it had no basis in truth. In fact, as long as demand keeps rising and supply remains the same, there's no reason why prices shouldn't keep on rising for ever. And, as it turned out, that was exactly what did happen. The bubble has never burst. In fact, quite the opposite has happened. According to ONS data, house prices have risen in London in every year since 1993 bar 2008 and part of 2009, with prices overall increasing more than ten-fold in that period. It's 30 years now since I bought my flat, but still today there is talk of a London property bubble from market analysts and estate agents. We'll see if these predictions prove any more accurate in the future than they have in the past.

Stats and Symbols

Different symbols, different reactions

These kinds of depictions matter. Michael Morris and colleagues at Columbia University in New York carried out a detailed study in 2007 looking at how metaphors of the market can impact behaviour. They found that metaphors broadly fall into two camps: agent metaphors and object metaphors. Agent metaphors suggest that the share has a life of its own: for instance, you might say, the housing market *leapt*, *rose*, *climbed*, picked up *pace*. Object metaphors, on the other hand, suggest that the share does not have a life of its own, so these were inanimate objects, like rocks or tools, being affected and shifted by physical forces such as gravity, resistance or external pressure. So you might say the housing market was *pushed* higher, *dropped off a cliff*, or it's *bounced* back, *plummeted* or *fallen*.

Michael Morris found that agent metaphors were more likely to lead investors to expect price trend continuance than object metaphors or no metaphors at all. So, if you said that yesterday shares in Apple *leapt* (using an agent metaphor) then people would expect that trend to continue. If you said shares in Apple were *driven* higher, people would be less likely to expect that trend to continue. This is an important finding, as much of the language which is used to describe market movements is metaphorical.

As Morris pointed out, anthropologists believe that we are hardwired to recognise the difference between the movement of living beings and objects. This is a protective mechanism to help us determine what kind of threats or opportunities might be in front of us. So it may be that sensitivity to these different kinds of trajectories are hardwired into us. We know, for instance, that the frog protrudes its tongue instinctively in response to stimulus that resembles the zigzag of a fly. So it may be that, by activating different schema, different reactions can also be evoked. In this way we can either depict numbers to represent an opportunity, or to represent a great threat.

There was a lot of this kind of rhetoric in the Brexit debate. Research from HM Treasury predicted that Britain's departure from the European Union would result in a fall in GDP of somewhere between 3 and 10 per cent. These numbers appear small. We can hold them on the tips of our fingers.

Those who did not want Britain to leave the European Union charged these numbers up by saying this represented a 'cliff edge'. Some went further and described it as an act of 'egregious self-harm' or 'suicide'. This narrative was referred to by many of the most senior politicians in Britain, from Tony Blair and Nick Clegg through to Nicola Sturgeon and Paddy Ashdown. Google 'Brexit' and 'cliff' and you get 4 million results. Google 'Brexit' and 'suicide' and you get 12 million results. This is a much more dramatic way of putting it than referring to the actual numbers.

As Hans Rosling wrote in *Factfulness*: 'There's no room for facts when our minds are occupied by fear.' Some metaphors can activate fear. Other metaphors can suggest something soothing.

Death waves

It was peculiar that during the coronavirus pandemic, large numbers of coronavirus deaths were depicted as waves. *First wave. Second wave. Third wave.* To speak about movement on graphs as waves is not uncommon – it can be a helpful way of visualising data – but when you look at the coronavirus deaths on a graph, they do not look like traditional waves on graphs: the rises are much more dramatic than that. They look more like mountains, spikes, surges, swells, steep rises, nails, or tsunamis. But the language never wavered, it was always 'waves'.

The idea of waves speaks to our instincts. The waves occupy a powerful place in our imagination. We never feel more in harmony with our natural environment than when we are within earshot of the sea's natural rhythms, with waves washing in and out, which is why these sounds so often appear on relaxation or sleep soundtracks. The sounds of waves connect with our own body rhythms and the rhythms of the world and are fundamentally soothing.

Waves have a huge symbolism in our mind, coming in at the intersection of sky, sea and land, representing the meeting point between the earth and the sublime. In terms of our perception, we also understand that waves hold a mighty power, they are unstoppable, the ultimate force of nature. The legend of King Canute tells us we cannot stop the waves coming in. They're subject to extra-terrestrial forces. We can do nothing about them. So, this primes us to think of the deaths as inevitable, part of the natural order.

Also, waves wash in, waves wash out; and we know waves are dangerous, but they are also fundamentally cleansing and liberating. This suggests the waves could represent a positive force, which I don't think really bears much relation to the death of millions of people from coronavirus.

Connect!

Yet during the pandemic, talk of waves was everywhere. In the British press alone, between March 2020 and the end of February 2021, there were more than 20,000 stories about coronavirus that referenced waves. Wave references in the press outnumbered tsunami references by a ratio of approximately 30:1. This was almost bound to have shaped how people feel about it.

Sarah Cobey, an epidemiologist and evolutionary biologist at the University of Chicago, said early on that she didn't think it was useful to think about the dynamics of coronavirus as waves. She said it was much bigger than that, with the capacity to hurt many more people much more quickly. She said, 'what we are seeing here is a massive epidemic that could burn through the population rapidly unless we do something to slow transmission.' Maybe it should have been talked about more as a *wildfire* than as a wave.

So facts, stats and data are not as free of rhetoric as we might imagine. We can connect stats with symbols in order to change how people feel, but also we should be confident enough to challenge when we believe people are looking at the wrong stats in the wrong way. Sometimes it can be a matter of life or death, as we saw with coronavirus.

When the pandemic broke out in early March 2020, I was working in Copenhagen. It was extraordinary to see the different ways that leaders in London and Copenhagen interpreted the data in front of them.

In the UK, on 9 March, Boris Johnson held a press conference in which he downplayed the threat. 'There have now been four deaths from coronavirus in the UK, and our deepest sympathies are obviously with their friends and families . . . It bears repeating that the best thing we can all do is wash our hands for 20 seconds with soap and water.' He announced no further restrictions. Mass gatherings continued. Schools stayed open. The Government line was literally 'business as usual'. Four deaths did not seem significant. You could count them on your fingertips.

In Denmark, on 11 March, Danish prime minister Mette Frederiksen called a press conference. She had a very different perspective. Not a single Danish citizen had died of coronavirus at that point, but she said, 'When I stood here yesterday, 157 Danes were infected with corona. Today, we have 514 infected. The number has more than doubled since Monday, when the number was 35 infected. Coronavirus spreads extremely fast . . . It's already going too fast. Too fast . . . We have a very great obligation to help especially the weakest in our society, the most vulnerable, people with chronic diseases, cancer patients, the elderly. For their sake, the infection must not spread.' She conjured up the image of exponential growth, like the grains of rice on the chessboard. She announced an immediate lockdown. She conceded there would be huge consequences to this but, as she put it, 'The alternative would be far worse.'

It was not until 23 March that Boris Johnson finally followed Mette Frederiksen and introduced a lockdown. As of December 2021, per capita, for every one Danish person who died of coronavirus, five British people died – 2,939 Danes died of coronavirus compared to 146,000 British people. The death toll in Britain would fill London's Olympic Stadium twice over.

Connect!

This is why it's so important that we tell our numbers well. It truly can be a matter of life and death. And that's why it was so vital that Sir David Attenborough used symbols to depict statistics when he addressed global leaders on the issue of climate change at COP26. It remains to be seen whether Attenborough's message will be heeded. As he said in his speech, the ultimate test of his success will be whether that vital number, the 414 parts of carbon in the atmosphere, started to fall after that conference . . . or not. Google that figure now. How are we doing? Is it coming down now? If not, what do you think? Is humanity heading over a cliff? Is our bubble about to burst? Is our house going up in flames? Or were we foolish to ever imagine that we could turn this particular tide?

Deeds and Dreams

'Best day ever!' cried Jeff Bezos as his New Shepard space capsule touched down in the Texan desert on 20 July 2021. He'd just led one of the most remarkable journeys in history, the first ever civilian flight to cross the Karman line, the point 62 miles above the surface of earth that marks the entry point into space. But that wasn't the only record broken that day. The crew also comprised the oldest person ever to fly into space – Mary 'Wally' Funk, an 82-year-old aviator – as well as the youngest person ever to fly into space: 18-year-old Oliver Daemen, whose father had paid for his seat on the capsule in an auction.

One of the most striking images from the day was the look on Jeff Bezos's face. He might be one of the wealthiest and most powerful people on the planet but he looked like a little boy at a fancy-dress party as he emerged from the capsule, beaming from cheek to cheek, jubilantly dishing out high fives, proudly wearing his cowboy hat and blue space suit. Indeed, his first words on touching down – 'Best Day Ever' – owed more to the world of kids' cartoons – *Spongebob Squarepants* or *Charlie and Lola* – than the pantheon of great oratory. It perhaps isn't surprising he seemed so childlike that day. He was literally living out his childhood dream.

Jeff Bezos was five years old when Neil Armstrong and Buzz Aldrin set foot on the moon on 20 July 1969. Over the years, he's described many times the effect that moment had on him, saying it left him obsessed with the idea that one day he might travel to space. Of course, he was by no means the only child to have that dream – most of the kids in my class also dreamed of being astronauts – but whereas most of us let our dreams slip away at different points, Bezos doggedly clung on and pursued his dream for more than five decades. Critically, he eventually accumulated the mountain of cash necessary to make it happen. And so it was that on 20 July 2021 his dream came true. Acknowledging where his dream began, he even timed his mission to coincide with the 52nd anniversary of the first moon landing.

We all have dreams. They can be profound or professional, long term or short term, smutty or sublime. We might dream of becoming astronauts, rock stars, prime ministers, Olympic champions or inventors. Maybe we dream about setting up a business, travelling around the world or going on holiday? We might dream of having a better partner, a better set of friends, a better life, a better home, a better job, a better body. We may simply dream of making it through to the weekend, having dinner with friends or enjoying a beautiful slice of cake.

Dreaming is one of the easiest and cheapest pastimes we can enjoy and the beauty of it is that we can do it anytime, anywhere and with anyone. And the evidence suggests we do it rather a lot! One study by Harvard University suggests as much as half of our day may be spent daydreaming. Some dreams can last a lifetime, while others can vanish as swiftly as they arrive, but when we have a really big dream in mind, something really clear in our mind that we're deeply connected to, it releases within us a phenomenal force, firing us up, energising us, giving us the drive to overcome any obstacles that get in our way.

The dream of one day being a rock star can (and very frequently does!) lead a teenager to spend thousands of hours practising the guitar in their bedroom, doing monotonous scales over and over again, investing huge time, money and effort into improving technique and performance in the hope that one day, just maybe, they might appear on stage bending or burning the strings like Jimi Hendrix. The prospect of landing the house of our dreams might lead us to spend thousands of extra hours at work, forgoing nights out with friends in the hope that one day we'll wake up in our dream house. The dream of one day having our own business can lead us to spend thousands of hours in higher education.

The power of dream

We're all prepared to make extraordinary sacrifices and invest incredible effort today for the promise of a better tomorrow. The clearer our dream is, the more connected we are to it – the more we can see it, hear it, smell it, taste it, feel it – the harder we'll work to achieve it. The dream doesn't need to be earth-altering. We're not all John F Kennedys or Martin Luther Kings. A simple dream of having sushi can keep me motivated enough to keep writing a speech on a sunny afternoon. But our dreams can enable us to endure all sorts of sacrifices and it all comes down to one simple molecule that we all of us have in our minds: dopamine.

Dopamine is one of the most important neurotransmitters. Dopamine is released whenever our brain is in pursuit of something. Say we are sitting at home and we smell cake baking in the kitchen. Our brain will produce dopamine in response to that familiar smell. This gets us thinking about cake and motivates us to get up and check what's cooking, in the hope we might get a slice. Then, when we do get a slice, more dopamine flows, reinforcing in our mind the connection between the smell of cake and satisfaction, which means that the next time we smell cake again, we'll be extra motivated to get up and get it.

You can see, from an anthropological perspective, why we have this reward mechanism within us. It motivates us to do what is necessary for our survival, ensuring our needs are met and that we have supplies in place for when things are scarce. Dopamine is often described in popular culture as the 'pleasure molecule' but, as Daniel Z Lieberman, a paleoanthropologist at Harvard University says, it would be better described as the 'molecule of more'. As Lieberman puts it, in his book *The Molecule of More* (co-written with my speechwriting brother-in-arms, Mike Long), 'From dopamine's point of view, having things is uninteresting, it's only getting things that matters. If you live under a bridge, dopamine makes you want a tent. If you live in a tent, dopamine makes you want a house. If you live in the most expensive mansion in the world, dopamine makes you want a castle on the moon.'

This is an important point: our reward system is never satisfied. It can never get enough. It always wants more, which explains why we can sit eating pretzels all night long on the sofa, eating far beyond the point when we are full. It explains why we can spend hours swiping on TikTok, constantly seeking out more and more pleasure. And it might also explain why Jeff Bezos, having already acquired control over pretty much everything imaginable on earth, ended up setting his sights even further afield, eventually leading him to boldly go to outer space.

Dopamine was discovered in 1957 by Kathleen Montagu, a researcher in a laboratory at the Runwell Hospital in London. Its discovery has proved critical to understanding the science of behaviour, explaining why we behave in the often-mysterious ways that we do. Not many of our brain cells produce dopamine – just one in two million – but those that do exert a powerful influence on our character, identity and sense of self. They determine what we care about and what we don't; which tasks we approach with gusto and which we approach half-heartedly; how we think and how we feel.

Our dopamine network governs much of our day. It gets us out of bed in the morning to make a coffee, have breakfast and brush our teeth. It also gets us thinking about what we don't have, creating new possibilities. We might be out driving, stop at some traffic lights and see an advert for a beautiful big Samsung TV with crystal clear vision. That might engage our dopamine system as we conjure up a picture of how wonderful that TV would look in our front room, with our family sitting around it. Then we realise we can't afford it, which causes our dopamine system to register this as a failure. So, our dopamine system is not so much a pure pleasure system as an accounting system, a bank account that can go into credit or debit, recognising success or failure. When we get what we want, our dopamine system goes into credit and makes us feel great. When we don't, our dopamine system goes into deficit, and we feel rubbish.

Some people are more dopaminergic than others. Entrepreneurs, immigrants, great leaders, creatives and geniuses all appear to have high levels of dopamine, which can drive them to discover more, constantly seeking out new ambitions, adventures and dreams to pursue. Such people play a critical role in the advance of civilisation. Their dreams can literally change the world. Thomas Edison's dream was affordable lighting for everyone. Henry Ford's dream was that every person should be able to afford a car. Bill Gates's dream was that everyone would have a home computer. These dreams aren't just exciting for the entrepreneurs, they inspire and energise everyone around them.

We've all experienced the force that flows around anyone who's pursuing a big dream. We all need the promise of a better future. We all need something to look forward to. When we're around people who promise us that, it's engaging, exciting and energising. And when you walk into a place where there are lots of people focused on a big dream, you can instantly feel the power and energy flowing all around, just as you can also feel swept away by the deadly feel of inertia and lethargy in a place where everyone is watching the clock, with no greater vision in their mind than making it through to the end of the day.

This provides an opportunity for us to make another great connection. Connect the dull, dreary deeds that need to be fulfilled throughout the day with a big, grand dream for the future and, all of a sudden, the whole world looks like a completely different place. If people are building a ship, don't just have them thinking about the trees they're chopping down, get them thinking about the infinite miles of ocean that lie out there which are waiting to be explored. If people are building a house, don't just have them thinking of the bricks they're laying down, get them thinking about the families who will live in those houses for centuries to come. If people are building a railway, don't just have them thinking of laying down tracks, get them to think about how they are making a country in which everyone is closer connected. Get them looking ahead, get them looking to the distance. Yes, we need to observe what we're doing through a microscope, but sometimes a telescope can be useful as well.

Connecting deeds and dreams

Novo Nordisk is the world's largest supplier of insulin. Their dream is to defeat diabetes for good. They want diabetes gone, done with, kaput, finito. The irony for them is that, if they do defeat diabetes, they'll also have defeated their own business, but they don't mind that so much because, for them, the defeat of diabetes is the ultimate and more noble ambition, and because so many of the people who work there either have diabetes or know people who have diabetes: indeed, many were inspired to work for Novo Nordisk in the first place because of that connection. I've met many Novo Nordisk employees over the years. All of them have felt deeply connected to that dream, whether they work in sales, strategy or HR. The dream keeps them motivated. It's the drive of dopamine, like the teenager practising guitar scales in their bedroom.

Nor do dreams need to be quite so grand or earth-altering. A farmer may dream of one day winning an award for organic farming. A Business School may dream of seeing their research showcased on the front page of *Harvard Business Review*. A small firm of ceramic workers in Stoke-on-Trent may dream of one day seeing their mugs for sale in John Lewis. They may never get that award, that front page or that deal with John Lewis, but the dream could keep them motivated for years, releasing within them an incredible energy. And that energy spreads to everyone around. Employers who can really get people visualising a clear future, something they're working towards, are able to get people working harder, being more focused, more collegiate, happier and more determined. They're giving them something to look forward to.

Leaders attract followers by setting out big dreams and always have done. We have a deep human need to know that our future is assured, and are instinctively drawn to leaders who offer that assurance. It's an emotional contract. The leader gives people a dream; in return the people do what is necessary to achieve that dream; The dreams the leader offers can take many forms.

Deeds and Dreams

Political leaders sometimes deliberately create visions that are ambiguous, to allow different people to project their own images and ideas on to that dream. *The great society. The honest society. The fair society.* Such slogans could have multiple meanings for multiple audiences, which means a broadest audience can connect with them. When Barack Obama said, 'Yes We Can', no one knew precisely what he was talking about, but everyone could connect with it in some way and find inspiration within. When I saw Barack Obama say 'Yes We Can' in 2008 I had lots of big dreams in my mind. *Creating a company. Having children. Moving to the countryside.* His optimism connected with my hopes and dreams, although I'm pretty sure he didn't have me in mind when he said it.

Metaphor is another way in which a dream can be communicated. *We're smashing through the glass ceiling. We're climbing a mountain. We're driving change. We're removing barriers. We're breaking free.* As we explored in earlier chapters, the brain struggles to differentiate between metaphor and literal communication, so metaphors can engage the brain very directly, creating powerful images in people's minds, especially when they are reinforced through physical imagery: either props or body language. I once attended an evangelical service in Malaysia in which 1,000 people simultaneously stood up and mimed breaking free from chains, prompted by a particularly exuberant and charismatic preacher. It was extraordinary to watch. The energy generated in the room was astonishing. Tragically, on the night of the 2016 US election, Hillary Clinton planned to make her victory speech beneath a glass ceiling at New York City's fabulous all-glass Javits

Center. As the news came through that Trump had won, it seemed the metaphor was all wrong. The ceiling seemed to be made not of glass, but iron.

When I'm working with leaders on their speeches, I'm always trying to help them articulate and paint a clear picture of the future. Sometimes they're literal, sometimes they're metaphorical. Sometimes they're specific, sometimes they're ambiguous. Sometimes they know what they're working towards, sometimes they don't. But I've never known an audience that didn't need to know where they were headed to. And that's why it's so important that leaders are able to articulate some kind of dream for the future.

One of the sectors which is best at communicating their dreams is the communication sector, based in Silicon Valley. It is full of people with big dreams. It's no coincidence that it is also famous as one of the hardest working regions on the planet, staffed with super-enthusiastic, wide-eyed, evangelical dreamers working through the night. That's the energy that is generated by a big dream (together with several crates of Red Bull).

In Silicon Valley, dreams can come in various forms. They can be metaphorical or literal, or sometimes a blurring between the two. It's almost no coincidence that the same people who have spent the last couple of decades explaining how they are pushing the frontiers in metaphorical cyberspace are now increasingly trying to occupy literal outer space.

Their dreams might be consumer oriented, perhaps reimagining a product or marketplace; for instance, a vision for how we interact with each other (Facebook) or a vision for how we can shop for everything in one place (Amazon). Their dreams might be commercially oriented: for instance, a desire to completely dominate a market.

Their dream might have more of a moral dimension. Mark Zuckerberg, founder of Facebook, aired a few possibilities in his 2017 Harvard Commencement Speech: 'How about stopping climate change before we destroy the planet and getting millions of people involved manufacturing and installing solar panels? How about curing all diseases and asking volunteers to track their health data and share their genomes? How about modernising democracy so everyone can vote online and personalising education so everyone can learn?'

Or their dream might be territorial. Peter Thiel (PayPal) has a dream of sea-steading, building new island paradises in oceans, free of government interference. Elon Musk has his dream to colonise Mars. Will there be life on Mars in our lifetimes? Who knows? But also, to an extent, who cares? It's exciting just thinking about it. And maybe that's the point. The energy comes from anticipation as much as accomplishment.

Duke University professors of pharmacology Wilkie Wilson and Cynthia Kuhn have carried out several experiments to understand how the dopamine system works, looking at how monkeys behave in anticipation of receiving a treat, such as sweet food. They found that dopamine production peaks not at the moment that the monkey receives the treat, but in the moments leading up to receiving that treat. So, the sweetest pleasures are derived in the moments leading up to success, rather than at the point of accomplishment.

Connect!

This explains why we frequently enjoy the run-up to Christmas more than the actual day; why we get more excited to see that a new message has come in on Facebook than actually reading it; why we can pursue a love interest for months and then find our interest wanes when our interest is reciprocated. The thrill comes from the journey not the destination.

When I was younger, aged 16 or so, my brother and I frequently used to buy lottery scratch-cards in our lunchbreaks. These were the highlights of the day as we decided what we would do with our millions. We never won, of course, but, in our imaginations, we'd spent those millions of pounds many times over. It's the Del Boy effect. *This time next year, we'll be millionaires.*

We all need dreams. The promise of better times tomorrow helps us get through today. So, if you are in a position of leadership, you have a responsibility to make sure you are presenting to people some dreams for the future, and making sure that your dreams are aligned with their own dreams. If you do so you will be meeting one of their deepest needs, and in return they will give you what you need. But you should also make sure that you have some dreams for yourself – that's assuming you want to get the best out of yourself.

Have a dream

We know how powerful our dopamine system is, but we also know that it's possible for other people to take control of it. The Netflix documentary, *The Social Dilemma* showed that social media platforms hack into our dopamine networks to keep us online, which might explain why the average social media user spends two hours a day on social media, with many spending even longer. They're distracting attention away from what we should be doing. We need to take back control of our own dopamine system, and this means putting our own dreams first. And this means creating some dreams for ourselves.

As I explained earlier, I've always been a firm believer in the power of positive visualisation. I've found a huge value in creating dreams to motivate me to get through things and be my best. I use this in all sorts of ways, to accomplish ambitions in the short, medium and long term. This might be as simple as dreaming of a nice plate of sushi with an ice-cold bottle of Asahi once I've finished writing a speech, or it might be a much bigger ambition.

Shortly after my wife and I got married, we spent a day walking beside the river Thames, going all the way from Hammersmith to Kew, talking about the kind of life we wanted to share together. At the time we were living in London, no children, but slogging our guts out in Westminster, working silly hours. As we walked, we conjured up a dream for the future: an image of us living in a big house on a hill in the country with two children, a dog and a cat. I was a published writer, with my own company, choosing who I worked for, and when I worked. We loved the prospect of that kind of life. When we got home, we literally drew that picture. We got out a pen and drew it on a scrap bit of A4 paper.

We had a vision of where we wanted to get to. We then made it our mission to make that dream come true. It didn't happen easily. It wasn't a case of clicking our heels together and it happened. We spent three years going to a clinic before we were given the go-ahead to conceive. I went to night school to study for a master's degree in mass communications, while still working full-time as a speechwriter. We then tried to buy a house in the country, which proved harder than we'd imagined, taking six years, and at one point we wound up living in a bed and breakfast with our then one-year-old daughter. But all the time we knew where we were heading, and that gave us the energy to power through the hardships. Today, almost 20 years after that riverside walk, we have everything we drew in that little A4 picture, and we still have that A4 picture too, which hangs in our office in our house on a hill in the country, with two children, a dog and a cat.

But, even though we've made it to the top of one hill, there's always another hill to climb. At the beginning of 2021, I felt like I needed something new to work towards. I always find New Year a bit of a tricky time – the weather's miserable, Christmas is behind and, in 2021, that feeling was exacerbated by the continuing pressure of coronavirus. The first stage of the pandemic had felt incredibly productive for me from a personal perspective – I'd made it my mission to learn to play the whole of the Beatles back catalogue by memory on the piano and I'd accomplished that – now, I felt like I needed something new.

I had in mind all sorts of *possible* dreams. Perhaps I could write a musical about the life of former Scottish politician, Jennie Lee? Maybe I should start up a charity promoting public speaking among disadvantaged youngsters? Maybe I should study towards getting a degree in piano performance.

I couldn't quite work out what I wanted to do, so I ended up doing very little, spending too much time on social media and snacking too much. By the time March came, I decided I needed to do something about it.

I did a stock-take on my life, looking at which bits I was happy with, and which bits I was not so happy with. I tried to think of my values, my strengths and my ambitions for the future. It was a variation on the self-affirmation exercises that you can find online. I wrote down the three things that I thought were most important to me, the things that made me happiest. It didn't take long for me to get my answer. Creativity, Curiosity, Connecting. (Obviously it was an alliterative three-part list). It didn't take long before the idea emerged of writing this book, which is in your hand now. *CONNECT.*

As soon as I got that vague image about writing a book, I started making it clearer and clearer. I threw my imagination forwards 18 months. I could visualise walking into Foyles on Tottenham Court Road and seeing my new book on the shelf. I could visualise myself hosting the launch party, signing books, with my lovely family around me. I could see how I would feel at that party: happy, healthy, confident.

Now I just needed to make it happen. Key to that was breaking it down into smaller chunks. I had long-term, medium-term and short-term targets. My long-term target was getting the book published. My medium-term target was to write the book. My short-term target was to get a book deal. To make all that happen, I needed to commit to at least three hours of writing, which I did every day. It was simple. I just took all social media off my phone and got on with it.

From that point on, it was actually fairly easy. And I loved the realisation that I was getting closer and closer to achieving my dream. I celebrated success. It was a joy watching the word count on my book increase and I marked each day of writing by putting a little orange dot on the wall to show the progress I was making.

It wasn't always easy. Every now and then I'd screw up and miss a day. When that happened, I tried not to be too harsh on myself. I just reconnected to my dream a bit more. I worked hard to keep my dream alive. I would imagine my book launch party when I was going to sleep. I'd draw it when I was doodling at my desk. I'd imagine it when I brushed my teeth in the morning. The more closely I was connected to my dream, the less likely I was to give it up.

It's what's known as the 'endowment effect'. Once we believe something is already in our possession, we don't want to give it up.

The endowment effect was discovered by Nobel Prize winner Daniel Kahneman and researchers at Cornell University who carried out an experiment where a class of students were all given a gift. Half were given a mug and the other half were given a bar of chocolate. They asked if any of them wanted to exchange their gifts for the other. The vast majority wanted to hold on to whatever they already had. The emerging insight: once we have possession of something we don't want to let go. It's the same with dreams. Once we've internalised ours, we will not let it go.

Dreams and desires

But that was my dream. What's yours? Literally, draw a picture of your dream. Then, to make your dream happen, you need to break it down. DJ Patil, the first ever US chief data scientist, summarised his method as dream in years; plan in months; evaluate in weeks; and ship daily.

So, take the time to:

- Draw a picture of your dream of where you want to be in one year's time. Literally draw it. Imagine it. Believe it.
- Now work back from that: if that's where you want to be one year from now, where must you be six months from now?
- If that's where you must be six months from now, what must you now start doing today and every day?

Finding your dream is the starting point and often the hardest bit. The reason most people's dreams don't come true is because they don't know what their dreams are, or they don't acknowledge them or can't properly commit to them. Know your dreams, feel your dreams and share your dreams. Tell people about your dream: tell the people you love, the people you care about. They will support and encourage you but, you never know, you may also inspire other people to make their dreams come true as well. The energy you emit can prove infectious.

Everyone needs something to look forward to. So don't be afraid to create dreams for other people as well. Give your friends, your family and your community something to look forward to. It doesn't need to be something big: a meal out, a night at the theatre, a weekend away. Create a vision, create expectation, activate the dopamine system. Boom! We all need something to look forward to.

Some people may feel intimidated by the energy you release when you are powering forward in pursuit of a dream. They may envy you, or mock you, or put you down. These are people who simply don't admire growth and change, which is more of a problem for them than it is for you. Try not to condemn or judge them as harshly as they may judge you.

Keep looking forward. Look forward to your sushi at the end of your writing, or your night out with friends at the end of the month, or your big ambitions for a year forward.

Or perhaps go the whole way. A good way to change your perspective on your life is to project yourself right forward. Imagine you are at the end of your life, looking back on what you're doing now. Are you doing the right thing? Are you making the right choices now?

Projecting yourself forward and then looking back is what Jeff Bezos has been doing for many years now. Whenever he is facing a difficult decision in life, he projects himself forward to the end of his life and asks, 'Would I regret doing what I want to do now?' That was why he decided to resign from his job on Wall Street to create Amazon. And that's why he kept his faith in Amazon, even while it was racking up eye-watering losses in its early days. And that was why he never gave up on his space mission which he achieved on 20 July 2021, which he described as his 'Best Day Ever!'

Deeds and Dreams

He calls it his 'regret minimisation framework'. So, fast-forward to the end of your life. Really connect with that future. Look back on what you're doing now. What would you say to yourself? Would you say you're doing the right thing with your life now or not? Would you say you're being true to the person you really are or did you take a wrong turn at some point? Would you say you're living your best life or is this the moment right now when you should commit to make a change?

Find your dream for the future and fight for your dream. You may not create a company as big as Amazon. You may not become the richest and most powerful person on the planet. But, you never know, you might just make the best of all of the talents you have available to you. And then you can make it your mission that, by the end of your life you can smile to yourself and say, like a kid emerging from a fancy-dress party, that you've lived your 'Best Life Ever'.

Connecting Connections

The coronavirus pandemic affected many people in different ways – for better and for worse. It changed me in at least one way that I'd never imagined. The first day I really noticed something was different was Friday 10 December 2021. I was just coming to the end of one of the most exhilarating and exciting years of my professional life, in which I'd gone from total lockdown and Zoom speeches at the beginning of the year to getting back on the road again, travelling around the world writing big speeches for my clients and the joy of once again making speeches of my own to audiences of 1,000+ in Helsinki, Copenhagen and Dubai. The holiday season was in touching distance, I'd finished the first draft of my book and the pandemic seemed almost beaten, although there was worrying news about a new variant emerging – Omicron. Everyone was trying to remain upbeat, but no one was quite sure they were doing the right thing. Messaging from the government was as ambiguous as ever. It was a strange period; as Dickens said, 'the best of times, the worst of times'.

Connecting Connections

I'd been working in London that week and, before driving home to Wales, I called my wife, Lucy, to say that I was going to pop into the Brentford Community Stadium on the way home to watch Brentford play Watford. The stadium was right by the motorway so it wouldn't be a huge diversion; I'd miss the worst of the traffic and, big bonus, I'd managed to grab a fantastic seat right by the dug-out.

'Wow!' she said. 'You're actually hooked!' I was a bit taken aback by her directness, but I couldn't argue. 'You're right,' I said. 'I am hooked. Weird, isn't it?'

It was true. I was hooked. And it was weird. Before the coronavirus pandemic, I'd never been in the slightest bit interested in football. Despite growing up within earshot of both Fulham and Chelsea's football grounds, I'd never been to a match as a youngster, nor had I wanted to. If friends started talking about football, my eyes would glaze over until the conversation turned to a different topic more to my liking (friends will confirm!). I literally couldn't think of anything more futile than a bunch of guys kicking a ball back and forth up a pitch.

But something had changed. Now I wanted to go to every game. Why? Truth be told, I think the 18 months of COVID had affected me more deeply than I'd realised at the time. It had been beautiful being in the Brecon Beacons during lockdown, just us, all together, our small family, doing our own little things, playing piano, baking, playing games. But I think I'd grown lonely, out of touch, disconnected and I needed to be among more people again. I was craving connection.

Connect!

And the more I think about it, the more I realise I value that connection between people. The more it seems central to the whole human race, to what's made us special, to what's given our species supremacy on this planet over other beings: it is our ability to connect.

And now, as I walk from the car park to the stadium, among other people chatting animatedly and optimistically, with big smiles on their faces, wearing their red and white striped scarves, hats and gloves, like me, I feel connected. I walk into the bar in the South Stand to see a lot of other people dotted around, but I'm quickly welcomed into people's conversations about the quality of the samosas, or our prospects in tonight's game, and I feel connected. Five minutes before the game starts, I take my seat, and I look around at the familiar multi-coloured seats, noticing the various spots in the stadium where I've watched games with my daughters over the last few months, and I feel connected.

'Hey Jude' starts ringing across the PA system, as it does at the beginning and the end of every game and, as 30,000 people join together in singing along with the rousing McCartney outro (Na Na Na Na-Na Na Na) I feel connected. After two years of wearing masks, we're not sitting down and shutting up, we're standing up and singing out and I feel connected. The familiar players come out on the pitch, I join the applause and, as they wave to the fans, I feel connected. The buzz and energy begins to build across the stadium as more and more people start coming in and I feel connected.

Connecting Connections

I see the familiar West London skyline in the distance and the Heathrow flight line that I grew up under, as a youngster living on a council estate, and I feel connected. The whistle blows for the game to start and, when all the players take the knee for Black Lives Matter and the crowd applauds, I feel connected to the players. I look around at the signs quoting Danish manager, Thomas Frank, 'Everyone deserves respect', and I feel connected.

The game proceeds. We go 1–0 down after a goal by Emmanuel Dennis in the first half and, although I feel the frustration along with 30,000 other people, I see the team fighting back, playing harder, showing the ferocious spirit of the perennial underdog, and I feel connected. At regular intervals, the crowd bursts spontaneously into the three-part chant, 'Come on, Brentford! Come on, Brentford! Come on, Brentford!' and I feel connected. We are all focused solidly on the action, the drama, for 90 minutes, and no one is checking their phone, and I feel connected. Pontus Jansson equalises in the 84th minute, there is a huge roar and a surge of optimism powers through the stadium, and I feel connected. Then in the 95th minute, in the fifth minute of extra time, Bryan Mbeumo scores a penalty, taking us to 2–1.

The referee blows the final whistle, and the crowd is ecstatic, leaping up and down. We've taken three points and we're now in the top half of the Premier League. 'Hey Jude' once again comes blasting out on the tannoy and everyone is on their feet, singing along, and I look around and see many grown men with tears streaming down their cheeks at this glorious comeback evening. I even feel my own eyes water, although it may be the cold. I feel connected.

My wife and daughters are watching the game live on Sky at home. They are trying to connect with me, seeing if they can spot me in the stadium. They don't, but they do hear Gary Neville, the former captain of Manchester United and England, commentating on the match for Sky Sports and describing the mood and feeling in the stadium that night.

'They're connected – the fans, the players, the manager, the owner, they're all connected. It's not the biggest club there's ever been in the Premier League, but they've got a massive spirit and energy to them. You see the players all walking around the pitch celebrating with the fans as football should be and it's fantastic. We've got "Hey Jude" again and, like I say, it's absolutely fantastic. They've brought a real energy and spirit to the Premier League.'

The world has been broken by coronavirus. Many of the connections we've relied upon throughout our lives have been broken. Our connections with ourselves. Our connections with each other. Our connections with who we are, what we stand for and where we're going.

But somewhere in this Brentford game I can feel the solution and see a glimmer of hope for how we rebuild. If 30,000 people can get connected over something as futile as kicking a ball around, then why shouldn't we be able to connect and create huge movements to tackle the problems in the world which really matter? Fighting poverty. Saving the environment. Promoting equality.

Connecting Connections

It was Leonardo da Vinci who said, 'Everything connects to everything else', and he was right. It was his ability to see connections that others had missed, between music and machinery, engineering and architecture, geology and geometry, which enabled him to come up with so many breakthrough inventions – the helicopter, aeroplane, and swinging bridge, to mention just three. He was a man with such a conviction that everything was connected that he barely even put full-stops in his writing. That ability to see, find and exploit connections is still critical to intellectual breakthrough.

But we also know that people need to connect today more than ever. Through the course of history we have always seen there is a clear correlation between the amount of connections there are between people in the world and the advance of civilisation. We need people to connect. And I hope this book has given you some inspiration for how you can do that.

Start by getting yourself connected. Connect with the things you really care about. Connect with where you've come from. Connect with where you're headed. Connect your mind and body, your thoughts and actions, your hopes and dreams.

Connect with people you admire. Connect what they do with why they do what they do. Connect who they are with who they want to be. Connect morality with meaning, emotion with logic, instinct with action, the past with the present, the present with the future.

This is what great leaders have done through the ages: they've made connections. And today people are looking more than ever for a new generation of leaders who can make

Connect!

connections and bring people together. The pandemic did make it feel as if the world was broken for a while. But it was only ever going to be temporary. You can't keep people apart. And you can't keep a great planet down. So get connected. Stay connected. And help make a better world.

Notes

CONNECTIONS

3 **these first impressions are very much guided by similarities to people we've known or met before**
A. Eggleston, E. Geangu, S.P. Tipper, *et al.*, 'Young Children learn first impressions of faces through social referencing', *Sci Rep*, 11, 14744 (2021), https://doi.org/10.1038/s41598-021-94204-6 <Accessed 23 March 2022>

3 **If someone looks like someone who gave us the creeps, we'll assume that they're a bit creepy too**
Alexander Todorov, *Face Value: The Irresistible Influence of First Impressions* (Princeton University Press, 2017)

5 **developing new computational technologies to map the neural connections in the brain**
Anna Gosline, 'Why your brain has a Jennifer Aniston cell', *New Scientist*, https://www.newscientist.com/article/dn7567-why-your-brain-has-a-jennifer-aniston-cell/ <Accessed 23 March 2022>

Connect!

5 **It was the Canadian psychologist Donald Hebb who established the idea that when neurons fire together, they wire together**
Donald O. Hebb, *The Organisation of Behavior: A Neuropsychological Theory* (1949)

6 **invented the roll-on deodorant after looking at a Biro and wondering if the same roll-on mechanism could be used to dispense deodorant**
Mary Bellis, 'The History of Commercial Deodorants', *ThoughtCo.Com* (2019), https://www.thoughtco.com/history-of-commercial-deodorants-1991570 <Accessed 23 March 2022>

7 **looking at his waffle iron over the breakfast table and wondering, 'What if I poured plastic in that . . .?'**
Sumedha Shra, 'Nike's first shoe was made using a waffle maker', *Inshorts.com* (6 June 2016), https://inshorts.com/en/news/nikes-first-shoe-was-made-using-a-wafflemaker-1465233184443#:~:text=The%20company's%20founder%2C%20Bill%20Bowerman,as%20the%20'Waffle%20Trainer <Accessed 23 March 2022>

7 **Can you put haggis and snails on the same plate . . .?**
Berklee College of Music, 'David Bowie | Berklee Commencement Address 1999', uploaded to *YouTube* (11 January 2016), https://www.youtube.com/watch?v=IZNEvTYVo4s <Accessed 23 March 2022>

8 **Steve Jobs once described creativity as 'just connecting things'**

Gary Wolf, 'Steve Jobs: The Next Insanely Great Thing', *Wired* (1996), https://www.wired.com/1996/02/jobs-2/ <Accessed >23 March 2022>

8 **Apple Stores have unusually high ceilings, helpful concierges and a 'bar' at the back**
Joshua Barrie, 'Apple is adding a "Concierge" service to its Genius Bar that priorities customer problems', *Business Insider* (24 February 2015), https://www.businessinsider.com/apple-adds-concierge-service-to-genius-bar-2015-2?r=US&IR=T <Accessed 23 March 2022>

10 **after watching an episode of *The West Wing* about gay marriage in which Bartlet had argued that it wasn't for politicians to define or ill-define love**
Manchester Evening News, 'Johnson: Don't moralise on marriage' (28 February 2007), https://www.manchestereveningnews.co.uk/news/greater-manchester-news/johnson-dont-moralise-on-marriage-981308 <Accessed 23 March 2022>

13 **An article in the *Daily Mail* argued, 'Bring on the Brixit!'**
Iain Murray, 'Bring on the "Brixit": EU withdrawal would bring benefits for both Britain and the US', *Mail Online* (2012), http://www.dailymail.co.uk/debate/article-2163244/Bring-Brixit-EU-withdrawal-bring-benefits-Britain-US.html <Accessed 23 March 2022>

13 ***The Economist* once warned 'Brixit looms'**
Bagehot, 'A Brixit looms' (2012), https://www.economist.com/bagehots-notebook/2012/06/21/a-brixit-looms <Accessed 23 March 2022>

13 *MoneyWeek* **pondered 'Why Britain's economy would prosper from a "Brixit"'**
Matthew Lynn, 'Why Britain's economy would prosper from a "Brixit"', *Moneyweek* (9 November 2012), https://moneyweek.com/17502/why-britains-economy-would-prosper-from-a-brixit-61414 <Accessed 23 March 2022>

19 **two reported campaign trips and both were to food manufacturers**
The Johnson Dossier, containing the 200,000 words that Boris Johnson said or posted publicly between 21 February 2016 and 22 June 2016, compiled by *Led by Donkeys*, https://johnsondossier.com/#h.2rb4i01 <Accessed 23 March 2022>

20 **We've lost control of our dough**
Nick Gutteridge, '"We've lost all our dough!" Boris tackles EU funding debate on visit to biscuit factory', *The Express* (2 June 2016), https://www.express.co.uk/news/politics/676281/EU-referendum-Boris-tackles-Brussels-funding-debate-on-visit-to-biscuit-factory <Accessed 23 March 2022>

20 **no one understands the intricacies and complexities of trade negotiations, everyone understands cake**
Tom Newton Dunn, '"WE'LL HAVE OUR CAKE AND EAT IT" Boris Johnson joins forces with Liam Fox and declares support for "hard" Brexit which will "liberate" Britain to champion free trade' (2016), https://www.thesun.co.uk/news/1889723/boris-johnson-joins-forces-with-liam-foxand-declares-support-for-hard-brexit-which-will-liberate-britain-to-champion-free-trade/ <Accessed 23 March 2022>

20   **in the British press between 2016 and December 2018 which featured Brexit in the title and a cake reference in the text**
Jonathan Charteris-Black, *Metaphors of Brexit: No Cherries on the Cake* (Palgrave Macmillan, 2019)

21   **'cakeism'**
'Cakeism', *Collins Dictionary*, https://www.collinsdiction-ary.com/dictionary/english/cakeism <Accessed 23 March 2022>

21   **'cakeist'**
'Cakeism', *Macmillan Dictionary*, https://www.mac-millandictionary.com/buzzword/entries/cakeism.html <Accessed 23 March 2022>

21   **'We can maximise the size of the cake and enjoy a much bigger piece.'**
Jon Stone, 'Philip Hammond mocks Boris Johnson over Brexit in front of German audience', *The Independent* (27 June 2017), https://www.independent.co.uk/news/uk/politics/boris-johnson-philip-hammond-brexit-have-our-cake-and-eat-it-joke-mock-german-cdu-economic-council-a7810571.html <Accessed 23 March 2022>

22   **It looks like the cake philosophy is still alive**
James Randerson, 'Donald Tusk: UK position is pure illusion', *Politico* (23 February 2018), https://www.politico.eu/article/donald-tusk-uk-brexit-position-is-pure-illusion/ <Accessed 23 March 2022>

22   **The fact they were refuting it didn't matter: the uncon-scious brain doesn't process negatives**

Dummies, 'Getting Acquainted with your quirky uncon-
scious mind' (26 March 2016), https://www.dummies.
com/health/mental-health/getting-acquainted-with-
your-quirky-unconscious-mind/#:~:text=goals%20seem-
ingly%20effortlessly <Accessed 23 March 2022>

22 **'even by negating an image, we're evoking that image'**
George Lakoff, *Don't Think of an Elephant!: Know Your
Values and Frame the Debate* (Chelsea Green Publishing
Co, 1990)

23 **Put it in. Err . . . [more laughter]. And then we can get
on . . .'**
Global News Live Streaming, 'UK election: Boris Johnson launches Conservative party campaign' (6 November
2019), https://www.youtube.com/watch?v=sZi4xvFINRE
<Accessed 23 March 2022>

24 **On the doughnut. In your mouth. Get Brexit Done . . .'"**
Robert Ford, Tim Bale, Will Jennings, and Paul
Surridge, *The British General Election of 2019* (2021),
p.221

24 **comparable with viewing figures for the UK's top-rated
TV show, *Strictly Come Dancing***
Conservatives, 'Boris Johnson's hilarious election advert
| 12 Questions to Boris Johnson', uploaded to *You-
Tube* (12 November 2019), https://www.youtube.com/
watch?v=97zPDojMWiQ

24 **Fox News reported on the British prime minister's
approach to tea-making**
Stephen Sorace, 'Boris Johnson shows off tea-making
skills, stirs outrage when he adds milk with bag still in

mug', *Fox News* (13 November 2019), https://www.foxnews.com/world/boris-johnson-tea-video-outrage-milk <Accessed 23 March 2022>

25 **delivering milk and groceries direct to the doorstep of a beaming voter in Leeds**
Heather Stewart and Aamna Mohdin, 'Boris Johnson hides in a fridge to avoid Piers Morgan interview', *The Guardian* (11 December 2019), https://www.theguardian.com/politics/2019/dec/11/boris-johnson-hides-in-fridge-to-avoid-piers-morgan-interview <Accessed 23 March 2022>

26 **The reward system is activated, hormones are released in the stomach and salivation occurs**
Charles Spence, Katsunori Okajima, Adrian David Cheok, Olivia Petit, Charles Michel,
'Eating with our eyes: From visual hunger to digital satiation', *Brain and Cognition*, Volume 110 (2016): 53-63, https://www.sciencedirect.com/science/article/pii/S0278262615300178 <Accessed 23 March 2022>

28 **delta means sleep, theta means drowsy, alpha means relaxed, beta means focused, and gamma means high insight**
'Brain Waves', *Science Direct*, https://www.sciencedirect.com/topics/agricultural-and-biological-sciences/brain-waves <Accessed 23 March 2022>

29 **a member of what's known in India as an OBC ('Other Backward Class')**
https://en.wikipedia.org/wiki/Other_Backward_Class (accessed 5 April 2022)

32 **Social psychologists agree that warmth is one of the prime factors determining trust and it's not hard to understand why**
Amy Cuddy, Matthew Kohut and John Neffinger, 'Connect then lead,' *Harvard Business Review* (July–August 2013), https://hbr.org/2013/07/connect-then-lead <Accessed 23 March 2022>

32 **Feelings of social exclusion can lead people to literally feel cold**
Chen-Bo Zhong and Geoffrey J. Leonardelli, 'Cold and Lonely: Does Social Exclusion Literally Feel Cold?', *Psychological Science*, Volume 19 Issue 9 (2008): 838–842

33 **Those who were given the warm drink said they believed the person had a 'warmer personality'**
Lawrence E. Williams and John A. Bargh, 'Experiencing Physical Warmth Promotes Interpersonal Warmth', *Science* (2008) 322(5901): 606–607, https://www.ncbi.nlm.nih.gov/pmc/articles/PMC2737341/ <Accessed 23 March 2022>

35 **Great things are never done by just one person, they're done by a team of people**
Paulinosdepido, 'Steve Jobs My Model in Business is the Beatles', uploaded to *YouTube* (2011), https://www.youtube.com/watch?v=1QfK9UokAIo <Accessed 23 March 2022>

35 **'A mind forever voyaging through strange seas of thought alone'**
Karen Haslam, 'Why is Apple called Apple?', *Macworld* (5 March 2020), https://www.macworld.co.uk/feature/

why-is-apple-called-apple-3783504/ <Accessed 23 March 2022>

36 **Maybe the logo had primed them to be more creative and think different?**
Gráinne M. Fitzsimons, Tanya L. Chartrand and Gavan J. Fitzsimons, 'Automatic Effects of Brand Exposure on Motivated Behavior: How Apple Makes You "Think Different"', *JOURNAL OF CONSUMER RESEARCH*, Vol. 35 (2008), https://faculty.fuqua.duke.edu/~gavan/bio/GJF_articles/apple_ibm_jcr_08.pdf <Accessed 23 March 2022>

36 **This might explain why the Apple brand is now the most valuable in the world, with a value of more than $355 billion**
Trevor Little, 'Apple retains most valuable brand crown as tech boom continues and TikTok soars,' *Trademark Review* (26 January 2022), https://www.worldtrademarkreview.com/apple-retains-most-valuable-brand-crown-tech-boom-continues-and-tiktok-soars <Accessed 23 March 2022>

MIND AND BODY

44 **He's just given England their first Rugby World Cup win in history**
Duncan Bech, 'Rugby World Cup 2003: Jonny Wilkinson recalls "that kick" against Australia', *Independent* (2013), https://www.independent.co.uk/sport/rugby/rugby-union/news-comment/rugby-world-cup-2003-jonny-wilkinson-recalls-kick-against-australia-8956710.html <Accessed 23 March 2022>

44 It helps your body to get used to performing well under pressure
Support, 'Use Imagery techniques to improve your performance!', *My PT Hub* (2016), https://support. mypthub.net/use-imagery-techniques-to-improve-your-performance/ <Accessed 23 March 2022>

47 'I never hit a shot, not even in practice, without having a very sharp in-focus picture of it in my head.'
A.J. Adams MAPP, 'Seeing Is Believing: The Power of Visualisation', *Psychology Today* (2009), https://www. psychologytoday.com/gb/blog/flourish/200912/seeing-is-believing-the-power-visualization <Accessed 23 March 2022>

47 With characteristic modesty, he replied, 'Yes, I did actually.'
Paul McKenna's interview with Gareth Southgate, '70- Gareth Southgate', Paul McKenna's *Positivity* Podcast (8 November 2021)

51 bringing up your oxytocin and serotonin levels, in other words, it reduces stress and makes you feel good
Xiao Ma, Zi-Qi Yue, Zhu-Qing Gong, Hong Zhang, Nai-Yue Duan, Yu-Tong Shi, Gao-Xia Wei, and You-Fa Li, 'The Effect of Diaphragmatic Breathing on Attention, Negative Affect and Stress in Healthy Adults', *Frontiers in Psychology* Vol 8, 874 (2017), https://www.ncbi.nlm. nih.gov/pmc/articles/PMC5455070/ <Accessed 23 March 2022>

53 **you open up the left frontal lobes of the brain, which puts you into challenge mode, so basically you feel more up for it**
Jenny Lee, 'A moderate amount of stress is good for you', *The Irish News* (2017), https://www.irishnews.com/lifestyle/2017/02/08/news/a-moderate-amount-of-stress-is-good-for-you-919327/ <Accessed 23 March 2022>

54 **Positive visualisation can help you reach your best too, and it can help in all sorts of professional contexts, not just speeches and presentations**
Tim Blankert and Melvyn R. W. Hamstra, 'Imaging Success: Multiple Achievement Goals and the Effectiveness of Imagery', *Basic Appl Soc Psych*, 39, 1 (2017): 60–67, https://www.ncbi.nlm.nih.gov/pmc/articles/PMC5351796/ <Accessed 23 March 2022>

56 **While some of Cuddy's peers cast doubt over her findings, a major peer review in June 2020 largely vindicated her**
Emma Elkjær, Mai B. Mikkelsen, Johannes Michalak, Douglas S. Mennin, Mia S. O'Toole, 'Expansive and Contractive Postures and Movement: A Systematic Review and Meta-Analysis of the Effect of Motor Displays on Affective and Behavioral Responses', *Perspectives on Psychological Science* (2020), https://journals.sagepub.com/doi/abs/10.1177/1745691620919358 <Accessed 23 March 2022>

57 **In actual fact, research shows this increases our stress levels**

Connect!

I.M. Lin, E. Peper, 'Psychophysiological patterns during cell phone text messaging: a preliminary study', *Applied Psychophysiology & Biofeedback*, Vol 34 (2009): 53–57

57 **which might explain why looking up is such a simple but affirmative act**
Mike Long and Daniel Lieberman, *The Molecule of More: How a Single Chemical in Your Brain Drives Love, Sex, and Creativity – and Will Determine the Fate of the Human Race* (BenBella Books, 2019)

57 **Even though the participants knew they were faking their smiles, it didn't take long before they were feeling great**
Marmolejo-Ramos, F., Murata, A., Sasaki, K., Yamada, Y., Ikeda, A., Hinojosa, J. A., Watanabe, K., Parzuchowski, M., Tirado, C., & Ospina, R., 'Your face and moves seem happier when I smile: Facial action influences the perception of emotional faces and biological motion stimuli', *Experimental Psychology*, 67, 1 (2020): 14–22, https://doi.org/10.1027/1618-3169/a000470 <Accessed 23 March 2022> https://psycnet.apa.org/record/2020-32759-001

57 **A "fake it till you make it" approach could have more credit than we expect.'**
University of South Australia press release, 'When you're smiling, the whole world really does smile with you' (12 August 2020), https://www.unisa.edu.au/Media-Centre/Releases/2020/when-youre-smiling-the-whole-world-really-does-smile-with-you/ <Accessed 23 March 2022>

58   **One study showed that wearing a lab coat increased people's attentiveness and care**
Hajo Adam and Adam D. Galinski, 'Enclothes cognition', *Journal of Experimental Social Psychology*,
Volume 48, Issue 4 (July 2012): 918-925, https://www.sciencedirect.com/science/article/abs/pii/S0022103112000200 <Accessed 23 March 2022>

58   **Another showed dressing up more professionally for interviews gave people extra confidence**
Chloe Levin, 'Dress To Impress; Does Suiting Up Bring More Confident?', *Psych Learning Curve* (2017), http://psychlearningcurve.org/dress-to-impress/ <Accessed 23 March 2022>

58   **Perhaps predictably, the group who said 'I feel excited' outperformed the group who said they felt anxious**
Ian Robertson, *How Confidence Works: The new science of self-belief, why some people learn it and others don't* (Bantam Press, 2021), p.28

ME AND WE

63   **I've changed my mind. I don't want to hang out at Power 106 FM . . .**
Ariana Grande Loves Ü, 'Ariana Grande spent this entire interview educating these lowkey sexist and homophobic interviewers!', uploaded to *YouTube* (2017) https://www.youtube.com/watch?v=XTtMQrSS_q0 <Accessed 23 March 2022>

63   **environment which 'urges us to approach the world, and the people in it, in an adversarial frame of mind'**

Deborah Tannen and Michael Leapman, *The Argument Culture: Changing the Way We Argue and Debate* (Little Brown Book Group Limited, 1998), p.5

64 **A study by YouGov in 2019 showed that today just 14 per cent of people think politics should be out of bounds in conversation**
Lloyds Bank, 'RELIGION, SEX AND POLITICS? THE M WORD IS BRITAIN'S BIGGEST TABOO' (7 March 2019), https://www.lloydsbankinggroup.com/assets/media/press-releases/lloyds-bank/2019/lloyds-bank---the-m-word-press-release_final.pdf <Accessed 23 March 2022>

65 **we know that soft textures encourage collaboration and generosity**
Sense, 'Sensebook, summary findings of Russell Jones' book', www.sensebook.co.uk/project/collaboration <Accessed 23 March 2022>

69 **two of the participants in his study, randomly put together, ended up marrying one another six months later!**
Arthur Aron, Edward Melinat, Elaine Aron, Robert Vallone and Renee Bator, 'The Experimental Generation of Interpersonal Closeness: A procedure and some preliminary findings', *The Society for Personality and Social Psychology*, Vol 23, No.4 (April 1977): 363-77, https://journals.sagepub.com/doi/pdf/10.1177/0146167297234003 <Accessed 23 March 2022>

70 **When we see people smiling, the instinctive response is to smile back, which gets all those beautiful hormones flowing which make us feel good**

Notes

Elaine Hatfield, John T. Caciopppo, Richard L. Rapson, Market Clark, 'Primitive emotional contagion', *Emotion and Social Behaviour, Review of Personality and Social Psychology*, Vol 14 (1992): 151-177

70 **Studies have shown this even works on online platforms like Zoom, Teams or TikTok**
Phoebe H.C. Mui, Martijn B. Goudbeek, Camiel Roex, Wout Spierts and Marc G. J. Swerts, 'Smile Mimicry and Emotional Contagion in Audio-Visual Computer-Mediated Communication', *Front. Psychol.* (5 November 2018), https://www.frontiersin.org/articles/10.3389/fpsyg.2018.02077/full

71 **And those who went to the happy face first spent longer there!**
Marc Silver, '"Goats Might Prefer A Smile to A Frown", Study says', *NPR* (29 August 2018), https://www.npr.org/sections/goatsandsoda/2018/08/29/643034723/goats-might-prefer-a-smile-to-a-frown-study-says <Accessed 23 March 2022>

73 **It only takes a tenth of a second but it creates a real intimacy**
Karen L. Schmidt and Jeffrey F. Cohn, 'Human facial expressions as adaptations: Evolutionary questions in facial expression research', *Yearbook of Physical Anthropology* 44, S33 (November 2001)

75 **This rises to 80 per cent on social media**
Mor Naaman, Jeffrey Boase, Chih-Hui Lai, 'Is it really about me? Message Content in Social Awareness Streams', Rutgers University (February 2010), http://infolab.stanford.

edu/~mor/research/naamanCSCW10.pdf <Accessed 23 March 2022>

75 **Harvard researchers found that talking about ourselves lights up similar parts of the brain to taking cocaine**
Adrian F. Ward, 'The Neuroscience of Everybody's Favourite Topic', *Scientific American*, (2013), https://www.scientificamerican.com/article/the-neuroscience-of-everybody-favorite-topic-themselves/

78 **with 38 per cent of us having talked about it in the previous hour!**
Linda Geddes, 'Why do Brits talk about the weather so much?', *BBC Future* (2015), https://www.bbc.com/future/article/20151214-why-do-brits-talk-about-the-weather-so-much <Accessed 23 March 2022>

80 **Ardern's go-to pronoun was 'we' while Boris's was 'you'**
Neil Vowles, 'Want, wants, want: How Boris Johnson's choice of language failed to bring the UK together', University of Sussex (2020), http://www.sussex.ac.uk/broadcast/read/52112 <Accessed 23 March 2022>

81 **flattery triggers the same reward centres in the brain that light up during sex**
K. Aleisha Fetters, 'Compliments Are Like Mini-Orgasms for Your Brain', *Vice* (6 February 2017), https://www.vice.com/en/article/mg9pex/compliments-are-like-mini-orgasms-for-your-brain <Accessed 23 March 2022>

81 **the recipient must have known the flattery was fake, and yet it was still found to have the same impact**
Elaine Chan and Jaideep Sengupta, 'Insincere Flattery Actually Works: A Dual Attitudes Perspective', *Journal*

of Marketing Research Vol. 47, No. 1 (2010): 122-133, https://www.jstor.org/stable/20618959 <Accessed 23 March 2022>

81 **It turned out to be somebody he went to school with, who had been sentenced to prison**

Ross Lydall, 'Sadiq Khan says his name should be pronounced as "Saad-ick", not "Sad-eek"', *Evening Standard* (2019), https://www.standard.co.uk/news/politics/sadiq-khan-says-his-name-should-be-pronounced-as-saadick-and-not-sadeek-a4233831.html <Accessed 23 March 2022>

MORALITY AND MUNDANITY

88 **They found a sense of morality often interferes with our rationality**

Corey Cusimano and Tania Lombrozo, 'Morality justifies motivated reasoning', *Cognition*, Volume 209 (April 2021), http://www.coreycusimano.net/docs/Cusimano_Lombrozo_cogsci2020.pdf <Accessed 23 March 2022>

91 **to check that the ventromedial prefrontal cortex, the part that deals with morality, is being engaged**

Jessica Hamzelou, 'Brain imaging monitors the effect of movie magic', *New Scientist* (2010), https://www.newscientist.com/article/mg20727774-000-brain-imaging-monitors-effect-of-movie-magic/ <Accessed 23 March 2022>

92 **he said he went there because he believed it was the 'honourable and right thing to do'**

Emily Maitlis, 'Prince Andrew's statement seems to contradict answers he gave me,' *BBC News* (16 February 2022), https://www.bbc.co.uk/news/uk-60407806 <Accessed 23 March 2022>

92 **His dying words were that the world would be 'eternally grateful for what he had done'**
Will Storr, *Science of Storytelling* (HarperCollins, 2019)

93 **'Hans! Are we the baddies?'**
Rootsrockbelgium, '"Are we the Baddies?" Mitchell and Webb Funny Nazi Scetch[*sic*]', uploaded to *YouTube* (7 February 2012), https://www.youtube.com/watch?v=hn1VxaMEjRU <Accessed 23 March 2022>

94 **that things are not simple, that the world out there is chaos**
Tom Jacobs, 'The Comforting Notion of an All-Powerful Enemy', *Pacific Standard* (2010), https://psmag.com/social-justice/the-comforting-notion-of-an-all-powerful-enemy-10429 <Accessed 23 March 2022>

95 **Studies show we are more forgiving to people who are close to us that behave immorally**
Rachel C. Forbes and Jennifer E. Stellar, 'When the Ones We Love Misbehave: Exploring Moral Processes Within Intimate Bonds', *Journal of Personality and Social Psychology* (2021), https://www.sciencedaily.com/releases/2021/07/210729095212.htm <Accessed 23 March 2022>

106 **Sanctity/degradation – which derives from our need to protect ourselves and our communities. *The body is a temple!***

Notes

Summary of moral foundations theory, on moralfoundations.org, https://moralfoundations.org <Accessed 23 March 2022>

111 **It's a moral argument that I strongly believe myself, but which also resonated with others**
Devin T. Stewart, 'Toward Understanding Our World's Moral Landscape: Carnegie Council's Centennial Projects on a "Global Ethic"', *Carnegie Council for Ethics and International Affairs* (2014), https://www.carnegiecouncil.org/publications/articles_papers_reports/0226 <Accessed 23 March 2022>

111 **The publisher of this book, Heligo, has a commitment to reach groups that have traditionally been underserved by publishers**
Heloise Wood, 'Bonnier Books UK unveils new imprint, led by Ubhi,' *The Bookseller* (8 December 2021), https://www.thebookseller.com/news/bonnier-books-uk-unveils-business-imprint-heligo-books-led-ubhi-1292764 <Accessed 23 March 2022>

STATEMENT AND STORY

116 **the narrow depiction of women in adverts as homemakers and sex objects, dependent on men and incapable of making decisions**
Alice E. Courtney and Thomas W. Whipple, 'Sex Stereotyping in Advertising', *Atlantis: Critical Studies in Gender, Culture, and Social Justice*, Vol. 10 No. 1 (1984), https://journals.msvu.ca/index.php/atlantis/article/view/4463 <Accessed 23 March 2022>

116 **you can really make a difference, for not just yourself but for lots of other people**
Marsellus Wallace, '12 year old Meghan Markle on Nick News in the 90s after protesting sexist commercial' uploaded to *YouTube* (19 May 2018), https://www.youtube.com/watch?v=YJce_HcXACQ <Accessed 23 March 2022>

122 **He can predict who will give money based on nothing more than their oxytocin and cortisol levels**
Paul J. Zak, 'Why Inspiring Stories Make Us React: The Neuroscience of Narrative', *Cerebrum* (2015), https://www.ncbi.nlm.nih.gov/pmc/articles/PMC4445577/ <Accessed 23 March 2022>

122 **you'll soon forget it, but you'll remember the story I told you about Alice**
Jennifer Aaker, 'Harnessing the power of stories', *Women's Leadership Innovation Lab* at Stanford University, https://womensleadership.stanford.edu/stories <Accessed 23 March 2022>

127 **Researchers at Ohio University found that after we listen to people's stories, we are more likely to follow their values and beliefs**
Melanie C. Green and Timothy C. Brock, 'The Role of Transportation on the Persuasiveness of Public Narratives', *Journal or Personality and Social Psychology* 100, vol. 79, No. 5 (2000): 701-721, http://www.communicationcache.com/uploads/1/0/8/8/10887248/the_role_of_transportation_in_the_persuasiveness_of_public_narratives.pdf

Notes

128 **It was the real deal – very forthright, very confident and very uncelebrity**
Sean Smith, *Meghan Misunderstood: The Truth about Meghan Markle*, (HarperCollins, 2020), p.155

129 **she made her points through amusing and frequently self-deprecating anecdotes, such as this story, told in her 2013 TED Talk**
TED, 'Why we have too few women leaders | Sheryl Sandberg', uploaded to *YouTube* (2010), https://www.youtube.com/watch?v=18uDutylDa4&t=196s <Accessed 23 March 2022>

130 **Let us work at it. Together. Starting now**
Sydney Morning Herald, 'The Girl Power Speech that put Meghan Markle on the map' (9 October 2018), https://www.smh.com.au/lifestyle/life-and-relationships/the-girl-power-speech-that-put-meghan-markle-on-the-map-20181009-p508lb.html

132 **The audience was shell-shocked, but her revelation encouraged many more people across Scandinavia to come out and share their stories**
'Sofie Linde – The speech provokes reactions', *News Beezer* (7 September 2020), https://newsbeezer.com/norwayeng/sofie-linde-the-speech-provokes-reactions/ <Accessed 23 March 2022>

132 **Sixty-five per cent of normal conversation is swapping stories and gossip**
Jeremy Hsu, 'The Secrets of Storytelling: Why We Love a Good Yarn', *Scientific American* (August 2008),

Connect!

https://www.scientificamerican.com/article/the-secrets-of-storytelling/ <Accessed 23 March 2022>

134 **things get worse and worse and worse, until finally they get better**
David Robinson, 'Examining the arc of 100,000 stories: a tidy analysis', *Variance Explained* (26 April 2017), http://varianceexplained.org/r/tidytext-plots/ <Accessed 23 March 2022>

PAST AND PRESENT

146 **It's why *Friends* is still the most watched show in the UK, a quarter of a century after it first aired**
Myfanwy Craigie, '24 years after it first aired Friends is the UK's most watched show,' *New Statesman* (10 August 2018), https://www.newstatesman.com/culture/2018/08/24-years-after-it-first-aired-friends-is-the-uks-most-watched-tv-show <Accessed 23 March 2022>

153-4 **almost one in five, of articles in *Time* magazine between 1982 and 2000 contained a war metaphor**
Michael Karlberg and Leslie Buell, 'Deconstructing the "war of all against all": The prevalence and implications of war metaphors and other adversarial news schema in *TIME*, *Newsweek*, and *Maclean's*', *Journal of Peace and Conflict Studies*, 12, 1 (2005): 22–39.

155 **up from 1,457 articles in February to 16,549 articles in March**
Jonathan Charteris-Black, *Metaphors of Coronavirus: Invisible Enemy or Zombie Apocalypse* (Palgrave Macmillan, 2021), p.43

Notes

155 **the rather extreme argument that 'never, ever, should a government use war as a metaphor in a time of peace'**
Simon Jenkins, 'Why I'm taking the Coronavirus hype with a pinch of salt', *Guardian* (6 March 2020), https://www.theguardian.com/commentisfree/2020/mar/06/CORONAVIRUS-hype-crisis-predictions-sars-swine-flu-panics <Accessed 23 March 2022>

157 **We will meet again**
BBC, '"We will meet again" – The Queen's Coronavirus broadcast | BBC', uploaded to *YouTube* (5 April 2020), https://www.youtube.com/watch?v=2klmuggOElE <Accessed 23 March 2022>

157 **and say they would put their whole household in quarantine**
Jonathan Charteris-Black, *Metaphors of Coronavirus* (2021), pp.48-9

157-8 **Even Simon Jenkins, reversing his previous position, started writing articles about the 'political battleground' of coronavirus**
Simon Jenkins, 'Pity a public that has so many questions about Covid. Who should be believed?', *Guardian* (20 December 2021), https://www.theguardian.com/commentisfree/2021/dec/20/public-questions-about-covid-evidence <Accessed 23 March 2022>

158 **nothing scary here, business as usual, which was the line taken by the UK government in the early days**
Stephen Grey and Andrew MacAskill, 'Special Report: Johnson listened to his scientists about CORONAVIRUS – but they were slow to sound the alarm', *Reuters*

Connect!

(7 April 2020), https://www.reuters.com/article/us-health-Coronavirus-britain-path-speci-idUSKBN-21P1VF <Accessed 23 March 2022>

159 **between the levels of uncertainty expressed in the conversation (measured by use of hesitant terms like 'I guess', 'I think' and 'maybe') and the use of analogy**
Joel Chan, Susannah B. F. Paletz and Chrisitan D. Schunn, 'Analogy as a strategy for supporting complex problem solving under uncertainty', *Memory & Cognition* issue 40 (2012): 1352–65, https://link.springer.com/article/10.3758/s13421-012-0227-z, <Accessed 23 March 2022>

159 **Likewise, when the Iraq War was debated in Congress, an astonishing 72 different analogies were used**
Two analyses of the debate in Congress over whether the US should invade Iraq on 10–12 January 1991 (Voss et al., 1992, Taylor and Rourke, 1995)

159 **Almost every article contained a new analogy**
Robert Axelrod, Larissa Forster, 'How historical analogies in newspapers of five countries make sense of major events: 9/11, Mumbai and Tahrir Square', *Research in Economics*, Volume 71, Issue 1 (2017): 8-19

160 **For example, take this medical dilemma**
Mary L. Gick and Keith J. Holyaok, 'Analogical problem solving', *Cognitive Psychology* Volume 12, Issue 3 (July 1980): 306–355, https://www.sciencedirect.com/science/article/abs/pii/0010028580900134 <Accessed 23 March 2022>

161 **92 per cent of people were able to find a solution to the problem**
Ronald T. Kellogg, *Cognitive Psychology* (SAGE Publications, 1995), p. 333

167 **Funari gave an interview with *Forbes India* in which he described Havaianas as the most iconic Brazilian brand after Pelé**
Samar Srivastava, 'We are the most iconic Brazilian brand after Pele: Havaianas' Roberto Funari, *Forbes India* (25 April 2019), https://www.forbesindia.com/article/leaderboard/we-are-the-most-iconic-brazilian-brand-after-pele-havaianas-roberto-funari/53205/1 <Accessed 23 March 2022>

168 **The video is breath-taking and of course this also makes an important point, about what we can all achieve when we do the heavy lifting together**
Tom Hayden, 'When 100 people lift a bus', *BBC News* (2015), https://www.bbc.co.uk/news/magazine-32993891 <Accessed 23 March 2022>
Sky News, 'Amazing Moment A Crown Lifts Double Decker Off Trapped Unicyclist', uploaded to *YouTube* (2015), https://www.youtube.com/watch?v=72-obuscJ-E <Accessed 23 March 2022>

THIS AND THAT

175 **love is war and even love is torture!**
Emma Gavelin, 'Conceptual metaphors: a diachronic study of LOVE metaphors in Mariah Carey's song lyrics', Umeå University (2015), https://www.diva-portal.

org/smash/get/diva2:902296/FULLTEXT01.pdf <Accessed 23 March 2022>

175 **It's not surprising to learn that Benny was known to enjoy a spot of gambling when he was away from the stage . . .**
'Benny and Björn appear in BBC Agnetha documentary', *icethesite* – Benny Andersson news site (12 June 2013), https://www.icethesite.com/2013/06/benny-and-bjorn-appear-in-bbc-agnetha-documentary/<Accessed 23 March 2022>

176 **"Bohemian Rhapsody" WAS Freddie's confessional.'**
Lesley-Ann Jones, 'Bohemian Rhapsody was Freddie Mercury's Coming Out Song,' *The Wire* (9 April 2017), https://thewire.in/culture/is-bohemian-rhapsody-really-all-about-freddie-mercury <Accessed 23 March 2022>

184 **against time to overcome the challenge of climate change**
United Nations Climate Change, 'Race to Zero Campaign', https://unfccc.int/climate-action/race-to-zero-campaign <Accessed 23 March 2022>

184 **and save the only planet we have'**
Transcript, Speech by SM Teo Chee Hean at the Virtual Temasek International Panel Meeting (4 October 2021), https://www.pmo.gov.sg/Newsroom/SM-Teo-Chee-Hean-at-the-Virtual-Temasek-International-Panel <Accessed 23 March 2022>

184 **Prince Charles called for nations to go on a '*war-like* footing', putting together 'a vast *military* style campaign'**

Notes

Transcript, A speech by HRH The Prince of Wales at the Opening Ceremony of COP26 Glasgow (1 November 2021), https://www.princeofwales.gov.uk/speech/speech-hrh-prince-wales-opening-ceremony-cop26-glasgow <Accessed 23 March 2022>

187 **I want you to act as you would in a crisis. I want you to act as if our house is on fire.**

Greta Thunberg, '"Our house is on fire": Greta Thunberg, 16, urges leaders to act on climate', *Guardian* (2019), https://www.theguardian.com/environment/2019/jan/25/our-house-is-on-fire-greta-thunberg16-urges-leaders-to-act-on-climate <Accessed 23 March 2022>

189 **'climate emergency' increased by a whopping 76-fold between 2018 and 2020**

Robyn Vinter, 'Language used to describe the climate becoming more urgent, study finds', *Guardian* (2021), https://www.theguardian.com/environment/2021/oct/21/language-used-to-describe-the-climate-becoming-more-urgent-study-finds <Accessed 23 March 2022>

189 **To protect ourselves, we process danger-related inputs faster and remember them longer**

Kristina Makansi, 'As Coronavirus-19 Disrupts Lives, Words Matter', *Research, Innovation and Impact* (2020), https://research.arizona.edu/stories/CORONAVIRUS-19-disrupts-lives-words-matter <Accessed 23 March 2022>

190 **a) far more likely to accept that there was a problem and b) far more likely to want to do something about it**

'How to build lasting support to solve UK poverty', *Joseph Rowntree Foundation* (2018), https://www.jrf.org.uk/report/how-build-lasting-support-solve-uk-poverty

190   **to show people how they can weave this imagery into their everyday language**
'Framing toolkit: Talking about poverty', Joseph Rowntree Foundation (2019), https://www.jrf.org.uk/report/framing-toolkit-talking-about-poverty <Accessed 23 March 2022>

191   *It's An Ocean's Life*
Nicky Hawkins, 'Reframing the ocean,' *FrameWorks* Guide (November 2019), https://www.frameworksinstitute.org/wp-content/uploads/2020/06/FRAJ7735-UK-Oceans-Impact-Brief-191119.pdf <Accessed 23 March 2022>

198-9   **Richard Branson has always personified Virgin and says he has always seen his company as a family**
Richard Branson, 'Surprising connections in the Virgin family', Virgin (2021), https://www.virgin.com/branson-family/richard-branson-blog/surprising-connections-in-the-virgin-family?utm_medium=social&utm_author=richard <Accessed 23 March 2022>

201   **the parts of our brains which actually deal with those actions will light up**
Lai, V. T., Howerton, O., & Desai, R. H., 'Concrete processing of action metaphors: Evidence from ERP', *Brain Research*, 1714 (2019): 202–209, https://doi.org/10.1016/j.brainres.2019.03.005 <Accessed 23 March 2022>

Notes

201 Her unique approach has led to an increase in the yield of palm oil estates on tropical peatland

Peter Sibon, 'For peat's sake, it's Sarawak's goldmine', *Borneo Post* Online (2013), http://www.theborneopost.com/2013/07/14/for-peats-sake-its-sarawaks-goldmine/ <Accessed 23 March 2022>

208 Both her mother and father have appeared in major public performances of *Romeo and Juliet*

'Svante Thunberg', *EverybodyWiki*, https://en.everybodywiki.com/Svante_Thunberg <Accessed 23 March 2022>

RHYTHM AND REASONING

217 There's something uniquely credible, compelling and convincing about an argument which comes in threes

Suzanne B. Shu and Kurt A. Carlson, 'When Three Charms But Four Alarms: Identifying the Optimal Number of Claims in Persuasion Settings', *SAGE Journals*, Vol 78, 1 (2014): 127–139, https://journals.sagepub.com/doi/10.1509/jm.11.0504 <Accessed 23 March 2022>

218 Three days of continual rises represents the point we see the pattern. It cannot be reliably deduced before then

Kurt. A. Carlson and Suzanne B. Shu, 'The rule of three: How the third even signals the emergence of a streak', *Organizational Behavior and Human Decision Processes*, Vol 104, 1 (2007): 113–121, https://www.sciencedirect.com/science/article/abs/pii/S0749597807000398?via%3Dihub <Accessed 23 March 2022>

219 **He found three-part lists generated applause so frequently he called it a 'clap trap'**
Max Atkinson, *Our Masters' Voices: The Language and Body-language of Politics* (Routledge, 1984)

219 **the phrase 'Woes unite foes' seemed more believable than 'Woes unite enemies'**
Matthew S. McGlone and Jessica Tofighbakhsh, 'The Keats heuristic: Rhyme as reason in aphorism interpretation', *Poetics*, Vol 26, 4 (1999): 235-244, https://www.sciencedirect.com/science/article/abs/pii/S0304422X99000030?via%3Dihub <Accessed 23 March 2022>

222 **And where there is despair, may we bring hope.**
Transcript, 'Remarks on becoming Prime Minister (St Francis's prayer)' (1979), https://www.margaretthatcher.org/document/104078 <Accessed 23 March 2022>

222 **The Office for National Statistics announced this in possibly the best-titled press release ever: '390,000 Jedi there are.'**
'Census 2001 Summary theme figures and rankings – 390,000 Jedi There Are', *The National Archive* (2003), https://webarchive.nationalarchives.gov.uk/ukgwa/20160105215239/http://www.ons.gov.uk/ons/rel/census/census-2001-summary-theme-figures-and-rankings/390-000-jedis-there-are/jedi.html <Accessed 23 March 2022>

231 **379 of the 821 scenes in Shakespeare's plays end in rhymes**
Patrick Spottiswoode, 'Programme Details for the 189th season 2012/13', *Shakespeare Club of Stratford* (2012),

http://www.stratfordshakespeareclub.org/shakespeare-club-Review-Patrick-Spottiswoode.html <Accessed 23 March 2022>

235 **he is the 'finest speaker [they] have ever heard', describing him as 'mesmerising'**
Andrew Adonis, *It's the Leader, Stupid* (Independently published, 2021), p.110

235 **speech he delivered at the Bharatiya Janata Party's Delhi headquarters after the vote count in the 2019 election**
'Full text of Modi's first speech after historic election victory', *Business Insider* (26 May 2019), https://www.businessinsider.in/full-text-of-modi-speech-lok-sabha-election-2019/articleshow/69467611.cms <Accessed 23 March 2022>

238 **And she ends with a three-part rhyme: *'Let's keep going. Let's keep rebuilding. And let's keep moving.'***
Transcript, 'Jacinda Ardern's Labour 2020 Campaign Launch Speech' (8 August 2020), https://www.labour.org.nz/news-speech-campaignlaunch <Accessed 23 March 2022>

242 **Because the boys watching today will be the men of tomorrow**
Simone Olesen and Karina Nyborg Jørgensen, 'The Constitution of Boundary Objects: An approach to the performance of Corporate Political Advocacy', Aalborg University (2 June 2020), https://projekter.aau.dk/projekter/files/335180683/The_Constitution_of_Boundary_Objects_An_approach_to_Corporate_Political_Advocacy.pdf <Accessed 23 March 2022>

242 **Gillette's online mentions had swung from 85 per cent positive to 54.8 per cent negative**
Tim Cross, 'Did Gillette's "The Best Men Can Be" Campaign Succeed? Here's What the Data Said . . .', *Videoweek* (2019), https://videoweek.com/2019/01/17/did-gillettes-the-best-men-can-be-campaign-succeed-heres-what-the-data-said/ <Accessed 23 March 2022>

SERIOUS AND SILLY

248 **An incredible ten million people did just that**
Brian Barrett, 'He made a viral Bernie meme site. Now he has to keep it going.' *Wired* (21 January 2021), https://www.wired.com/story/bernie-sanders-meme-street-view-site/ <Accessed 23 March 2022>

252 **Trying to explain social justice to the Conservative Party is like trying to explain origami to a penguin**
Hansard report of the debate on the Draft Part-Time Workers (Prevention of Less Favourable Treatment) Regulations (2000), https://publications.parliament.uk/pa/cm199900/cmstand/deleg3/st000518/00518s04.htm <Accessed 23 March 2022>

254 **No one, however smart, however well educated, however experienced, is the suppository of all wisdom'**
Sky News, 'Tony Abbott – No One is the suppository of all wisdom', uploaded to *YouTube* (12 August 2013), https://www.youtube.com/watch?v=oep_DPDy6xw <Accessed 23 March 2022>

Notes

254 **Momentarily uncertain whether he wanted to say that he spat at the television or shouted at the television, he blurted out, 'I shat at the television.'**
This Morning, 'Holly Willoughby Phillip Schofield David Cameron laughing at slip of the tongue I Shat' posted on *YouTube* (19 September 2019), https://www.youtube.com/watch?v=1y-qevPXNQI <Accessed 23 March 2022>

258 **He once roared so loud, his vocal cords required surgical repair**
Mark Leibovich, 'Alter Egos', *Washington Post* (December 31 2000), https://www.washingtonpost.com/archive/politics/2000/12/31/alter-egos/91b267b0-858c-4d4e-a4bd-48f22e015f70/?utm_term=.a893731292f8 <Accessed 23 March 2022>

259 ***Laughter: An Investigation*, found we're 30 times more likely to laugh in company than we are on our own**
Robert R. Provine, *Curious Behaviour: Yawning, Laughing, Hiccupping, and Beyond* (Belknap Press, 2012), p.56

263 **Jerry Seinfeld talks about the 'silly putty of the mind that enables you to reform what you see into what you want it to be'**
Jerry Seinfeld, *Is This Anything?* (Simon & Schuster, 2020)

263 ***"Because African elephants can weigh up to 330 pounds at birth."***
Dan O'Shannon, *What Are You Laughing At* (Bloomsbury Academic, 2012), p.225

267 **Sloss said he had no idea it was going to have that kind of impact**
Daniel Sloss on *The Graham Norton Show* (January 2021)

STATS AND SYMBOLS

271 **60 per cent of the people being admitted to hospital with coronavirus had *not* been properly vaccinated, a big difference**
'COVID 19 press conference', streamed live by 10 Downing Street (19 July 2021), https://www.youtube.com/watch?v=3EkYBeoGgV8 <Accessed 23 March 2022>
Sir Patrick Vallance (@uksciencechief) Twitter (July 19 2021) at 8.26pm, https://twitter.com/uksciencechief/status/1417204235356213252?lang=en <Accessed 23 March 2022>

272 **On immigration, most people think around a quarter of their population is immigrant when the actual figure is less than half of that**
'Perils of Perception', *IPSOS* Mori (April 2021), https://perils.ipsos.com/slides/index.html <Accessed 23 March 2022>

273 **'This is partly because we over-estimate what we worry about.'**
'Perils of Perception', *IPSOS* MORI (2015), https://www.ipsos.com/ipsos-mori/en-uk/perils-perception-2015 <Accessed 23 March 2022>

273 **As he's pointed out, we are all born with an innate instinct for processing numbers and scale**

Jim Holt, 'The Numbers Guy – Are our brains wired for math?' *The New Yorker* (24 February 2008), https://www.newyorker.com/magazine/2008/03/03/numbers-guy <Accessed 23 March 2022>

273 **This suggests that even at just a few weeks old, a baby can recognise the difference between three and four dots**
Sue Ellen Antell and Daniel P. Keating, 'Perception of Numerical Invariance in Neonates', *Child Development*, vol. 54, 3, Wiley, Society for Research in Child Development (1983): 695–701, https://doi.org/10.2307/1130057 <Accessed 23 March 2022>

275 **Studies have shown a correlation between the sensitivity of a child's fingertips and their ability in maths**
Robert Reeve and Judi Humberstone, 'Five to 7 year olds' finger gnosia and calculation abilities', University of Melbourne, *Frontiers in Psychology* (8 December 2011), https://www.frontiersin.org/articles/10.3389/fpsyg.2011.00359/full <Accessed 23 March 2022>

276 **So, they were still thinking through their fingers, even though they were not using them**
Ilaria Berteletti and James Booth, 'Perceiving fingers in single-digit arithmetic problems', *Frontiers in Psychology* (March 2016), https://www.ncbi.nlm.nih.gov/pmc/articles/PMC4360562/ <Accessed 23 March 2022>

277 **so the perception is reversed in cultures where writing moves from right to left, such as Arabic**
Bodo Winter and Jeff Yoshimi, 'Metaphor and the Philosophical Implications of Embodied Mathematics,' *Frontiers in Psychology* (2 November 2020), https://www.

frontiersin.org/articles/10.3389/fpsyg.2020.569487/
full#ref26 <Accessed 23 March 2022>

281 **even though the latter offered better value**
H. (Allan) Chen, Marmorstein, H., Tsiros, M., & Rao,
A. R., 'When More Is Less: The Impact of Base Value
Neglect on Consumer Preferences for Bonus Packs over
Price Discounts', *Journal of Marketing*, 76, 4, (2012):
64–77, http://www.jstor.org/stable/41714499 <Accessed
23 March 2022>

282 **I felt quite nervous when I bought my flat**
Jonathan Charteris-Black, *Metaphors of Coronavirus:
Invisible Enemy or Zombie Apocalypse?* (Palgrave Mac-
millan, 2021), p.190

286 **Wave references in the press outnumbered tsunami
references by a ratio of approximately 30:1**
Jonathan Charteris-Black, *Metaphors of Coronavirus:
Invisible Enemy or Zombie Apocalypse?* (Palgrave Macmillan, 2021), p.82

286 **So maybe it should be talked about more as a *wildfire*
than as a wave**
Maria Broadfoot, 'Mispalced Analogies: COVID19 is
more like a wildfire than a wave,' *Scientific American* (29
June 2020), https://www.scientificamerican.com/arti-
cle/misplaced-analogies-Coronavirus-19-is-more-like-
a-wildfire-than-a-wave <Accessed 23 March 2022>

DEEDS AND DREAMS
289 **The crew also comprised the oldest person ever to fly
into space**

Notes

NBC News, '"Best Day Ever!" Watch Highlights from Jeff Bezos Launch to Edge of Space', https://www.youtube.com/watch?v=pPuFuJAusv8 <Accessed 23 March 2022>

289 **18-year-old Oliver Daemen, whose father had paid for his seat on the capsule in an auction**
'Oliver Daemen, Youngest Astronaut Candidate to Fly with Jeff Bezos,' VOI (19 July 2021), https://voi.id/en/technology/68321/oliver-daemen-youngest-astronaut-candidate-to-fly-with-jeff-bezos <Accessed 23 March 2022>

290 **saying it left him obsessed with the idea that one day he might travel to space**
Andrew Buncombe, 'Musk, Branson and Bezos: Why are three billionaires determined to go to space – and what's the danger to planet Earth?' *Independent* (19 July 2019), https://www.independent.co.uk/news/science/elon-musk-space-jeff-bezos-richard-branson-apollo-11-moon-landing-a9011591.html <Accessed 23 March 2022>

291 **One study by Harvard University suggests as much as half of our day may be spent daydreaming**
BBC News, 'People spend 'half their waking hours daydreaming' (12 November 2010), https://www.bbc.co.uk/news/health-11741350 <Accessed 23 March 2022>

292 **If you live in the most expensive mansion in the world, dopamine makes you want a castle on the moon'**
Daniel Z Lieberman and Micheal E Long, *The Molecule of More,* (BenBella Books, 2018) p.16

299 **How about modernising democracy so everyone can vote online and personalising education so everyone can learn?**
'Mark Zuckerberg's Commencement Address at Harvard' (25 May 2017), https://news.harvard.edu/gazette/story/2017/05/mark-zuckerbergs-speech-as-written-for-harvards-class-of-2017/ <Accessed 23 March 2022>

300-1 **the average social media user spends two hours a day on social media, with many spending even longer**
'Daily Social Media Usage worldwide, 2012-2022', *Statista Research Department* (21 March 2022), https://www.statista.com/statistics/433871/daily-social-media-usage-worldwide/ <Accessed 23 March 2022>

304 **The emerging insight: once we have possession of something we don't want to let go**
D. Kahneman, Knetsch, J. L., & Thaler, R. H., 'Experimental Tests of the Endowment Effect and the Coase Theorem', *Journal of Political Economy*, *98*, 6 (1990): 1325–1348, http://www.jstor.org/stable/2937761 <Accessed 23 March 2022>

306 **That was why he decided to resign from his job on Wall Street to create Amazon**
'Jeff Bezos: Regret Minimisation Framework', YouTube, https://www.youtube.com/watch?v=jwG_qR6XmDQ <Accessed 23 March 2022>

Acknowledgements

They say writing a book is like having a baby. This is my fourth and now, as I stand here holding my newborn in my hands, every inch the proud father, all that's left is to thank all those who helped me from the elation and excitement of conception through the ups and downs of gestation to the final pain of the delivery room.

First and foremost, big thanks to Lucy, who, as well as being my wife, is also my consigliere and counsellor, comrade and compadre, constant companion, co-creator and total BFF. Thanks also to my inspirational daughters, Lottie and Alice; my ever-encouraging mum – who is still the best proofreader on the planet; my dad, for all his support; and the endless source of energy that is my brother, Brendon, to whom this book is dedicated.

I also want to thank all those who checked the baby's health along the way. Martha Rolley, for initial research and final fact checking. Paul Rainey, who has now illustrated three of my books (*onmi trium perfectum* and all that). And thanks also to Lord Adonis, Professor Jonathan Charteris-Black, Dr Lyndsey Jenkins, Dr Giulia Maltagliati, Mette Fjeldhoff,

Connect!

Greg Simpson, Stewart Price, Laurian Hubbard, Miguel Veiga Pestana, Ian Dench, Kate Stanley and Neil Mullarkey for reading over various bits of the book at different stages.

Finally, thanks to the expert team of doctors, nurses and midwives who ensured a smooth and successful delivery. Sally Holloway at Felicity Bryan Associates, my brilliant, straight-talking and always on-point agent. Super-positive, super-smiley Rik Ubhi and the rest of the team at Heligo who powered through the process. And eagle-eyed editor/midwife Justine Taylor, who discreetly disposed of the messy sheets without anyone noticing.

I hope you find my baby as adorable, enchanting and irresist-ible as I do. And I hope that, in some small way, the book makes a little difference to the way you live your life. I hope you get con-nected, not least by connecting with me anytime on LinkedIn, Twitter, TikTok or by email: simon@bespokespeeches.com.

Business and smart-thinking books for curious readers and business leaders.

Designed to inspire, energise, and encourage.

Heligo
Books

Sign-up for exclusive content:
www.heligobooks.co.uk